CREATING KILLER WEB SITES

I have my own web design company and everything was going along just fine until I read your book. It changed my life! Now, because of you, I have to go back and redesign all my web sites! — **Bob**

For the longest time I couldn't find any decent books on web design. I sat in the book store transfixed for half an hour before finally my wife snapped her fingers a few times to bring me out of it. Yours is the first book on web site design that I've completely agreed with. — **Eric**

You've made a good thing here. The writing is clear and concise. The design is excellent. The illustrations are outstanding. And all that other stuff everyone else probably tells you. Tell your Verso team that I complement them on their work with the book. — **Jay**

My wife and I just purchased your wonderful book Creating Killer Web Sites. *We found it on Friday night at the local book store. Bridget read it cover to cover on the remainder of Friday night and all day Saturday. I could not get her away from it – your book is that wonderful!* — **Ed**

Your book Creating Killer Web Sites *has been an inspiration to me; I immediately realized that I was heading totally in the wrong direction (frames, horizontal rules, scrolling, blinking stuff, etc.). Being a former student of architecture, I instantly learned to admire the approach you take in designing simple, yet amazing web sites.* — **Eugene**

Your book, your web site, and your attitude are a wonderful sort of mentoring that must be benefitting thousands of people. I finished Chapter 3 over breakfast today and am busily (and with a touch of embarrassment) compressing all my 8-bit GIFs. Thanks again! — **Naomi**

I started designing sites about six months ago when I bought your book Creating Killer Web Sites. *I thought it was great and always keep it by my side. I also love your High Five site as it enables me to compare myself with others out there and to try and better myself.* — **Anthony**

CREATING KILLER WEB SITES

The Art of Third-Generation Site Design

David Siegel

Hayden
Books

CREATING KILLER WEB SITES
SECOND EDITION

Copyright © 1997 David Siegel

Excerpt from "SGML Buyer's Guide" © 1998 Charles F. Goldfarb. Reprinted with permission.

Trademark Acknowledgments

Library of Congress Catalog Number: 97-073902
ISBN: 1-56830-433-1

Printed in the United States of America
1 2 3 4 5 6 7 8 9 0

This book was produced digitally by Macmillan Computer Publishing and manufactured using computer-to-plate technology (a film-less process) by GAC/Shepard Poorman, Indianapolis, Indiana.

HAYDEN BOOKS

The staff of Hayden Books is committed to bringing you the best computer books. What our readers think of Hayden is important to our ability to serve our customers. If you have any comments, no matter how great or how small, we'd appreciate your taking the time to send us a note. You can reach Hayden Books at the following:

Hayden Books
201 West 103rd Street
Indianapolis, IN 46290
317-581-3833

Email address:

hayden@hayden.com
Visit the Hayden Books web site at http://www.hayden.com

President	*Richard Swadley*
Publisher	*John Pierce*
Managing Editor	*Lisa Wilson*
Director of Marketing	*Kelli S. Spencer*
Product Marketing Manager	*Kim Margolius*
Development Editor	*Beth Millett*
Publishing Coordinator	*Karen Williams*
Marketing Coordinator	*Linda B. Beckwith*
Cover and Book Design	*Studio Verso*
Manufacturing Coordinator	*Brook Farling*
Production Team Supervisor	*Brad Chinn*
Production Team	*Mark Walchle*
Indexer	*Chris Barrick*

Contents at a Glance

Acknowledgments and Credits

The second edition of this book was driven and edited by Doug Millison, whose professionalism and positive attitude motivated the entire team. Doug coordinated and conducted research, wrote drafts, edited my rough drafts, and kept track of thousands of miscellaneous details that always crop up. Doug worked closely with Verso's design technologist Todd Fahrner, production manager David Cullinan, and designer Purvi Shah. Todd, David, and Purvi meticulously combed the first edition for details to update and new information to include, and kept us all informed of the latest evolution of the 4.0 browsers. Joe Silva put the book together and gently reminded the team that he couldn't lay out any chapters if the editors hadn't given them to him. Amy Wilkins filled in on writing miscellaneous chunks, updated the Creative Design Solutions, and edited and proofed each chapter – twice. David Cullinan took charge of production, wowing and soothing the team with his organization and competence, while Jennifer Wolf and Geoff Gladden took the lead on producing illustrations and ideas for new sites to include. Michel Milano produced the wonderful chapter divider illustrations. Thanks also to the tireless dedication of Hayden Books, especially publisher John Pierce and development editor Beth Millett.

The second edition could not, of course, have been written had the first edition not been such a success, and this success reflects the efforts of the first-edition team. Although the book is written in first person, almost everyone at Studio Verso wrote some part of it. They designed most of it. They illustrated all of it. Finally, my deepest thanks go to designer and mentor Gino Lee, who served as the spiritual guide for the first-edition group, keeping us on course and focused. It is a privilege to be part of the Web with these remarkable people during these remarkable times.

Executive Editor to the Second Edition:	*Doug Millison*
Copy Editors:	*Louise Galindo, Amy Wilkins*
Writers:	*Todd Fahrner, Doug Millison, Amy Wilkins*
Readers:	*Henry McGilton, John Giannandrea*
Special Contribution:	*Todd Fahrner*
Illustrators:	*David D. Cullinan, Todd Fahrner, Robert Frank, Geoff Gladden, Matthew Johnson, Jennifer H. Wolf*
Divider Illustrations:	*Michel Milano*
Production Coordinator:	*David D. Cullinan*
Production:	*Todd Fahrner, Matthew Johnson, David Siegel, Ilsa Van Hook*
Contributors:	*Ray Guillette, Hussein Kanji*
Layout/Design:	*Todd Fahrner, Gino Lee, Joe Silva*
Cover Design:	*David Siegel*
Book Site Team:	*David D. Cullinan, Brian Dame, Robert Frank, Matthew Johnson, Hussein Kanji, Gino Lee, Joe Silva*

The principal typefaces used in this book are FFScala, Meta, and Matrix Script.

Preface to the Second Edition

In 1996, I wrote a little book called *Creating Killer Web Sites*. It was a labor of love for me and the people who work at Studio Verso. Back then, we were just seven people, and we were desperate to change the Web. It wasn't that we wanted to build the best looking web sites for our clients. We wanted to reach out a hand and pull all the designers onto the Web with us, so we could make the Web more beautiful together. Another reason was that, as designers, we love to hold things in our hands. Many of us have book backgrounds. We're drawn to bookstores like magnets. We spend way too much money on design books.

I think the person most surprised by the success of *Creating Killer Web Sites* is my father. (I mean, his son may be a designer and a computer geek, but a writer?) I was the second most surprised. When the book became the number-eight best-seller at Amazon.com, I thought I had reached some sort of peak. Then came the email messages from people all over the world. Even after it became Amazon's best-selling book for 1996, and after it was translated into 10 languages, I think the most important thing to us has been the email messages. They still come in every day, and I can think of no more appropriate response than providing this updated edition.

I'm proud to say this is a complete rework of the book, built on the same strong foundation. My goal in writing this edition of *Creating Killer Web Sites* was to make sure that anyone who had the first edition would get her money's worth from this one. We've rewritten every chapter. We've gotten rid of most of our single-pixel GIFs! This book represents a new approach to web-site design, one that takes over where the previous edition left off. There are more than 100 new pages and 150 new illustrations. And the new chapter on style sheets is the most reality-based piece of writing you'll find on the subject. Revisiting the example chapters will show you how our approach has changed.

Because a book is not a web site, it travels backward in time as everything else moves forward. Yet there's something reassuring about its consistency, about the fact that it will always be right here in human-readable format, and that you can open it even if your provider isn't providing.

This is it. There will not be another edition of this book. I hope you'll find it worthy of your time and that you'll write to tell me what you think. I look forward to seeing you on the Web.

David Siegel
San Francisco, California

This book is dedicated to the surfers from around the world who visit my web sites regularly. Keep the cards and letters coming!

Introduction

The Book Site: http://www.killersites.com

New software emerges on the Web daily. Any CD-ROM included with this book would be hopelessly out of date before pressing.

My company, Studio Verso, maintains a site, http://www.killersites.com, which serves as an up-to-date companion reference to this book. There you will find all the files you need to follow these chapters from your own desktop, as well as pointers to books and software useful for making third-generation web sites.

You'll also find three chapters that appeared in the first edition of this book: "A Hot List," "A PDF Primer," and "A Catalog in PDF." It is generally referred to as the "Book Site" throughout the text. We hope it will serve you well!

About this book and its contents

This is not a first book on HTML. In addition to a good book on basic HTML, I recommended the following books on design principles:

The Form of the Book by Jan Tschichold, edited by Robert Bringhurst (Hartley & Marks, Vancouver, BC, 1991).

The Visual Display of Quantitative Information by Edward R. Tufte (Graphics Press, Cheshire, CT, 1983).

Envisioning Information by Edward R. Tufte (Graphics Press, Cheshire, CT, 1990).

Visual Explanations by Edward R. Tufte (Graphics Press, Cheshire, CT, 1997).

WE DON'T MAKE WEB SITES the way our parents did. The typical welcome-to-my-home-page, menu-driven, icon-encrusted model is fast being replaced by a model I call third-generation site architecture. Though third-generation sites rely heavily on today's browser technology, the difference is not technology per se – the difference is design. This is the first book about the conception, design, and construction of third-generation sites.

Now in its second edition, this book reinforces the importance of third-generation design and resisting the urge to build sites with the latest browser features and technical gizmos.

I have written this book in three parts. Part I covers the nuts and bolts of making third-generation sites, from theory and structure to implementation and tools. Part II contains case studies that take you through the design and construction of four third-generation sites, ranging from introductory to advanced.

For space reasons, three chapters from the first edition of this book are not included. You'll find them in PDF format at the book site.

This section ends with a chapter that showcases several real-life design solutions from around the Web, all updated with new methods and illustrations. Part III includes a thrilling jeep-drive through the Style Sheet landscape, with pitfalls, pinnacles, and perilous browser implementations around every corner. Then I cover several transitional strategies that will help designers while the Web slowly migrates from 3.0 to 4.0 and 5.0 browsers. Finally, I discuss issues beyond HTML as we know it today, presenting a vision for the future of online design.

Although this book is more than a survey, it is far from complete. I have tried to cover graphic design as applied to the Web, and that necessarily involves a great deal of technical detail. There is much to know and learn about information design, form design, internationalization, and user interfaces. I touch on these subjects briefly. These are substantial subjects, too big for any one person to put into a single book.

We must start somewhere. The days of paper used frivolously are over. The Web is here to stay. I hope this book helps designers to make the transition. In her essay entitled "Electronic Typography," Jessica Helfand, a brilliant designer who has turned her modem into a design tool, wrote:

Here is the biggest contribution to communication technology to come out of the last decade, a global network linking some 50 million people worldwide, and designers – communication designers, no less – are nowhere to be seen.

With the freedom of the Web comes new responsibility; it will take new thinking and the continual desire to sharpen our tools and discard old tools as necessary. The designer's goal should be to add to the beauty and usefulness of the content of the Web as it continues to change our lives.

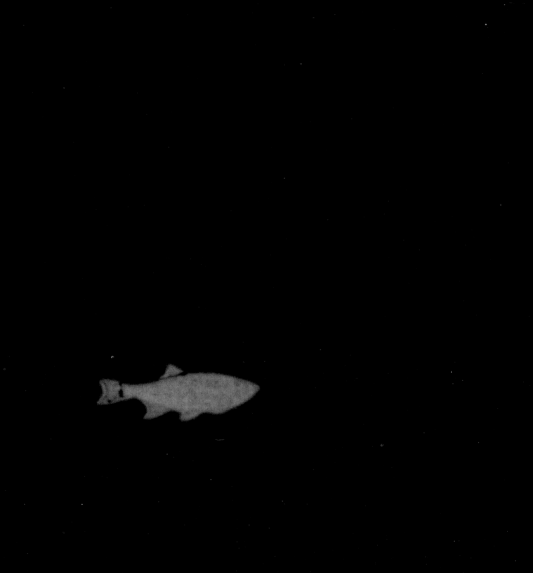

Part I

CHAPTER 1

Form versus Function

My web site. A playground for reinventing layout and learning about HTML. It hasn't changed much since 1995, but it showed a generation of designers how to think out of the box.

IN 1994 I HAD my first experience on the Web. In early 1995, I made my first web site. The first time I saw the same web page through two different browsers at the same time, a feeling of panic swept through me. Why should the pages look so different? I knew various systems had different color spaces and resolutions, but these programs actually presented the pages in different ways. As a graphic designer, how could I design web pages if I didn't know how they would look? Could I let a piece of software reinterpret my work as it wanted?

That was precisely what the Framers of the Web had in mind. They saw browser differences as beneficial. Because every document is marked with *structural tags* (headers, paragraphs, list items, emphasized phrases, and others), they believed users should control the presentation of documents they see. HTML (HyperText Markup Language) lets the visitor choose how her browser displays the page.

That's like telling the artist how to hold the brush! I wanted more control. It was either toss in the mouse and go back to print design, or jump into the Web and color outside the lines.

I threw my HTML book in the trash and started from scratch. I figured out a bunch of tricks to get around structural markup and make pages the way I wanted them to look. I began using images to lay out pages in two dimensions, rather than one. When tables became available, I poured columns of text in them. I reduced the colors and made the file sizes small and – guess what? – people came! The numbers actually broke my access counter.

I wrote a book – the first edition of this book – and people bought it. So many people adopted the tricks and techniques I explained that many people said I had single-handedly ruined the Web. I was just one of many people who wanted to have more control over the layout of pages, mostly to make more attractive sites for my clients. The web-development community eagerly shares new discoveries. Collectively, we steered the Web in a direction the Framers hadn't intended to go, and I'd like to think we contributed in a positive way to the development of new standards.

When they write the big book on the history of Web development, I would like to be seen as someone who fought hard for absolute positioning and more precise control over the layout of page elements. It may take a few more books and a few more browser versions before we can say we have accomplished that.

Of course, there has been no head-on collision between the designers and the structuralists. Instead, we are headed toward a set of standards to give designers more control while giving users and search engines more flexibility in the way they "consume" information. From richer markup languages and Cascading Style Sheets to the new object model, designers and members of the w3c – the UN of the Web – are now working hand-in-hand to build a more flexible foundation for online authoring, publishing, and consumption of content. Now, if we can just get the browser companies to care more about visual issues, we'll all live happily ever after.

Browser History

Originally, the HyperText Markup Language was meant to show the *structure* of a document, without much regard to its meaning or presentation. Thus, you were supposed to identify a paragraph not by a line break, or an indent, but simply by marking it with a `<P>` tag. It was up to the browser (the so-called *user agent*) to decide how to present the paragraph.

`<P>`

Paragraphs were meant to be marked with this special tag. The `<P>` tag was meant to be a *container*, meaning it had beginning and ending forms (as shown here). Browsers didn't enforce the closing tag, and most browsers rendered a blank line between paragraphs, so people started using the `<P>` tag as a *separator*, rather than as a *container*.
`</P>`

Headers were enclosed in `<H>` tags: `<H1>` through `<H6>`, just in case you needed that many levels of logical subdivision. You were supposed to emphasize something by using the `<EM>` tag, with its corresponding `</EM>` counterpart. Most browsers, I think, italicized that tag's contents, while the `<STRONG>` tag usually rendered as bold. These are called *structural tags*. Early HTML also included some *visual tags*, also called *procedural tags*, like `<B>` for bold and `<I>` for italic, so it was never exactly clear whether you should use structural or visual tags.

With the Netscape 1.1 extensions, people began adding ugly (but "cool") background images to their sites.

Consumers have come to the Web.

By the middle of 1997, more than 31 million PCs in the U.S. were regularly connected to the Internet, according to market researcher Computer Intelligence, a 108 percent increase over the previous year. FIND/SVP estimated between 40-45 million total U.S. adult users of the Internet in April 1997 and estimated that some 25 million people use the Web at least weekly in the U.S. alone.

Most consumers surf the Web on their lunch hour, which means they want to be entertained. They have 640 x 480 screens, but more are starting to log in with 800 x 600 screens, which will be the new entry-level standard. Unfortunately, consumer systems will continue to display only 256 simultaneous colors for some time to come.

While lots of designers would like to design for high-bandwidth users, the majority – a full 70% of surfers – still dial-up to the Web using 14.4 or 28.8kbps modems, according to e-stats (www.eland.com/e-stats). Seventy percent of surfers view the Web through the Netscape Navigator browser, but market research shows that Internet Explorer has been steadily gaining market share at Netscape's expense, and will continue to do so. A final statistic worth noting – FIND/SVP found that 42% of surfers are women, well up from a very low percentage just a few years ago.

Perhaps the most important addition was the <TABLE> tag, which finally let people publish their tabular information they'd been dying to properly display. Of course, web designers took tables and immediately poured columns of text into them, something tables weren't really intended for. By putting text into tables, we found we could get margins and shorter line lengths, providing better typographic layout control. Everyone poured text into tables, even the people who designed the Netscape web site. It was naughty and fun, and it gave designers hope that we could start doing real typography on the Web.

Netscape took a proprietary, tag-based approach to extending HTML. They released new tags with every version of their browser, giving people new toys to play with and further mixing structural markup with presentation tags. The release of their 2.0 browser went even further, showing several web pages at a time, using a new device called frames. Anyone without a frames-capable browser would not see what the author intended. For better or worse, people readily adopted these new tags. Netscape enjoyed a virtual monopoly on the browser market.

Enter Microsoft

The only browser with any chance of competing was Microsoft's Internet Explorer, and Microsoft had a long way to go to catch up. But they did something smart. They started working with the w3c and its various committees to develop and publish public-domain open standards they hoped would level the playing field.

In time, Microsoft's IE 3.0 became a huge success. They had worked hard to implement frames, add more font choices, and build a more robust, compact browser than Netscape's Navigator. While Microsoft had worked hard to contribute to the W3C's specification of style sheets, the browser's implementation was more a proof of concept than a tool for web developers. Navigator 3.0, on the other hand, had more marketing than performance features.

The big showdown came with the 4.0 browsers. Netscape knew Microsoft was going to use IE 4.0 as a front-end for Windows, so people could actually use the browser to see and use the files on their desktops. Netscape fired back with a suite of groupware and email tools to let people in corporations do more for their intranets and collaborative projects. Both 4.0 browsers implement style sheets, but, as we'll see in Chapter 11, "A CSS Primer," the implementations are less than ideal. I'll talk about the 5.0 browsers and the future of HTML in the final chapter, where the light at the end of the tunnel is just starting to glow.

The Virtual Melting Pot

The Web is a bouillabaisse of information providers and consumers. On one hand, we have the structuralists. To them, a good web page is marked up perfectly. They actually have programs to "validate" how well you've marked up your content, and they think that's important. In fact, standard HTML markup benefits the search engines,

visually impaired people, and those who surf with images turned off. Their ideal world consists of even more structure to include more information about their content (extra information that describes content is called *metadata*, see Chapter 13), so the search engines can make even more sense of their sites.

Structuralists want everyone to be able to access web content with any browser. They don't worry much about typographic niceties or the visual layout of a page. To them, web pages are documents, and when you have millions of documents, you need structure to make them indexable, searchable, and maintainable.

Then we have designers. On one end of the spectrum are information designers, and on the other end are people determined to break the rules (for example, www.jodi.org and www.superbad.com) no matter what they are. All designers want to be able to create an online experience. They are used to working with programs like Illustrator, Photoshop, and Page-Maker. Many of them have worked in television or on CD-ROMs with movement and time-based events. They want to create online galleries, games, theme parks, movie sites, TV-channels, underground 'zines, community centers – web sites that grab people's attention and give them a good time, so they'll want to come back for more. Shock value and fresh content may be more important to many sites than verifiable markup. Designers know that if people don't consume their content, it doesn't matter how well structured it is.

In the middle, we have clients and we have surfers. Clients want their sites to reach their audience appropriately. Would I tell a marketing executive from Pepsico that I was going to make sure her web site conformed to strict structural markup standards? She doesn't care! She wants people to have more fun at her site than they do at the Coca-Cola site. Surfers want whatever they're looking for – sometimes they don't even know or care. The only consistent thing we know about surfers is that they want it now! They're looking for travel tickets, a restaurant, a date, a joke, a story – or maybe they just want to look at pretty pictures for a while. Some are visually impaired, some have small monitors, some have big monitors, some surf on their TV. Some have slow modems, others have T1 connections. Surfers are not all graduate students, nor are they all just looking for a good time. There are tens of millions of people surfing the Web, and there are many good reasons and ways to do it.

The Emphasis on Design

This book tries to balance the equation by emphasizing design. Designers put design above structure. Designers have taken the structuralists' HTML and bent it horribly to suit their visual needs. I believe design drives the user's experience of the content; it is the designer's responsibility to present content appropriately. Who cares how powerful your database is if people can't use the interface? Who cares how great your content is if people aren't attracted to it or don't find it pleasurable to read?

I have a traditional typographic training, so I care whether paragraphs are indented or not. I think it's crazy that paragraphs aren't indented on the Web, and structuralists think it's crazy that I use markup hacks to insert indents into my paragraphs. To quote hypermedia visionary Ted Nelson:

"Multimedia must be controlled by dictatorial artists with full say on the final cut."

The Web is no different from the rest of the world. From legal documents, newsletters, and the *Wall Street Journal* to *USA Today* and *Wired* magazine, a successful format completes the communication link between content producers and intended audience. The difference between the Web and real life is that in real life, the structuralists and the designers don't often show up at the same parties.

At some point, web designers and structuralists will meet in the middle. Every few months, each group takes another step toward the other. It's up to the browser companies to determine how quickly we converge.

Summary

With these concepts in mind, I hope you'll enjoy the new material we've put into this edition. There are plenty of tricks and hacks, but you'll also note a more sober approach to web design, one that lets us take advantage of some of the structural capabilities new browsers offer without losing the universal accessibility the Web was designed to provide in the first place.

As I predicted, we can now swing the pendulum back toward structure and layout, whereas before the choice was structure or layout.

We're not there yet, however. Many of the techniques in the middle of this book are workarounds, showing how designers can cope with the lack of visual tools in today's browsers. As you'll see in the final chapters, there is much more to do before designers and structuralists can appreciate each other's contributions.

Finally, although this book mostly covers techniques of visual layout control and seeks to frame the discussion around new web-based protocols, its real emphasis is on design. Because this book is not a web site, there will be a day when almost every technique I describe here is obsolete. I hope the design lessons and the sense of visual balance will remain valid for years to come.

A University Web Site

Look at a web site for a university, where the variety of content and consumers spans a wide spectrum. The physicists want to communicate and share data with other physicists. The drama department wants to create "play spaces" on the web. The dorms want to use a database to assign students to rooms. The administration wants forms people can fill out to sign up or apply for anything, maybe even pay their tuition through the site. Various live "cams" sprout up around campus. Labs have ongoing experiments people around the world can participate in. The athletic department wants to sell tickets to games. The library wants people to search for and find books, put a few thousand volumes online, and save money by putting a huge amount of video material online for people to see directly, rather than handling and checking out fragile video tapes.

Fraternities want to announce their parties. Student groups want live web-casts for their events. Disabled students want all course material online. The robotics group has wired the vending machines up to the Web. Students in remote locations want to participate in class discussions. The Student Union wants to create a mall, while the food-service group wants to put menus online and let people design their own pizzas. Meanwhile, the people who provide web access want all students, even those with impaired vision or those who are blind, to experience everything. The administration wants to make sure the entire site is branded, navigable, searchable, and that no one's rights or reputation are violated in the process. And HTML is supposed to do all of this?

CHAPTER 2

Third-Generation Sites

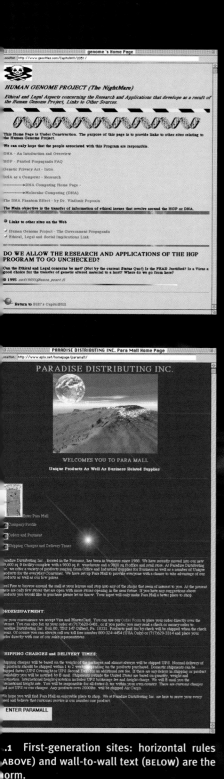

.1   First-generation sites: horizontal rules
ABOVE) and wall-to-wall text (BELOW) are the
orm.

WHAT IS A THIRD-GENERATION web site? A third-generation site combines typographic and visual layout principles with creative design solutions to provide a complete experience to the visitor. Third-generation sites use metaphor and visual theme to entice and guide. They strive to make a site feel familiar and easy to navigate, with quality content and high production values. Third-generation site designers carefully specify the position and relationships of all elements on the page, retaining fine control of the layout.

This chapter covers the evolution of third-generation sites and discusses their structure in relation to well known models of consumer behavior. This chapter also addresses the design needs of information-based sites.

First-Generation Sites

First-generation sites were linear. They were bare-bones functional, so scientists around the world could share their findings. Looking at a typical first-generation page, you can see the restrictions imposed by slow modems, monochrome monitors, and the default browser style sheets. The page displays a top-to-bottom, left-to-right sequence of text and images, interspersed with carriage returns and other data-stream separators like bullets and horizontal rules. All the initial HTML constructs were designed around this teletype model for laying out pages.

First-generation sites were designed by technical people [2.1]. Some sites had headline banners and were well organized; most had edge-to-edge text that ran on for pages, separated by meaningless blank lines [**2.1**]. At best, they looked like slide presentations shown on a cement wall.

Second-Generation Sites

In the spring of 1995, Netscape announced a set of extensions to HTML. People played with the extensions and had fun with the `<BLINK>` tag (aren't you glad this is a book?). Second-generation sites are basically first-generation sites with icons replacing words, tiled images replacing the gray background, buttons with beveled edges, and banners replacing headlines [**2.2 A–C**]. They use a top-down, bullet-list, menu-driven model to present a hierarchy of information [**2.3**].

Technology has always driven the Web. Exciting new capabilities appear weekly, urging site owners to try them. Second-generation site design continues to be menu-, icon-, and technology-driven. These sites tend to follow the home-page model, where the first page you see is encrusted with icons and 3-D graphical representations of buttons, windows, and pictures. At worst, gelatinous backgrounds and rainbow graphics make these sites unbearable. At best, they are nice white sites with color-coordinated icons.

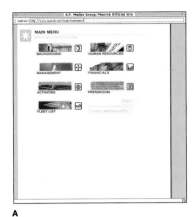

A

B

C

2.2 A-C Second-generation sites push visitors by using simile and hierarchy.

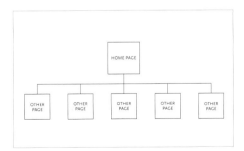

2.3 First- and second-generation sites start with a home page and a list of options.

The Restaurant Model

I use a restaurant metaphor when thinking about sites. You hear about a restaurant from an advertisement or a friend, or you discover it while passing by. You check out the daily specials chalked on a board out front and smell the aroma in the doorway.

Once through the door, you make a quick stay-or-bail decision. In a popular restaurant, you might have to wait for a table. If you stay, someone shows you to a table and hands you the menu. You make your selection.

When the food arrives, you have no urge to rearrange the various items on the plate. The food and presentation are the creations of the chef. You sample the various items, skipping among them, mixing flavors and textures.

When you are finished, you have dessert, ask for the bill, and pay. You leave a tip, pick up the card next to the cashier, and maybe exchange a few pleasant words with the owner. Later, when you are hungry again, you return or you don't, based on the quality of that first experience.

2.4 Early third-generation sites.

2.5 Third-generation sites pull people in the front door and guide them through.

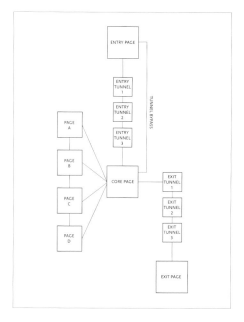

At this point, the majority of web sites are somewhere between jazzed-up first-generation and poorly executed second-generation designs. Legibility and visitor-consideration give way to "cool" technical tricks.

Third-Generation Sites

A third-generation site is wrought by *design*, not technological competence. Third-generation sites give visitors a complete experience, from entry to exit. The cleverness of third-generation designers is not technical but visual. Design is the difference. Creative people have made third-generation sites with all generations of graphical browsers **[2.4]**.

Third-generation sites pull visitors through using metaphor and well-known models of consumer psychology. Just as retailers spend a lot of time tuning their environments to the customers passing by, third-generation site designers spend hours and days making their pages enticing to the audience they seek. Rather than providing a list of out-and-back trips from the home page, third-generation sites are a complete experience – the more you explore, the more the entire picture of the site comes together. Third-generation design turns a site from a menu into a meal.

Think of the Web as a cozy little town with half a million restaurants.

Fourth-Generation Sites

Everyone wants to know whether we've gone past the third generation or not.

Some people say fourth-generation sites are database-driven with plenty of dynamic content. Others say we've already gotten to the sixth generation.

Many people thought the term *third-generation design* was tied to a particular technology. They thought second-generation design was for 2.0 browsers, and third-generation design was for 3.0 browsers.

Third-generation design has nothing to do with browser version releases or technology.

The term third generation has always been, for me, a way to describe a particular attitude toward site design. Most of the good third-generation sites have been or get reviewed at the High Five site (www.highfive.com), and I can report that at this writing there are only a few hundred well designed third-generation sites. I think the Web has a long way to go before third-generation sites are the norm. We have an even longer way to go before we can discuss fourth-generation design (the subject of the upcoming sequel to this book).

Building third-generation sites is hard. It takes time, dedication, and a sense of what excites your visitors. Third-generation sites usually require several people working together, pushing themselves to make every page beautiful and the entire site "work" as a surfing experience. If you want to use next-generation browser features, that's fine, but a third-generation site has nothing to do with specific technologies.

Case Study: Joe Boxer

Baiting the hook means giving something away. With the commercialization of the Web, fish food can be found on many sites. Whether it's QuickTime videos, screen savers, or a joke of the day, sites often reward surfers for coming back.

One of the best gimmicks I've seen is Joe Boxer's email interface to the "Zipper" electronic billboard at Times Square. You send email to timesquare@joeboxer.com, and they add your message to their email hour, which runs four times a day across the bottom of their big billboard. Needless to say, plenty of underwear-buying people show up to type in their messages, and they end up exploring the entire site, soaking in the Joe Boxerness and becoming unbearably hip with every click.

Who will be next to come up with a "killer" fish-food idea?

At www.joeboxer.com, people can actually send email to the zipper display in Times Square.

Site Structure

Millions of people surf the Web. You don't need all of them in your site. You want to reach a select group and turn window shoppers into customers who will take some action that benefits you both (send email, order a product, give feedback, and so on). Telling people to order your products doesn't work. You must welcome them and make them feel at home in your site. Most third-generation sites have an entry, a center area with a core page for exploration, and a well-defined exit [2.5]. Third-generation sites pull visitors through by tantalizing them with something exciting on every page.

Entry

An entry to your site tells people where they are without serving your whole smorgasbord of delights at once [2.6 A, B]. More and more sites have *front doors* for just that purpose. A front door, also known as a *splash screen*, loads quickly and tells people what's going on inside. A good front door should be hard to walk away from, yet it should tell people what they're getting into.

Above all, splash screens should load quickly. Your first screen should take no more than 15 seconds to load at prevailing modem speeds – faster if possible. Present your visitors with a tedious download, and they'll be at Yahoo! before your access counter can tell you what happened.

Fish Food

As people wander by your site, hold out a basket of goodies to tempt them. Gossip, news, sports scores, weather information, stock quotes, promotional sales, package-tracking services, pictures of Marilyn Monroe, free software, recipes, and sound files routinely lure potential audience members to third-generation sites.

"You give; you get. You no give; you no get."
– Harvey Mackay, author of Dig Your Well Before You're Thirsty

A

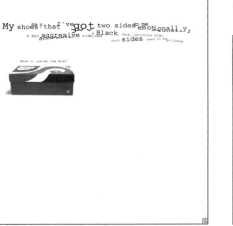

B

2.6 A, B A front door targets your audience.

A

B

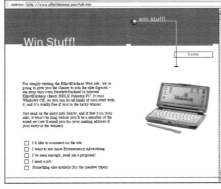

C

2.7 A-C The goal of free stuff is to generate a buzz on the Web.

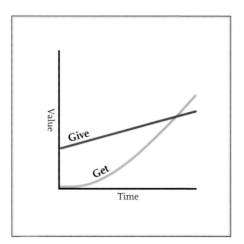

2.8 Only a constant effort to give people what they want can reap rewards later.

This is what I call *fish food*. If you want to attract investors, put up either current stock prices or some lively, timely investment advice. If you're looking for dog owners, put up "The anatomy of the flea," or have a "Name That Breed" quiz. You want a gimmick that reaches out to the people you hope will form your community.

The technical term for fish food on the Web is *free stuff* [**2.7 A-C**]. Give new visitors free stuff and a percentage of them will wander into your site. Use your imagination. Think of something your crowd would like to hear about, tell each other about, and go see. When people send your URL to their friends, you know you're serving something they want. Not surprisingly, the more you give, the more people want, so be prepared to keep giving [**2.8**].

As any advertiser knows, there are no rules for getting people's attention

[**2.9**]. Use any means at your disposal, even Java. Put up games, stunts, live video feeds, soap operas, a club for lefthanders – anything that generates a buzz. Vandalize your own site, challenge another site to a contest, ask people to vote on something. Things like this work better than filling out forms and asking the search engines to list your site because of its great content.

Entry Tunnels

Many third-generation sites have splash screens. A few have entry tunnels. As visitors enter your site, you may want to give them the option of taking a short ride rather than going straight into the site. I call these rides *entry tunnels*. They help build anticipation [**2.10**] as people approach the heart of the site.

Entry tunnels are not appropriate for most sites. They can be appropriate for consumer sites [**2.11 A-F**]. Limit them to 2-4 screens and make them entertaining.

The Core Page

The ultimate goal of many web sites is to create a community. A good site pays off when people return again and again to purchase or participate. Core pages make this process enjoyable.

In contrast to the second-generation concept of a home page, third-generation sites can have either one or several core pages to organize and present the contents. Some third-generation sites have no core page at all. Core pages direct and guide the visitor

2.9 (ABOVE) Collecting free stuff is actually a serious hobby on the Web.

A

B

C

D

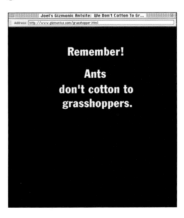

E

F

2.11 A-F (ABOVE) The Gizmonic Antsite entry tunnel sets the mood as you "crawl" into the site.

2.10 (LEFT) Entry tunnels build anticipation.

19

2.12 A core page doesn't have to be a bulleted list of items. An active core page encourages bookmarks.

by providing links to the various neighborhood pages. Core pages hold content while continuing to entice the visitor through the site **[2.12]**.

Don't be afraid to guide your audience. Give them choices, but also make suggestions. Give them lots of intrasite links and few external links. Put something interesting on every page.

Traditional home pages easily degenerate into an endless vertical list of links. Core pages use content to lure and tantalize. Use details of images and excerpts of text to guide your visitor. Otherwise, your work remains buried behind flat, uninformative links.

Take the example of a mail-order site, where the goal is to get your user to call an 800 number or fill out an order form. A direct link to that order form or the 800 number itself should be available on almost every page. Most people won't click the first time they see it, but clicks are a function of exposure. Put the links to these final action pages everywhere, and your audience will get there when they are ready.

Exit

Paradoxically, a well-marked exit entices visitors to stay. Showing visitors the door to an exit page or tunnel informs them that this is the way out of the site. If they come to an area that doesn't hold their interest, they shouldn't just type "www.cirquedusoleil.com" and surf on. They should visit any areas that might be interesting before taking the exit.

Announcing the exit builds a sense of expectation, like announcing the names of the guests on the talk show at the beginning. It's worth your time to make an interesting exit. Cap their visit with a bang, but don't overadvertise it. Links to your exit should be subtle, without encouraging people to leave before seeing the rest of the show.

The exit page is a good place to ask for something from your visitors. You might want to have them fill out a form, call your 800 number, make a purchase, sign your mailing list, give feedback, or take some other action. They are willing to work with you at this point, because you've rewarded their expectations.

The big finish may be as simple as a list of related sites on the Web, or it may be as lucrative as a chance to enter a drawing for prizes.

Net Equity

If people talk about your site, if they come back often, if your metaphor starts a buzz and the front door is enticing, you will be on your way toward building *net equity*. Simply put, net equity is audience mindshare. You build mindshare by making things that either are or will become familiar to your audience.

Change Is Good

You have a site. You want bookmarks. People don't need to bookmark the entrance to your site – they can probably remember that. But if you have a compelling core page, they just might bookmark it. The free stuff gets them there, but they come back regularly to the core of the site to see what's new.

If your site changes every month, it might as well be static. If it changes weekly, people might bookmark the pages with interesting things going on. If it changes daily, you could be in for some big numbers on your access counters. Make sure to provide links from your active pages to more static areas, especially if you are trying to drive visitors to a particular page.

How many sites have "What's New!" on the front page? We don't need to know how to get to what's new. If it's new, and it's important, it should be in our faces. Put some content on your core page – don't bury it under a "What's New!" link.

Metaphor: Vehicle of Exploration

Third-generation sites often make efficient use of metaphor. A strong metaphor can guide a visitor and glue a site together. Metaphors must be familiar, consistent, and appropriate for the modem speeds of the Web. Metaphors pull in visitors, making them feel at home while giving them features to explore. Examples of metaphors include galleries, comic strips, television channels, TV remote controls, magazines, tabloids, store

Barriers to Entry

Third-generation sites lure, seduce, coax. New visitors might not wait for a lengthy download on a high-bandwidth front page. Even the entertaining free stuff will irritate serious, repeat visitors if alternate points of entry or direct links to the core of the site aren't easily accessible. The best sites hook an audience before the audience even knows it.

In entry tunnels, it's no longer practical to ask people to register. Some entry tunnels say, "Register here free!" Who wants to register for free? If you really want people to register, you'll have to give them something major in return. Registration is a barrier to entry – be sure you need it before putting it in.

New approaches to registration will replace today's pleas for marketing information from surfers. The Web is advertising-driven. The advertisers will figure out a way to get what they want to know. In the future, your browser will be able to keep a fairly rich profile on you and automatically tell sites much more about you than they do today – subject to your approval, of course.

Case Study: Klutz Press

John Cassidy, owner of Klutz Press, asked me to create a web site for his company, a leading publisher of children's books. He wanted to put a few of the books' chapters on the Web to illustrate how much fun they are. My original design for Klutz included a long entry tunnel, a dark room with a light switch, then a four-walled room. Each wall had a book on or near it. When you clicked on a book, you found yourself at the book's title page. Clicking on the title page took you to the book's table of contents, from which you could finally begin to play.

People loved the site, but few even reached the books. Most left after the entry tunnel. The book chapters were 14 clicks from the front door! Our redesign for Klutz is much more direct, without sacrificing fun (www.klutz.com).

As you arrive at the Klutz treehouse, an animated GIF automatically opens the door and beckons you in. Seconds later, a script sends you into the treehouse automatically – you haven't even clicked yet. Now you're in a room that contains a book, with its table of contents below. Selecting a chapter – your first click – takes you right into the content. We used a Perl script to randomize the books, so you get to a different level of the treehouse every time you enter. It's easy enough to go up and down the ladder to find a particular book, but it was more important to get right into the content. This design completely eliminated the core page! We could have put one in, but it would have gotten in the way. This is an example of how to design a third-generation site with no core page at all, just content and a sense of exploration.

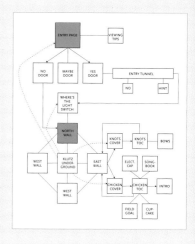

The first sequence (ABOVE) and the revised sequence (BELOW).

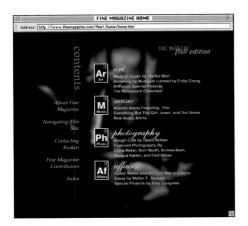

2.13 Fine Magazine uses a wonderful visual metaphor – a periodic table of the elements.

2.14 Some sites get caught up in their metaphors and forget the content.

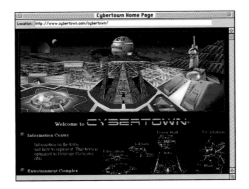

environments, museums, postcard racks, amusement parks, going inside things (computers, human body, buildings, ant farm, and so on), safaris, cities, and cupboards. These can be done well [2.13], or they can be overdone [2.14].

Metaphors are vehicles of exploration. Make it simple, consistent, and easy to get around. A good metaphor puts the light switch where you expect to find it. A bad metaphor makes you learn a whole new set of commands to enter. Well-executed metaphors make it difficult to get lost.

Some sites try to present arcade-like interfaces or physical-space metaphors that rely heavily on 3-D graphics. You find yourself wandering down hallways, through doors, up staircases, and so on. These can work at high bandwidth or on CD-ROMs, but not with modems. Keep your metaphors light and effective. (*See Chapter 10, "Creative Design Solutions," for a selection of good metaphors.*)

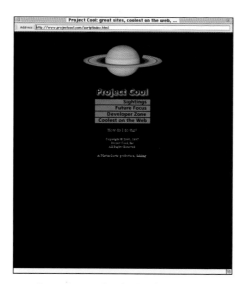

2.15 A good metaphor is simple and well executed.

Metaphors come in all shapes and sizes. This book should inspire you to seek new ways of representing your work, to think outside the constraints of HTML. Think of ways to make your visitors feel at home. Make the metaphor appropriate for your audience. Geologists might enjoy a virtual coal mine tour, but canaries won't.

The trick to presenting a successful metaphor on the Web is to couch it in HTML so it loads quickly, yet doesn't look cheap. Key visual elements of your metaphor will have to be small enough to reinforce the metaphor over and over again.

Graphic designers are a largely untapped resource on the Web. They learn to use metaphor in school and apply those lessons in making everything from business cards to TV commercials. Take advantage of them!

Collaborate with a designer rather than trying to become one. Graphic designers who make sites should apply the visual lessons they've learned on paper to create effective metaphors on the Web. Designers often check their visual skills at the door when entering the Web. Don't fall into the trap of making second-generation sites at first, just because they are easier to make. Start with third-generation design and the skillful use of metaphor.

Once you choose a metaphor, stick with it. It may sound easy, but once you get going, there will be temptations to overdo it or stretch it. Keep it simple. A good metaphor helps select your audience. This proposal **[2.15]** for an entry tunnel was meant to be mysterious and inviting, setting up a metaphor for the entire site: outer space. (Compare this image to the Cybertown concept on the previous page.)

Theme:
Interior Design for the Web

You don't need a metaphor to make a third-generation site. A consistent theme can work just as well. A theme can be visual or conceptual. Examples of themes: painterly, primitive, photographic, juvenile, art deco, typographic, futuristic, and so on. As with metaphor, themes can either enhance or get in the way **[2.16]**.

A theme can be almost anything. The best are subtle and consistent. Think of storefronts. Retail stores differentiate themselves by presenting a thematic environment. Some – particularly toy stores – use metaphors

When Is a Metaphor Not a Metaphor?

When it's a simile. Simply replacing words with icons does not a metaphor make.

While international menu bars are very helpful to surfers from other countries, if your visitors can't speak English, they probably won't get much out of your site unless you also provide a translated version. Don't turn words into pictures and call it a site.

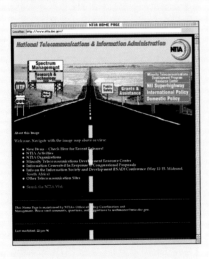

This is not to say you shouldn't have any symbols or icons on your site, or that you shouldn't be clever in presenting them. Icons play a supporting role in third-generation sites. Mixing metaphor and simile requires balance and restraint.

(castles, playhouses, and so on), but most use colors, textures, lighting, and graphics to uniquely identify their stores.

Commercial interior designers know about theme. They make a space functional and interesting, not cartoonish or repetitive. They must create both tangible and intangible value, pleasing the senses while serving the needs of the business.

Thematic sites are more difficult to create than you might think. There is a great temptation to throw in more of everything: sound, animation, fonts, and graphics, leading to clutter and confusion. Using quality photography, for example, can make a difference on

2.16 Color, type, and visual theme can give a site a distinctive look.

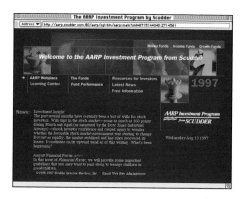

a theme-based site. Using the few colors available to site designers is a big challenge. Defining a subset of those colors to create an individual palette that expresses a particular identity is nearly impossible. A good thematic site is an exercise in subtlety, good information design, and consistency.

Information-Based Sites

Many sites are not geared toward consumers. In the information realm, sites must satisfy impatient, directed visitors. These sites can't afford to put too much glitter in front of the information. Nevertheless, they can be compelling without using a lot of icons and banners.

Most information-based sites present endless pages of text and bulleted lists, with a predictable home page up front (NEWS | ABOUT US | CATALOG | FAQ | HELP). Many have a search engine enabling visitors to find things immediately, but if a customer doesn't know exactly what she wants, she is lost.

Presenting database-driven information is a daunting task. Sites like c|net must coordinate search results with banner ads, site navigation, different levels of users, and enticing offerings on every page. Designers of such sites work with templates that are supposed to put everything together on the fly. They must make enough templates to create a robust architecture, yet not so many that they get out of hand and the rules get too complicated.

Forms design is another specialty. While most people seem to do fairly

HotWired Style

Jeff Veen, interface director at HotWired.com, has written an excellent book on site-design strategy and implementation. *HotWired Style: Principles for Building Smart Web Sites* is a valuable tool for any third-generation site designer. It is filled with great lessons from HotWired's journey as a nexus for nerds, hip net surfers, digerati, and future digerati.

With their finger on the pulse of the Web, Jeff and designer Barbara Kuhr share their thoughts and aspirations for what the Web can accomplish. The detailed studies show an inside look at one of the Web's most influential sites. Jeff gives plenty of real-world suggestions for applying what he has learned to your site. There aren't many killer books on site design. This is one of them.

Information Design

Many sites have information-based pages. While this book discusses good typography and presentation of textual information, a thorough treatment of information architecture and design is beyond its scope. People like Edward Tufte have devoted their lives to the field. User-interface designers and information architects are constantly working on new ways to present data. Some people are even starting to use VRML to model information spaces in 3-D.

Information designers talk about *granularity* — putting just the right amount of information in front of the user at any one time. The more expert people become, the more an information space should adapt to give them the power tools they need. Systematic, well thought out approaches consider the user and her environment and provide easy, step-by-step transitions from one data set to the next.

2.17 Good user interfaces are clean and uncluttered.

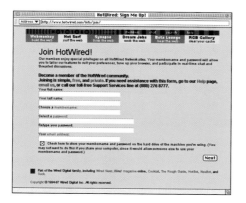

2.18 HotWired has always done an excellent job of keeping their forms easy to understand (RIGHT), unlike a lot of other sites (BELOW).

well with forms on the Web, some are better than others. A few leave the user stranded, disoriented, and not knowing how to order a product. The best way to design forms is to find well designed examples and start with those. It's okay to take people's HTML, as long as you modify it to suit your own purposes. Don't make the mistake of thinking forms are easy and can be done quickly. In general, I prefer forms that have borderless field names on the left and fill-in boxes on the right, grouped carefully as you go down the page **[2.17]**. Present only a few categories per page, then move on to the next screen. Forms demand as much attention to detail as graphics do **[2.18]**.

Many forms solicit information from people who are generally impatient with or afraid to fill out a long form. While the process of buying your product is very familiar to you, it won't be obvious to people coming to your site for the first time. Numbering the steps and breaking these sections out separately helps people overcome their fear of filling out complicated forms. One good reason to break the order process into steps is that you can find and correct errors more easily if you do it a few at a time **[2.19 A, B]**. Use colors and visual feedback elements consistently to guide the user through the process **[2.20]**.

Information-based sites must offer both browse and search capabilities. Regular customers need a page they can bookmark, preferably listing the features of the site and providing the shortest path to any given page. There should be a search window, or at least a button to a search page, on every

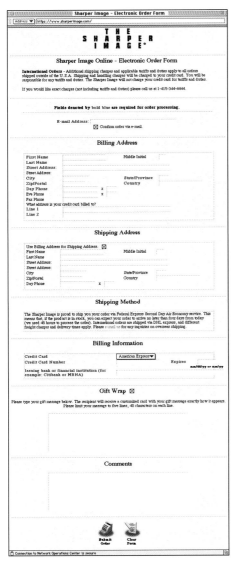

A

B

Client/Server Computing

Servers are computers connected to the Internet around the clock, serving information. Clients are programs, like Internet Explorer (a browser) and Eudora (a mail reader). When I use the word *client*, I mean a program that resides on your computer as you use the Internet.

An Internet Service Provider (ISP) gives you access to the Internet. A server sits somewhere and sends files to everyone. You don't need to locate your site on the server of your service provider. Your site can be hosted on a server in Zurich, but your ISP should be a local company that gives you good access to the Internet for a good price.

The View Info Command

Netscape's browser has a little-used feature that gives you information about the pages you see.

While most people are used to the View Source command that shows the HTML of any file you see on the Web, Netscape Navigator will also give you quantitative statistics for any given image. This includes the size of each image, both when compressed (content length) and in memory (decoded size).

2.19 A Numbering the steps of a long procedure can help. Some designers break the process into several pages, while others use one long page to collect all information. Use logical grouping and provide status information to help guide the user through the process.

2.19 B Information-based sites must be balanced. They must pull in new people, while giving the regulars an easy way to get exactly what they came for.

2.20 Information-based sites can't take anything for granted. Designers must continually refine their offerings to suit the audience.

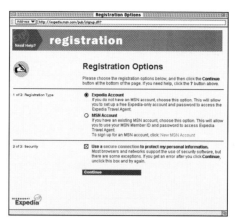

2.21 Frames-based catalogs show your shopping cart throughout your entire shopping session.

Webmasters & Webmistresses

A webmaster or webmistress is the person responsible for keeping the server running properly. Site designers are not webmasters any more than ship designers are first mates.

page in the site. More and more, these sites are providing a custom profile the user can fill out to help filter content the way he wants it.

One way to present a lot of continually changing data is to use the browser's frames feature. Frames can help, especially for presenting large sets of pages that users should compare. Information-based sites do not need frames, but they are candidates for frames. Catalog designers are starting to combine frames and scripts to create persistent shopping carts that update as you choose items [2.21].

Dynamic sites are becoming the norm in the information realm. Rather than bookmarking a static page, frequent users fill out a form telling the site about their needs. The site goes to work for them, sending them e-mail messages when new items of interest arise, providing a custom, made-on-demand page just for them when they log in, and generally keeping their interests in mind as they cruise the site. A good dynamic site presents opportunities to learn new things and see new offerings while trying to meet 90 percent of the frequent surfer's needs on the first two pages.

While the rest of this book discusses more consumer-based models of design, many of the principles of third-generation site design apply to information-based sites as well.

Summary

People tend to surf with their shortest attention spans turned on. Think of the center of your site as the kitchen, where you're serving meals all day. Once visitors have been lured in by the aroma of good food, they start prowling around, opening cupboards, and raiding your cookie jar. A commitment to fresh daily content is often the best way to attract and keep a crowd. Invite the critics over for a taste. Keep handing out samples and don't present the bill until after the meal. Cook up a good site, and you'll always have a line of hungry customers waiting to get in your front door.

As Joseph Squier, author of *The Place*, states, "Independent of medium or tool or technique, there are timeless aspects of art that endure. Artists communicate."

The Currency of the Web

A *hit* is any file downloaded. A hit can be a page of text, an inline graphic, or a downloadable movie or sound file. Thus, if you have a page with 10 pictures on it, a person coming to that page will generate 11 hits (if her browser can see images). Many people confuse hits with accesses or visitors, which makes 10,000 of them around noontime sound as though their site is packed with people (when it really isn't). Hits are the pennies of the Web.

An *access* is an entire page served. Accesses (also called *page hits* or *page views*) are the smallest unit to track, because they can help you determine where people go in your site.

A *visitor* is the true one-dollar bill of the Web. Unfortunately, *unique visitors* are more difficult to define. That's why there's so much incentive to get visitors to register – people are anonymous as they view your site. In general, I simply make educated guesses about the number of unique visitors to my sites. Programs are now available to help webmasters track visitors going through their sites.

A *repeat visitor* is the ten-dollar bill of the Web. If a visitor bookmarks your site, it means she is willing to come back. In the mail-order business, such a person is called a *responder*.

If people order things on your site, they turn from visitors into *customers*, the ultimate goal. A customer is the highest level of status a visitor can attain. A good web site strives to turn a small percentage of random surfers into customers.

Histogram

Channel: Gray   ▼

OK

Mean: 111.89   Level:
Std Dev: 99.58   Count:
Median: 49   Percentile:
Pixels: 5216425

CHAPTER 3

Preparing Images

COMPUTER IMAGES come in two fundamental types: raster and vector. *Raster images*, also called *bitmaps*, are made up of individual dots (pixels) arranged in a grid *x* pixels wide by *y* pixels high by *z* pixels deep (where *z* is known as *pixel depth* and determines the number of possible colors for each pixel). Raster images have fixed dimensions; their file size goes up with the size and resolution of the image. The screen image on your monitor is one large raster image, updated continuously.

Resolution refers to the physical information space of a given output device. A computer display typically has between 72 and 120 pixels per inch and ranges from 13 to 21 inches diagonally. This is changing constantly, with high-end displays getting bigger and the low-end displays shrinking, as palmtop computers take to the Web and as web-phone browsers give consumers access to the Internet from their kitchens. *Color depth* defines the number of colors in each pixel. The total amount of information your screen can display is the product of x times y times z, and this is determined by the amount of video RAM in your computer. (Video RAM, or VRAM, is separate from main memory, known as RAM.) With a given amount of VRAM, you can usually trade screen space for bit depth, sacrificing color fidelity for more pixels, and vice versa. Other devices, like printers, have much higher resolution. Most laser printers have 300-600 dots per inch (DPI). Some day, computer displays will, too.

Vector images are mathematical descriptions of an image (the formula for a circle is an example) rendered on your computer screen by a program that reads the description and builds an image. This makes them resolution-independent – they can be scaled to any size and resolution for display on screens, printers, and so on. Because they consist of instructions, rather than pixels, these files are usually much smaller than those of comparable raster images. In traditional graphic design terminology, raster images represent *screen art*, while vector images represent *line art* (for example, photographs versus blueprints) **[3.1 A-D]**.

Although vector formats are popular among print designers, they are just starting to appear on the Web. This chapter discusses preparing GIF and JPEG images for browsers.

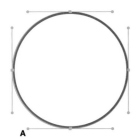
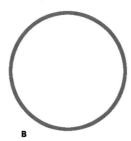
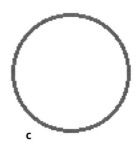
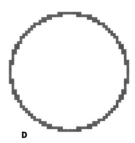

3.1 Vector images (A) are resolution-independent, while bitmaps (B-D) are tied to resolutions.

BIT DEPTH	EXPONENTS	NUMBER OF COLORS
1	2^1	2
2	2^2	4
3	2^3	8
4	2^4	16
5	2^5	32
6	2^6	64
7	2^7	128
8	2^8	256
16	2^{16}	16-BIT TRUE-COLOR
24	2^{24}	24-BIT TRUE-COLOR (8x8x8)
32	2^{32}	24-BIT TRUE-COLOR + 8-BIT ALPHA CHANNEL

3.2 Indexed images are 8 bits or fewer; true-color images have 24 bits or more.

Most of the material in this chapter applies to GIFs; there is a section on photographs and the JPEG format toward the end. (*See Chapter 12: "Transitional Strategies," for more on vector formats and new raster formats.*)

Please note that the techniques described in this chapter have been developed for Photoshop version 4.0.1.

Color Depth

The number of colors in a raster image determines its color depth. One-bit images have only two states – on (white) and off (black). More bits per pixel means more colors [**3.2**]. However, more colors make larger image files, which means it takes more time to download them. Smaller is better.

The number of colors your system displays depends on the amount of VRAM installed. While professional designers usually have machines that can display 24-bit images, most consumer machines have 8-bit color, which means they can display only 256 colors at a time. Many web surfers use 8-bit color settings. Even if their systems have higher color capability, they may not know how to change the color setting, or they may use 256 colors because that is what games require. Don't assume that visitors to your site will share the same high color settings your system has.

The high end of the scale includes 32-bit images, which have an associated alpha channel. An *alpha channel* is typically used for transparency and overlays. (*Although neither of the formats covered in this chapter supports an 8-bit alpha channel, I cover the subject in more detail in Chapter 12, "Transitional Strategies."*)

It's not true that file size goes up dramatically as you increase the number of colors or the dimensions of images, because on the Web, no one ever sends an uncompressed image. The biggest factor affecting file size is *compressibility*, which I explain in more detail later in this chapter.

3.3 Indexed images have associated palettes that determine the color range for the image.

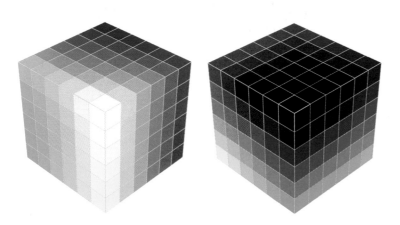

3.4 The color cube. See this image on the Book Site.

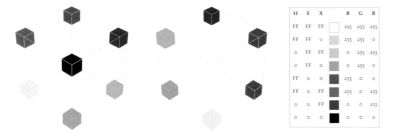

3.5 The corners of the color cube.

Palettes

The two ways of storing color raster images are *indexed* and *RGB*. Images in RGB format – also known as *full color* or *true color* – use 8 bits (0 to 255) of Red, Green, and Blue values to form a 24-bit pixel (8+8+8= 24). Images with 256 colors (or fewer) are called indexed. They have an associated color palette, called the *color lookup table*, or CLUT, as part of the file. The palette defines up to 256 colors, giving each one a number. The image then refers to each color by its position in the palette [3.3]. Images with more than 256 colors do not have an associated palette.

The Color Cube

Because so many people have systems that can only see 256 colors, Netscape originally came up with a single set of colors, or *color cube*, that would work well enough in all situations [3.4]. The only problem with the cube is that it has persisted when other methods are superior. This six-sided color cube has 216 colors. Why not the full 256? Windows needs 20 colors for itself, other programs (and wallpaper) use another 20, and the remaining 216 colors are available to the browser. Why force every web page to the same limited set of colors? Because it simplifies considerably the task of designing browsers. It was an easy way to dodge the problem of providing the best 256 colors for any particular page.

At the corners of the cube are all eight possible combinations of 255 (full on) and 0 (full off) in RGB space [3.5]. The internal colors of the cube are the four evenly spaced colors between each corner, for a total of 216. This simple approach results in a *dithering palette*. Other palettes might have been more useful – this one has only four internal gray values, for example – but the color cube is easy to program. Microsoft's Internet Explorer browser now uses Netscape's primitive color cube.

On a display set for 8 bits, browsers automatically dither the image using this default palette or shift colors without dithering. Images in the foreground will dither; images in the background map to the nearest color-cube color without dithering (for faster display). Setting your display to 256 colors shows how your images will likely appear to these systems. (If you are designing web sites, your system should display at least 16,000 colors.)

Note: Only browser programs use this color cube. Do not look at an image in Photoshop using 8-bit color to simulate the image in a browser window.

Pick from the Cube

Here's how to load the color cube's palette into Photoshop's color picker:

1. Get the color cube image from the book site.

2. Open the image.

3. Change mode to indexed color using "exact palette" and color depth of 8 bits/pixel.

4. Open the color table (in the Image menu).

5. Load the palette as "color_cube.tbl" onto your hard disk.

6. Cancel out of the Color Table dialog.

7. Go to Swatches in your colors window.

8. Click on the right arrow to pop up a submenu, and choose "Load Swatches."

9. Search your hard disk to find "color_cube.tbl," and open that color table.

10. Quit Photoshop and restart it to make sure it has saved this table as your default set of swatches. You may now use it to choose colors for creating and manipulating images.

11. Because the arrangements of these colors can be confusing, you may want to create or download a separate Photoshop document that has the colors arranged in a more useful way than you can get here in the picker. Then use the dropper tool to pick up colors. I use both methods, but I know my way around the picker's arrangement now, so I use that most often.

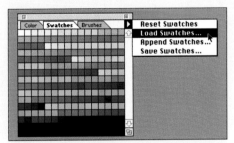

Loading the color cube into the picker.

3.6 How many colors in this image? Photoshop adds many subtle shades to achieve anti-aliasing. Make sure your main colors come from the color cube.

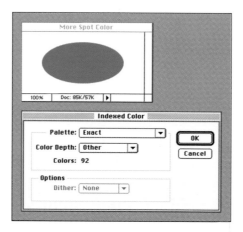

The bottom line: Use these 216 colors when you create images, or low-end browsers will impose them on your design.

Spot Color

If your image contains areas of solid colors (type, shapes, sky, and so on), you should try to make them viewable at the highest color quality by as many web surfers as possible. People who have 8-bit systems will see your images dithered to the color cube no matter what. The idea is to provide a higher quality image to those surfers who can see more colors without increasing file size (download time).

As you work in layers, Photoshop automatically generates many intermediate colors that aren't in the cube [3.6]. That's okay. Using colors from the cube for large areas but not for transitions is called *dithering on the client* (*see Chapter 5, "Rendering Type"*). Once your image looks good with this strategy, you can proceed to make it more compressible.

Dithering

Dithering is the process of using colors from the available palette to synthesize other colors. Available colors are sprinkled throughout to simulate unavailable colors. If you need a color one-third of the way from color A to color B, a program that dithers simply sprinkles 33 percent pixels of color B on top of 100% color A. Visually, it works fairly well for photographic images but not for most other types.

Web designers dislike pre-dithering because it makes images less compressible. The viewer's browser will automatically dither if the system can show only 256 colors and it encounters colors outside the color cube. While variable dithering leads to larger file sizes, *regular dithering* is not the same animal. If you can dither an image regularly – using predictable patterns of colored pixels – your file will compress nicely. (*See "Spot Color" elsewhere in this chapter for more on regular dither patterns.*)

Avoid pre-dithering as much as possible; it makes your files much bigger, and it makes your images look speckled.

Mapping Images to the Color Cube

When you have no control over how an image is created, and your audience is likely to have 8-bit systems, you'll have to decide whether to convert to the color-cube colors or let the visitor's browser do it for you.

The first thing to do is reduce the number of colors and work to make the image as compressible as possible, using methods outlined below. After it's as small as you can get it, try converting it to color-cube colors and see

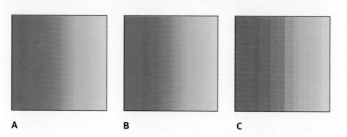

A   B   C

how you like it. (Photoshop 4.0 has a wonderful "Web Palette" feature that maps to the color cube and removes all the unused colors in one step.) If it's any good, you're done.

If mapping to the cube presents too many problems (banding, dithering, bad colors), you may want to make a JPEG (see below), or you may want to leave it as it is. By leaving it as it is, people with more color capability will see the true image, while people with 8-bit systems will see it dithered. That could be the best tradeoff you can make, given your audience and the particular image.

There are several different methods for mapping your images to the cube. A program like DeBabelizer offers the most choices (*see Appendix 3: "Image Optimization for the Web"*). In Photoshop, you can precolor certain parts of the image, then use adaptive-palette reduction from there.

The big choice here is to dither or not to dither. It's always best not to pre-dither your images if possible.

Color Blending

Because we are going to be stuck with the color cube for a while, people are finding interesting ways to work around it. Bruce Heavin, co-author of *Coloring Web Graphics*, showed me an interesting trick to get non-cube colors. The idea is to blend colors visually by alternating color-cube colors either in checkerboard or in stripe patterns.

Checkerboard patterns work quite well. If you choose two colors that are quite different in value (darkness or lightness), you'll get a checkerboard

Ditherbox

Ditherbox is a Photoshop 4.0 plug-in that creates blended colors (both checkerboard and interlaced) automatically. It's the brainchild of Hal Rucker of RDG Tools in San Mateo, California. This handy plug-in application is available at www.ditherbox.com – it's a killer tool for anyone trying to break out of the color cube to do real-world design. Simply enter two browser colors, and it gives you any combination to get various blends.

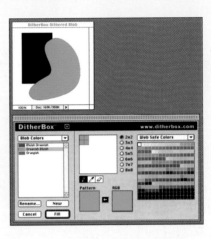

Or, specify a non-cube color, and Ditherbox will change the appropriate colors to mix. You can then save your custom blends as "colors" and use them to fill any selected area, saving lots of time cutting and pasting.

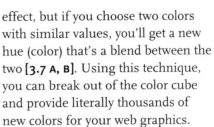

A   B

effect, but if you choose two colors with similar values, you'll get a new hue (color) that's a blend between the two [3.7 A, B]. Using this technique, you can break out of the color cube and provide literally thousands of new colors for your web graphics.

3.7 An interlace pattern (A) and a crosshatch pattern (B) and their respective color-cube pattern generators.

Hex Values and the Rule of 51

In HTML, the <BODY> element permits *hex values* to specify colors for background color, text color, and link colors. If you specify one, make sure you specify all – otherwise your selection might interact badly with user settings, leading to black text on a black background, for instance. Hex numbers are a way of specifying values from 0-15 with a single character (from 0-f). Use any 2-digit combination (for red, green, and blue) of "hhh" where h is in the set (00, 33, 66, 99, cc, ff). A light blue is "#CCCCFF" and a middle orange is "#996600". As long as you use only these values, any combination will produce a color-cube color. If you're aiming for a broad audience, stick with these combinations.

Color values are specified in the range 0-255. All color-cube colors are triple RGB combinations of the hex value 51. So color values like (0,102,51), (153,153,204), and (51,255,0) are all valid color cube colors. Anything slightly off [e.g., (53,102,51) or (105,251,3)] is not browser-safe and will behave unpredictably on low-end systems. Furthermore, if you're specifying in percentages, use only RGB values of 0%, 20%, 40%, 60%, 80%, and 100%.

660000	660033	660066	660099	6600CC	6600FF

The Golden Rule of File Size Reduction

Always start with the best image possible. Then reduce the size, colors, and quality of the image to below acceptable quality, then Undo. Reduce and Undo again and again, gradually raising the settings until you just break through to visual acceptability. Use this method any time you prepare indexed GIF images for the Web.

Interlaced patterns use alternating horizontal rows of single-color pixels. Using an interlaced pattern, you can easily make a nice pastel background, for example. I recommend checkerboards for backgrounds, rather than interlacing. After doing some experiments, I found checkerboards blend better, causing less interference with any type you might display on top. Play with these new color combinations and watch the possibilities open up.

Blended colors compress wonderfully. You'll find that a 20 (pixels high) by 1000 (pixels wide) background image compresses into just a few kilobytes for a quick download.

Anti-Aliasing

Many books explain anti-aliasing in detail; a good book on color theory will add immensely to this discussion. In a nutshell, anti-aliasing is the process of adding intermediate colors to smooth out the jagged edges seen in digital images [3.8].

Site designers should strive to anti-alias all but the simplest images. Anti-aliasing adds more colors, increasing the size of the palette. Open Photoshop or Painter and make a large solid color circle on a new layer. How many colors have you used? Chances are, over 100. The bigger the circle, the more colors you'll see. Because you want to have the smoothest edges possible, programs like Photoshop add extra colors to the edges to blend them into the background. Overlapping even simple shapes adds extra intermediate colors to the palette [3.9].

Anti-aliasing not only adds more colors, it makes images much less compressible as it adds more intermediate colors. To reduce file size, you must anti-alias with the fewest number of colors possible.

Some shapes do not need anti-aliasing. Rectilinear shapes are immune to anti-aliasing, because they have no jaggies to fix. A 45° degree line can be made either aliased or anti-aliased. An aliased 60° line can work, but it can also look jagged. Other angles or curves must usually be anti-aliased [3.10].

3.8 Anti-aliasing helps prevent the jaggies.

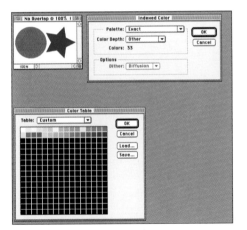

3.10 Some shapes need no anti-aliasing, others are borderline.

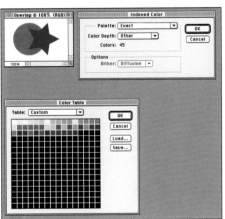

3.9 When shapes overlap, new colors are created.

Choosing GIF and JPEG Tools

Photoshop 4.0.1 does a great job producing good quality results at acceptable file sizes. But with Photoshop alone, you'll find yourself spending a lot of time going back and forth between modes, dialogs, files, and windows to determine file size and judge results. For sustained production of GIF and JPEG images, a plug-in with a live view of quality and size is essential. Two Photoshop plug-ins provide superior feedback during the process and can sometimes produce higher quality images, smaller file sizes, or both: BoxTop Software's PhotoGIF and ProJPEG (www.boxtopsoft.com/) and Digital Frontiers' HVS JPEG and HVS Color GIF (www.digfrontiers.com/). Compare the test results and file sizes below to get an idea of the subtle range of differences these tools provide.

The original image.

JPEG compression

Photoshop 4.0.1 – 17,141 bytes.

HVS JPEG 2.0 – 16,168 bytes.

BoxTop ProJPEG 2.1 – 21,577 bytes.

DeBabelizer 1.6.5 – 16,501 bytes

GIFF compression

Photoshop 4.0.1 – 26,945 bytes.

HVS ColorGIF 2.0 – 39,539 bytes. Looks best, but biggest file. Settings allow for smaller, less "compensated" files, too.

BoxTop PhotoGIF 2.1 – 33,546 bytes. Better shading than Photoshop, but a larger file.

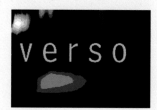

DeBabelizer 1.6.5 — 28,234 bytes. Of all these tools, only Debabelizer has not shifted the colors from their original values during reduction/compression.

42

Avoiding anti-aliasing is especially helpful if you have a patterned background, but in many cases reducing the noise or contrast of the background image works just as well.

Background Correction

A special case of anti-aliasing occurs when you use a foreground image over a given background in HTML. As you'll see later in this chapter, GIF images have only one color you can designate as transparent, so you must predetermine these transition colors. This means the images are anti-aliased into place. If you change the designated background color of an anti-aliased image, you'll get a halo around it. Keep everything on layers in Photoshop, so if a background changes, you can quickly make a new image and avoid halos. Take the background into consideration every time you make an image and anti-alias it properly for that particular background [3.12].

Background correction is different for simple and complicated backgrounds. With simple backgrounds using solid or nearly solid colors, make sure the edges blend into the background color. This works only for star fields and other almost-solid patterns.

Complicated backgrounds with large color transitions are another matter. To prevent halos, you must have either perfect registration between foreground and background (*see "Offsets and Alignment" in Chapter 4*) or have no anti-aliasing [3.11].

Keep It Simple

Good page design shouldn't rely on complex backgrounds – get rid of complicated backgrounds, and you solve the halo problem.

File Sizes on the Macintosh

To find out how big your file really is on the Macintosh, select the file in the Finder, use the Get Info command, and look for the number in parentheses. This is the file size as it will be on your server. On Windows, the file size shown in the File Manager is the same as the size you'll see on the server. Note that this applies only for files with no preview icon or other Macintosh-specific resources attached to them.

3.11 Halos. One of the Seven Deadly Sins of the Web.

3.12 Anti-aliasing against complicated backgrounds requires perfect registration, currently impossible across browsers.

The GIF Format

GIF (with a hard g) is the acronym for Graphics Interchange Format, the ubiquitous image format of the Web. GIF's LZW data compression technology is owned and licensed by Unisys Corporation. GIF handles indexed images of up to 8 bits (256 colors). A little known fact is that you can have higher-bit GIFs, but current browsers do not support them. As I write this second edition, I am disappointed to see that we are still using GIFs, when other, better formats exist. Unfortunately, GIF remains the dominant format, so we must work with it.

GIF Compression

The GIF format uses a compression algorithm called *Lempel-Ziv-Welch*, or LZW. This compression scheme is lossless, which means the resulting decompressed image looks exactly the same as the original. The average compression ratio for GIF images is 4:1. In general, use GIF compression for anything that isn't photographic or highly shaded. I use it for type, line art, and even small photographs.

The LZW scheme uses pattern-recognition techniques to achieve *run-length encoding*. The essence of the algorithm is to replace horizontal runs of same-colored pixels with a number indicating how long the sequence is [**3.13 A-D**]. Identical horizontal lines compress from line to line for even more savings. Study the images and file sizes to get a feel for how GIF compression works [**3.14 A1–H2**].

The compression scheme is quite powerful and can go beyond simple run-length encoding to reduce the file size of complex images. A good implementation of the algorithm looks for repeated patterns of pixels as it creates the image file. It builds a table of the patterns found as it processes the file and replaces each repeated sequence with an index entry that refers to the original pixel sequence, now stored in the table.

In particular, this means any horizontal regularity will be compressed, even if it occurs on separate lines in the image. An exact circle stores in almost the same amount of space as its top half only, because the runs are identical on top and bottom halves. It

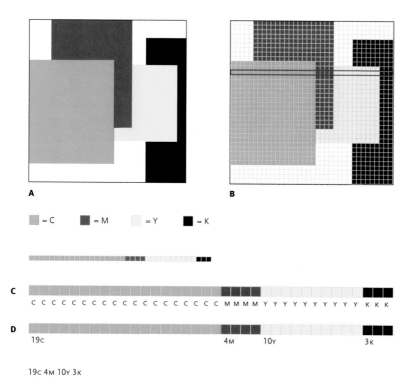

A
B

= C   = M   = Y   = K

C
C C C C C C C C C C C C C C C C C C C M M M M Y Y Y Y Y Y Y Y Y Y K K K

D
19C   4M   10Y   3K

19C 4M 10Y 3K

3.13 A-D The original image (A) is divided into scan lines (B) and the pixel patterns analyzed. Any repeating pattern (C) is compressed by reducing it to a single unit and noting how many times it occurs in the line (D).

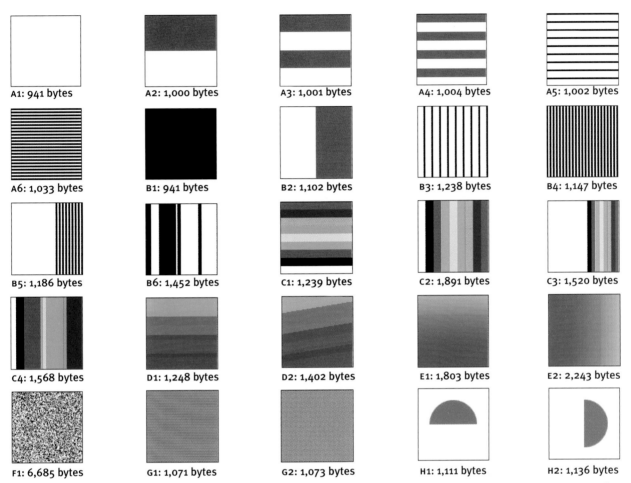

3.14 A1-H2 All images are 8-bit, 90 x 90 pixels (8,100 bytes uncompressed). Longer horizontal runs result in better compression. Note LZW's ability to recognize patterns.

doesn't have to be just a run of same-colored pixels; any sequence of colors that repeats will be compressed by LZW.

LZW compresses A5 and B3 down to almost the same size, for completely different reasons. Different implementations use slightly different approaches, but here is the basic idea. In A5, there are two primary entries in the table: one for the black line and one for the white line. These patterns are then called alternately down the page: 2 black lines, 8 white lines, 2 black, 8

white, and so on. In B3, there is only one line to store. It has all the alternating black-and-white sequences for the entire line. This single line is then repeated 92 times by reference, not by actual pixel values. Similarly, the two full blends (E1, E2) compress to almost the same size for the same reasons as the two images explained above. Though the details are missing, you can look at the images in this illustration to determine more or less how LZW pattern recognition works.

45

Designer's Tool Kit

Photoshop plug-ins, filters, GIF and JPEG tools, and other production software used at Studio Verso:

Netscape all versions http://www.netscape.com/	Quality assurance testing
Internet Explorer all versions http://www.microsoft.com/ie/	Quality assurance testing
Eudora Pro 3.1 http://www.eudora.com/	Client communication
DeBabelizer 1.6.5 http://www.equilibrium.com/	Raster image manipulation
Photoshop 4.0.1 http://www.adobe.com/	Raster image creation/manipulation
ScreenReady 1.0 http://www.adobe.com/	Batch image rasterization
Illustrator 6.0 http://www.adobe.com/	Vector image creation/manipulation
Freehand 7.0 http://www.macromedia.com/	Vector image creation/manipulation
Acrobat 3.0 http://www.adobe.com/	Formatted document portability
Excel 5.0 http://www.microsoft.com/	Quick and dirty large table creation
PageMaker 6.5 http://www.adobe.com/	Layout
Quark XPress 3.1 http://www.quark.com/	Layout, typography
BBEdit 4.5 http://www.bbedit.com/	HTML creation, editing, scripting, heavy text work
Word 6.0 http://www.microsoft.com/	Text content development
BoxTop Photogif 2.0 http://www.boxtopsoft.com/Photogif/	GIF export plug-in for Photoshop

When making GIF images, any recognizable regular feature will be compressed. Increasing the lengths of solid color runs will help make your files compressible.

Always end your gif file names with the suffix ".gif" as in "sparky.gif".

GIF89a

GIF89a builds on the original (GIF87a) format with a few additional features, like transparency. Photoshop's GIF-making process initially had numerous problems. To remedy the situation for Photoshop 3.0.5 or below, Adobe released the GIF89a Export plug-in [3.15]. Photoshop 3.x users will find this plug-in at www.adobe.com. Photoshop 4.0, Fractal Painter, Paintshop Pro, and DeBabelizer all save images in the GIF format correctly.

Interlacing

Normally, GIFs store pixels from the top of the image to the bottom. An interlaced image stores pixels out of linear order. *Interlaced images* arrive at your browser in evenly spaced blocks. Once the first block downloads, the browser repeats the data from that initial block, delivering a rough version of the final image so surfers get a quicker preview of the image. Subsequent blocks then complete the image in three more passes. This is a good example of a standard designed specifically for online transmission.

To interlace an image, check the Interlaced checkbox on the software that does your GIF compression. I hardly ever do this, because it adds slightly to the size of the file. I only do it for large images that people don't need to see completely before moving on. I never do it for text GIFS, because people can't read the text until the GIF finishes downloading.

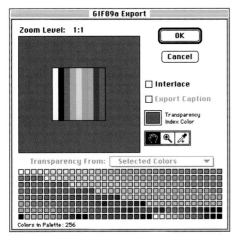

3.15 The GIF89a Export filter makes GIFS reliably.

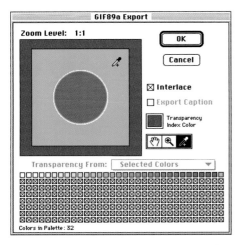

3.16 Transparency is essentially a chroma-key operation.

Designer's Tool Kit (continued)

BoxTop ProJPEG 2.0   JPEG export plug-in for Photoshop
http://www.boxtopsoft.com/Projpeg/index.html/

HVS JPEG 2.0   JPEG export plug-in for Photoshop
http://www.digfrontiers.com/

HVS Color GIF 2.0.6   GIF export plug-in for Photoshop
http://www.digfrontiers.com/

DitherBox 1.0   dither-pattern generator
http://www.ditherbox.com/

Flash 2.0   Splash animations, vector graphics
http://www.macromedia.com/

GifBuilder 0.4 (version 0.5 is buggy)   Animated GIF assembly
http://iawww.epfl.ch/Staff/Yves.Piguet/clip2gif-home/GifBuilder.html/

ImageMapper 2.5   Image map creation
http://www.cis.ohio-state.edu/~sabatino/imlaunch.html/

Fetch 3.0.3   File transfers via FTP
http://www.dartmouth.edu/pages/softdev/fetch.html/

Internet Config 1.3   Global Internet preferences setting
http://www.stairways.com/ic/

SmallScreen 1.2   Different screen/monitor checking
ftp://ftp.amug.org/pub/amug/bbs-in-a-box/files/prog/s/small-screen-1.3.sit.hqx

ScreenRuler 2.0.4   Screen measuring
http://www.infinet.com/~microfox/

Flash-It 3.0.2   Screen capture utility
ftp://ftp.amug.org/pub/mirrors/info-mac/gst/grf/flash-it-302.hqx

Gamma 2.0   Monitor calibration utility
packaged with Photoshop

Adobe Type Manager Deluxe 4.0 Font management and enhancement
http://www.adobe.com/

Adobe Type Reunion Deluxe 2.0 Font management and enhancement
http://www.adobe.com/

3.17 Animated GIFs are easy to make and fun to use.

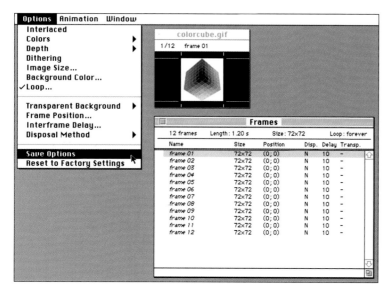

3.18 Making animated GIFs is easy with Yves Piguet's GIFBuilder 0.4. Get the new 0.5 version on the Web.

Transparency

In GIF89a images, one color can be designated as transparent; a browser that supports GIF89a will make all pixels of that particular color in the image transparent, allowing the background to show through. This is a *chroma-key operation;* that is, you must choose a single color in your image that will become transparent. That single color value will be replaced everywhere it occurs. Any pixels that are very close to this color – even indistinguishably close – will not become transparent [**3.16**].

Properly anti-aliased images with transparency are the basic building blocks of a third-generation site. They let designers visually break the bounds of rectangular images.

Animation

The GIF format includes the capability to embed multiple GIF images into a single file for animation. Animated GIFs are easy to make using many tools *(see "Designer's Tool Kit" in this chapter).* They even have different display options – for either continuous animation or a slide-show effect [**3.17**].

All animation programs specify which file types they'll accept. These programs change frequently, so I won't catalog them here.

Animated GIFs can delay between individual frames in 1/100 second increments, as well as finite and infinite looping. Once the image file downloads into the client's memory, it will continue to run, even if the connection gets interrupted or closed. You can use transparency in your images and specify how each image behaves as the next one loads [**3.18**].

Animated GIFs can (and should) also be optimized. Optimizing removes redundant pixels from one frame to the next. It isn't perfect, but for most animated GIFs it's worth

48

doing. Most animated GIF programs allow you to optimize your images.

Note that Internet Explorer will not begin playing GIF animations until the entire file has downloaded. While this assures accurate timing, it means the first frame of your GIF sequences should make sense without immediate animation. A fade-in from black is not a good idea.

You can make a poor-man's video by converting QuickTime movies to GIF animations using GIFBuilder or Smart Dubbing on the Macintosh.

Reducing File Size

Compression is the key to reducing file size and thus, download time. A common misconception is that you should reduce the number of colors to reduce the file size. While this often works, it is not a cause-and-effect relationship. Smaller file size is a matter of reducing an image to the fewest number of colors necessary while making it as compressible as possible.

Reducing the Palette

In general, palettes themselves aren't very big (the biggest palette is only 800 bytes – less than 1K), so reducing the size of the actual palette doesn't have much effect. Reducing the number of colors usually increases the compressibility of the image by lengthening the runs of same-color pixels.

When working with compressed images, don't think in terms of three dimensions (x by y by z). Think in

Adobe Photoshop Liabilities

Adobe Photoshop is an indispensable program for making images on the Web. But for web designers, it's less than ideal. Let me show you a problem. If you make a circle in which the most prominent color is a certain red (say, 204, 552, 153) and you reduce the colors using an adaptive color palette, Photoshop returns a palette in which that same color, which should be unchanged, has shifted to a similar looking, but different, shade of red (in this case, 201, 51, 19). This occurs because Photoshop reduces colors from a 24-bit (8 x 8 x 8) color space to a 15-bit (5 x 5 x 5) color space before executing its median cut algorithm to find the best palette. After the reduction, the resulting 15-bit palette gets a few extra bits tacked on to show the final palette colors as RGB. Those extra bits cause the color shift you detect, and the color shift causes a dithered area when displayed on a browser with only 256 colors.

The only colors not affected are the eight at the corners of the color cube. Every other color will experience some shift after adaptive color reduction in Photoshop. If you are in a pinch, you can open the color table and type in the real values. While this works, it's tedious and no one should have to do it. For now, I use DeBabelizer to do my final color reductions, because DeBabelizer does not shift colors.

Finally, Photoshop doesn't let the user see the color palette and the histogram while viewing the image.

Note the slight color shift in this color-cube color after adaptive-palette reduction in Photoshop.

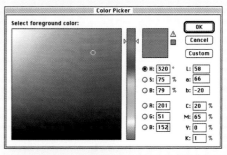

8-Bit Images

Many people use 8-bit images on their web sites. I've never had to use a full 8-bit (256-color) image on any site I've created. Most of my images fall in the 15-35 color range, with 35 being quite a few colors. Even without dithering, you'd be surprised how small a palette you need.

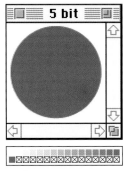 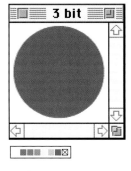

731 bytes   531 bytes

3.19 Reducing colors helps increase the lengths of the runs, making the compressed image even more compressible.

3.20 Photoshop makes extra colors for good anti-aliasing.

3.21 Photoshop builds a histogram behind the scenes to help with adaptive-palette reduction. This histogram corresponds to figure 3.20 (not to scale).

terms of the compression scheme and what makes an image compressible.

When does reducing the number of colors help make a GIF image more compressible? As it turns out, most of the time. The average image you want to put on a web page has some anti-aliasing on it, and that's where reducing colors can help. Because anti-aliasing introduces too many subtle color shades, reducing them will form many horizontal runs of more than one pixel [3.19].

Adaptive Color Palettes

Although you can reduce colors several different ways, I normally use an adaptive color palette to let the computer help me reconstruct the image using fewer colors. Remember the circle with lots of colors? Reducing colors will make it more compressible. To understand exactly how the color-reduction process takes place, start with a normally anti-aliased image.

When you do color reduction using an adaptive color palette, Photoshop goes through an elaborate scheme to preserve the colors in your image. Behind the scenes, Photoshop builds a *histogram* of all the colors in the image, rated by popularity. In practice, simple images [3.20] reduce well because Photoshop's *median cut* algorithm searches for areas of different color and does its best to preserve them (at the expense of intermediate colors). The histogram [3.21] helps the program determine how much weight to give certain colors in the resulting palette.

DeBabelizer

Equilibrium Software in Sausalito produces DeBabelizer, the Swiss Army Knife of the Web, offering amazing capabilities in opening and transforming graphics files.

DeBabelizer is much better than Photoshop at creating a common palette for several images, reducing colors, and working directly with palettes in general. It also has a very powerful scripting feature that lets you perform pre-scripted actions with a single command. Their web site has several free scripts for making web graphics (www.equilibrium.com).

DeBabelizer has been a necessary arrow in the web designer's quiver, but its complicated and obscure user interface has made it a challenging application for many designers. Fortunately, Equilibrium Technologies introduced a vastly improved interface with DeBabelizer Pro for Windows 95 and NT. A new version of DeBabelizer Toolbox for the Mac, scheduled to be available by the end of 1998, sports a new interface that promises to silence the complaints of those designers who found the previous interface hard to master.

DeBabelizer makes up for Photoshop liabilities by doing adaptive color reduction correctly. One of my favorite programs, DeBabelizer puts real power in the hands of all designers. I strongly recommend you get DeBabelizer and see how much easier it is to reduce colors and manipulate images.

Paul Vachier offers an online service to run DeBabelizer scripts (if you don't own the program) at www.transmitmedia.com/debabit/.

This invisible histogram is not the RGB histogram you find in the "Image" menu. It's a special color-popularity histogram Photoshop uses to help make an adaptive palette. While the adaptive palette machinery is quite complex, I want to show how you can influence the histogram to get a different palette than you get simply by asking for a reduced-color image.

How to Influence a Histogram

When the adaptive color palette method eliminates an important or favorite color, I don't have to increase colors. Instead, I can influence the process and make the histogram provide a better palette.

I will demonstrate this process using an image that dramatizes the situation. As an example, I'll show how to prepare a small-size photo, which I hope will turn out to be a smaller file than I can get with JPEG. I start with an RGB image and reduce it to 32 colors [**3.22 A, B**].

After indexing with an adaptive color palette, Sabine's lips have lost their color. A quick look at the palette shows

A

B

3.22 A, B The original picture in RGB color (A), and after indexing to 32 colors (B).

A

B

3.23 A, B Selecting an area of the picture (A) influences the histogram. The resulting image has been influenced by the red pixels (B).

A

B

3.24 A, B By selecting more areas (A), you have more control over the colors that make it into the final palette (B).

too many dark values for reproducing her hair and too many light values for the background. The skin tones show banding and the image looks flat. I can try again with more colors, or I can try to influence the histogram.

This time I want the red pixels, which aren't very numerous, to have a place in the final palette. In Photoshop, it is easy to influence the histogram. It's a little-known secret, but Photoshop uses the current selection at the time of reducing the palette as the area from which to build the histogram. Reducing colors with no selection builds a histogram for the entire image. If I choose areas of relative importance, I can effectively block outside areas from inclusion in the histogram, skewing the resulting palette toward the colors I want. I draw a rectangle around Sabine's lips and index again [3.23 A, B].

Now the lips look great, but her forehead looks banded. After undoing, I Shift-select another area and try to bring back some of the tones in her forehead [3.24 A, B].

After a few tries, I find a combination that results in the optimum 5-bit palette for this image. It's a matter of taking colors from one area to put into another, but it doesn't take too much time and the results can be worth it *(see "Eyeballing the Palette" later in this chapter)*.

DeBabelizer's methods for reducing colors are much more powerful. Past versions of DeBabelizer sported an interface that some designers found challenging, but the new interfaces are much better. The upside is that if you have 1,000 images to reduce, DeBabelizer will make them in minutes after you figure out how to do it once. For large-scale web sites, DeBabelizer's scripting functionality is a life saver. (*See Appendix 3, "Image Optimization for the Web" and Chapter 5: "Rendering Type" for details of two powerful automated production systems based on DeBabelizer.*)

As you can see, there are trade-offs. I might have added a few more colors, settling on a 34-color image, but then I would have had a six-bit palette and the file size would go up more than necessary on a small picture like this. It comes out to 8k, which is pretty good for a GIF. The same quality JPEG is 9k. (This example dramatizes the general approach to getting the palette you want for a GIF; it does not imply that you should go to all this trouble to shave 1k off one file.)

Eyeballing the Palette

It's important to get used to looking at palettes, because if you see two colors that are very similar to each other, you're not done reducing yet.

No matter which program you use, the program can't determine which areas of your image are important. Only you can look at the palette and decide if it's the right one. A good rule is that prominent main colors should have three or four intermediate transition colors between them.

Now I want to do a more practical experiment, showing how to dial in a palette for the absolute minimum number of colors necessary for the Web. I start with an RGB image and reduce it to 64 colors [**3.25 A**]. Because this is more than enough colors, I take

Why Web Designers Should Upgrade to Photoshop 4.0.1

Adobe Systems added a host of new features when it upgraded Photoshop to version 4. Here are a few of the things in the new version web designers will really appreciate.

1. Version 4 creates a new layer each time you do anything so you won't mess up art work or superimpose things by accident. This means you have to keep track of all the layers and name them as soon as possible, or you may wind up with a very big file. The key is to keep merging layers down to prevent layer overflow.

2. Version 4.0 supports new Web formats, including Progressive JPEG and PNG, plus PDF.

3. You can drag and drop between Netscape and Photoshop (while you could do this in 3.0, too, I mention it because we do it so often).

4. Use the new "Artistic" filter to achieve different kinds of painterly effects. There's also a new "Smart Blur" filter. Take advantage of some of the new features in "Texture" and "Stylize."

5. The new "Actions" feature lets you record anything you do, so you can repeat sequences of steps automatically – sizes, color depth, rotation, blur, feathering.

6. The new Navigator tool lets a web designer zoom smoothly all the way down to the pixel level, letting the designer see where she is at any time.

7. The new version lets you scale with numeric data, simply by punching in numbers.

8. The new version supports color correction.

9. In earlier versions of Photoshop, "Undo" actually caused the loss of some pixels. Now, you can do everything in *Adjustment Layer* and never damage the original.

10. Grids and guides let you align elements precisely, a big help when preparing to cut up a prototype and implement it in HTML.

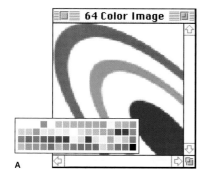

A

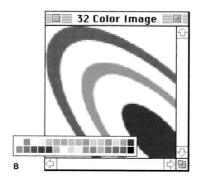

B

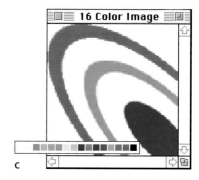

C

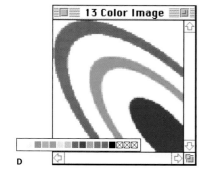

D

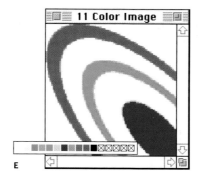

E

3.25 A-E For the Web, the 64-color image and the 32-color image look alike. The 16- and 13-color images are still acceptable, while the 11-color image shows problems.

it down to 32 and 16 colors **[B, C]**. The image is still acceptable. (For the purposes of this demonstration, I'm going from more colors to fewer, the opposite of the way I normally work.)

The 16-color image looks fine and gives me reason to believe I can do even better. I re-index the original to thirteen and eleven colors **[D, E]**.

Looking at the palettes for 13 and 11 colors, I can't help but wonder if I can squeeze this image to 11 colors with better color distribution. I go back to the RGB image and begin selecting areas to influence the histogram. I choose the top area as a baseline, to try to get more blues, but the red still dominates, so I include the bottom area to boost the green. Finally, selecting the middle area turned a pink to a light blue, and I had the palette I

was looking for **[3.26 A, B]**. Without showing all these intermediate experiments, the final selection gave me a well balanced palette in just three tries. The third image shows that 9 colors plus white is the theoretical limit for this image, as anything less shows unsightly artifacts of aliasing **[C]**.

The Mac version of Photoshop adds the black, which isn't necessary. I can either strip it in DeBabelizer or forget about it. Because the palette for this image contains 16 colors, the black entry isn't taking up any extra room. The resulting file is 2197 bytes.

This shows you can get away with only two intermediate colors if you choose them well. Influencing histograms and eyeballing palettes usually results in the smallest file for optimum download times. This experiment does

54

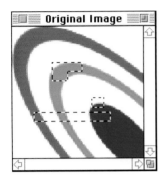
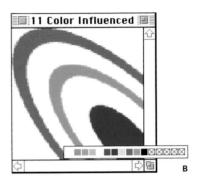
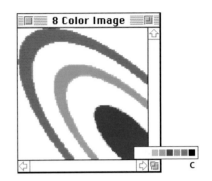

About Caching

3.26 **A-C** The area select-ed (A) results in a well-balanced minimum pal-ette of 11 colors (B) for a final size of 2,197 bytes. An 8-color palette (C) is simply not sufficient.

Your browser program keeps web pages and images in memory, so you don't have to wait to see things you've already downloaded. Your browser has two kinds of caches: a *memory cache* and a *disk cache*. The memory cache keeps all the images in a page in memory. Scrolling is fast because the whole page is in memory. It is the memory cache that gets overloaded by image inflation.

The disk cache keeps previously visited pages on disk, so you don't have to wait when you hit the Back button. For surfers, this is good. For developers, this is a problem, because if you update your images and redisplay the page, you want it to read the new description of the image, not the older, cached version. Fortunately, most browsers come with a Check Documents preference setting to update images a) Every Time, or b) Once Per Session. Checking a document means to compare the date on the file with the date stored in the cache; if the file date is newer, it reads the image again. If the date is the same or older, it keeps the cached version as is.

Surfers should use "Once Per Session" to avoid frequent checking with sites that aren't likely to change that often. In this case, a cache size of 5-10 megabytes is fine. Developers must use the Every Time option to make sure their pages change as they make updates to local images. If your pages aren't chang-ing, and they should, check this option and restart your browser. Unfortunately, developers who use this option must reduce the size of their disk cache to 2 megabytes to avoid sluggish performance, as the entire cache is checked each time you reload a page.

not mean that you can use two intermediate colors for every image. Using a vector technology like Flash (*see Chapter 12, "Transitional Strategies"*) for line art, combined with anti-aliasing on the client, will reduce this image to under 100 bytes. *(See Appendix 3, "Image Optimization for the Web," for a semi-automated approach to getting a good palette.)*

The JPEG Format

JPEG (the common name for the raster image format defined by the Joint Photographic Experts Group) is the most common way to compress photographic and rendered images. Because of the overhead involved, it doesn't work well for small images or line art.

To reduce file size, JPEG separates the brightness information from the color hues. It essentially keeps a good copy of the black-and-white version of an image, to which your eyes are sensitive, and compresses most of the subtle color differences your eye can't distinguish. Your computer then puts it back together after re-rendering the colors from the shorthand notation in the file. Rather than doing it line by line, as GIF does, JPEG breaks the image into zones.

JPEG Compression

JPEG is a lossy process – information is always lost in the compression. Once compressed with JPEG, even using the

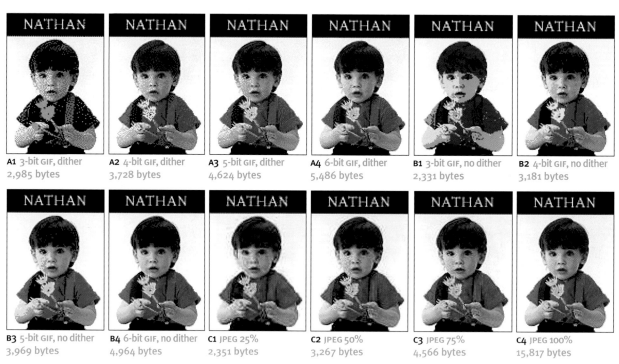

A1 3-bit GIF, dither
2,985 bytes

A2 4-bit GIF, dither
3,728 bytes

A3 5-bit GIF, dither
4,624 bytes

A4 6-bit GIF, dither
5,486 bytes

B1 3-bit GIF, no dither
2,331 bytes

B2 4-bit GIF, no dither
3,181 bytes

B3 5-bit GIF, no dither
3,969 bytes

B4 6-bit GIF, no dither
4,964 bytes

C1 JPEG 25%
2,351 bytes

C2 JPEG 50%
3,267 bytes

C3 JPEG 75%
4,566 bytes

C4 JPEG 100%
15,817 bytes

3.27 A-F Images A-C are 92 × 132 pixels; D-F (facing page) are 166 × 238. JPEG files have several kilobytes of extra information, called *overhead*, that make them unsuitable for small pictures.

D1 3-bit GIF, dither, 7,446 bytes

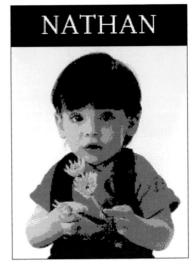

E1 3-bit GIF, no dither, 5,097 bytes

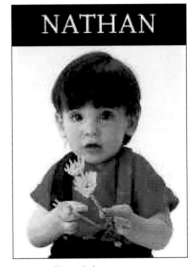

F1 JPEG 25%, 4,264 bytes

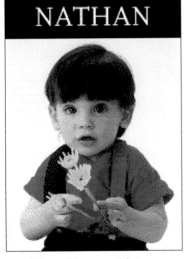

D2 5-bit GIF, dither, 11,498 bytes

E2 5-bit GIF, no dither, 9,692 bytes

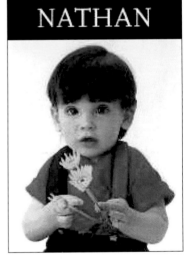

F2 JPEG 50%, 6,107 bytes

highest quality settings, the image will not be identical to the original RGB version. It might look the same, because your eyes can't tell the difference, but the file is smaller. At higher compression ratios (lower quality settings), the image is noticeably different, whereas high quality JPEGS can be substitutes for the original. Use low-quality JPEGS on the Web,

because they compress so well and look fine.

Compression ratios for JPEG range typically from 10:1 to 100:1, depending on the quality setting. The greater the compression, the smaller (and lossier) the file will be. In general, sharper images make larger files. Blurry pictures make smaller files and download quickly. Because of the overhead in the JPEG format, GIFs are a better choice for small pictures. I usually don't go to JPEG until my images are larger than 100 x 100 pixels [**3.27 A-F**]. When using JPEGs, your object isn't to reduce colors, it's to reduce file size. That's what the quality settings are for. Different software gives you different choices. All of the tools we use now have live previews of the actual image quality (*see the "Designer's Tool Kit" sidebar in this chapter*). Like Photoshop, many programs analyze each photograph and choose one of several methods before reducing, so you don't have to worry about the details. Set the quality level, look at the result, and decide to keep it or try again.

Don't reduce colors or pre-dither before making JPEGs!

Perform a few experiments on your images to see what makes them compress better. Reducing the color palette alone usually won't help make the image more compressible. Unsharp Mask sharpens the image and makes the resulting JPEG file bigger; Gaussian blur makes it smaller. Blurring JPEGs is equivalent to reducing colors in GIFs.

Always start with the lowest quality JPEG setting you can, throwing away the most information and reducing file size as much as possible. If your program says: Worst, Okay, and Best, choose the Worst option. You'll be surprised at how acceptable low-quality JPEGs are.

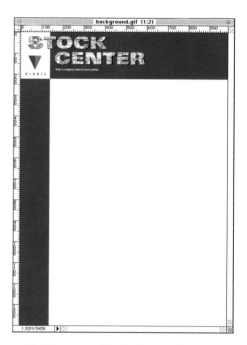

3.28 A large non-tiling background is tempting to third-generation designers.

Progressive Display

Like the interlaced GIF format, progressive JPEGs decode in successive passes, working in a grid to continually refine the quality of the image. Progressive JPEGs take more client-side computing power to decode. Various programs now create progressive JPEGs. As with interlaced GIFs, progressive JPEG files are usually slightly larger than non-progressives. All major browsers can now see progressive JPEGs. (*See Chapter 13, "Looking Forward," for more on progressive image formats.*)

Image Inflation

You have worked to get your file sizes as small as possible. You now want a large background image that compresses well and makes your page look distinctive [**3.28**].

You reduce the colors in this huge GIF image, compressing it to just 12K, so it loads like greased lightning. On your machine, it works beautifully. Yet certain visitors complain that your page causes their browser either to crash or to load incredibly slowly! What's happening? *You've got image inflation problems.*

Your browser doesn't display GIF images. In fact, you've never seen a GIF image. Think of GIF as the freeze-dried state of an image, when it's packed up for shipping as small as it can be. When you see a web page, your browser downloads the GIFs and decodes them, reconstituting them to full strength (x by y by z) to display on

your screen. The decoded version can take up a lot of memory, much more than the GIF itself. How much memory? The answer: it depends on the user's system.

GIF images always inflate to the size of the image (in x and y) times 8 bits (1 byte) or more. (With Netscape on Macintosh, GIFs inflate to 8 bits, but PC GIFs inflate to the color depth of the client.) Thus, if you have a 500 x 500-pixel image that contains only 2 bits of color, it will usually inflate to 500 x 500 x 8-bit = 244 kbytes, even if it compresses down to only 10K [**3.29**].

JPEG images are worse. They always inflate to fill the receiving system's color depth. If you can see millions of colors and you download that same 500 x 500 x 2-bit file, it will inflate to

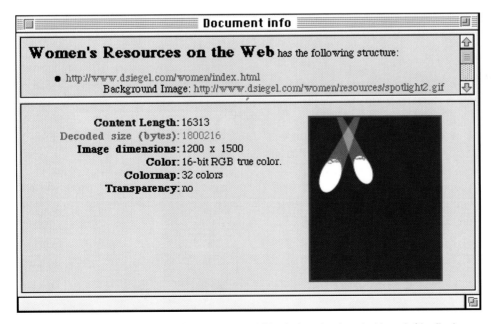

3.29 Compare the content length (the compressed file size) to the decoded length (the final inflated size.)

500 x 500 x 24-bit = 750 kbytes. Images that are 1200 x 1600 x 2-bits can compress to 18K, yet inflate to over two megabytes! This is 2 megabytes of main memory, which can cause a system with not much memory to crash. Many browsers run in 4-12 megabytes of RAM, so an image that accounts for two megabytes by itself can cause problems.

There is a solution, but it's painful. The solution is to completely avoid large-area images, no matter how small they compress. Stay calm. The people who build browsers will find a way out of this. There are two possibilities. First, the browser makers can try to control GIF inflation, which is possible, but tricky. Second, the real solution is to get rid of this two-layer model and go to z-axis layering (*see Chapter 13, "Looking Forward"*).

A good rule is to keep the total image area on a page smaller than about 600 x 800 pixels, unless you know your surfers have plenty of RAM.

Note: In the year since the first edition of this book was released, I have noticed many good designers using huge background images to get a desired effect. It seems few designers understand how image inflation can cause problems for low-end surfers. Many people who read the first edition of this book are still making sites with huge background images, causing low-powered systems to crash.

Summary

A good image comes in a small package. Always strive for the minimum number of colors absolutely necessary for your image, following the Real Golden Rule of file size reduction (*see Tip, opposite page*).

Page sizes tend to get smaller the more you work with images and try different strategies and approaches. Image inflation is a problem for the third-generation site designer. Future browsers and protocols should give us features that alleviate these issues, but for now, be wary of using large-area images, no matter how small they compress.

I'll go through several real examples of file size reduction, anti-aliasing, setting type, and making GIFS and JPEGS in Part II.

See Appendix 3 for more details on processing images using an automated script.

Number of Images vs. Image Size

In this chapter, I place great emphasis on making images as small as possible to reduce the time required to load them. Although this represents a good starting point, there is more to it than that.

Another way to lighten your page load is to achieve the desired effect with the fewest images possible. Reducing the number of server requests helps reduce the transaction overhead involved in serving a page. One page with many small images can take much longer to load than a page with fewer, larger ones.

The situation should improve. One improvement in a new version of the HTTP 1.1 server protocol is that multiple requests for images on a page are consolidated as one transaction. As the HTTP 1.1 protocol becomes more widely deployed on servers and in browsers, designers will be able to consider the total bandwidth load of the page, rather than just the number of images.

The Real Golden Rule of File Size Reduction

Reduce the size and complexity of your GIF images, then lengthen the runs, hand edit, and influence the histogram if necessary before adding more colors.

CHAPTER 4

Laying Out Pages

The Revo Shapes® Collection offers the superior visual performance of Revo's renowned Classic™ lens technology in an exclusive group of frame designs that are both stylistically ambitious and technologically advanced. The lenses, made of optical-quality glass, are polished to the standards of fine cameras and telescopes.

These lenses, combined with precisely stacked layers of thin film coatings, block potentially harmful ultraviolet light—UVA, UVB, UVC—and control infrared and shortwave blue light, while actually enhancing vision. This means you'll see better in any kind of light, be it full sun, flat light, fog or haze.

Did you know... *that the multi-layer coatings of Revo's Classic lens technology are actually clear? Their iridescent appearance is caused by the way they reflect light. You can actually see this if you cup your hand over the lens and look at it.*

Among the advanced features that set our Shapes frames apart are optical spring hinges, silicone nosepads, carefully engineered bridges and pantoscopic angles, lustrous antique finishes, subtle cloisonné accents, engraved detailing and custom logos. Their fit is uniquely comfortable and luxurious. Shapes represents a combination of frame and lens attributes that no other sunglass offers. Style by style, they give the discriminating owner something as rewarding to look at as through.

4.1 Look carefully at how third-generation type designers use vertical white space to convey meaning.

HERE IN THE TRENCHES of the browser wars, no one is safe. Designers must improvise to provide the basic tools, supplies, and even the duct tape they need to build their sites. Although the strategy is the same – good typography doesn't evolve as quickly as the Web does – the tools have changed since the first edition of this book came out. Now that the 2.0 browsers are mostly out of circulation, we can reassess the workarounds, hacks, and other tricks we use to make nice-looking pages.

The first edition of this book relied heavily on the single-pixel GIF trick, explained toward the end of this chapter. It was the only thing that provided reliable control of white space across browser versions and platforms. Although we still occasionally use that trick, I consider it a rather old bandage. It adds to the server load, confuses people surfing with images turned off, and it doesn't make editing HTML any easier. It is still in wide use around the Web, but now we have other hacks with fewer liabilities. When Cascading Style Sheets (css) are consistently well implemented in browsers (which may even happen within our lifetimes!), I hope we will throw away most of these hacks and begin, finally, to do things right. For now, use these tools (and those in later chapters) when appropriate, and tell your local Netscape or Microsoft representative that designers are tired of being used as human shields in the browser vendors' struggle for supremacy.

The browser companies make good typography more than a challenge. They continue to make it near impossible.

While I can show you today's work-arounds for achieving the desired result, I cannot guarantee that these methods will work on all versions of the two major browsers on three platforms. This chapter represents the best of my knowledge and research in the Fall of 1997. No technique is without compromises. Anyone who tells you he has all the answers is lying.

The Layout Problem

A web designer's central challenge is to have as much control as possible over the layout of elements on the page. In a program like Adobe Page-Maker, you place text and graphics where you want them. You balance visual elements with white space – the areas with no foreground elements – by grabbing elements and moving them. This is called *direct manipulation*. Though programs like NetObjects' Fusion imitate this paradigm, the underlying language – HTML – is fundamentally ill-suited for visual layout.

Using HTML does not give site designers a framework for direct two-dimensional manipulation. Instead, designing a web site is like working with Silly Putty. As soon as you hand it to someone, it snaps into some other configuration. The designer can't know the dimensions of the viewer's screen, the size or style of her fonts, the number of colors she has, or how fast her connection is. Designers must focus on the things they can influence and hope for better standards in the future.

Web design techniques are changing rapidly, as the changes to this book attest. Because the fundamental

standards of the Web keep mutating, no one can build visual design tools that are stable enough to be very useful. By the time we get a new tool, we have moved on to a new way of designing sites. For that reason, hand-coding remains state of the art, and the principles of this chapter will remain valid for some time to come.

Note: See also the new CSS Primer (Chapter 11) for a completely different approach to page layout using *Cascading Style Sheets*.

Typographic principles come first. In this second edition, I've put the discussion of vertical and horizontal white space first, followed by explanations of table tricks, single-pixel GIFs, and frames.

Controlling Vertical White Space

Good typography enforces a hierarchy of vertical white space throughout a document to convey meaning [4.1]. White space – the space between visual elements – is an integral part of the message. Magazines break paragraphs into groups with subheads; novels use successive paragraphs with breaks only at chapters or subchapters. In both instances, as in this book, the white space tells you where one section ends and another begins. On a third-generation site, systematic use of white space can vastly improve the presentation of text for easier reading and better comprehension.

The Non-Breaking Space

Now that the 2.0 browsers are gone, the non-breaking space has become a popular hack to induce white space – slightly less caustic than the old single-pixel GIF trick. You'll see it used throughout this chapter. Specify a non-breaking space using   (always add the semicolon at the end). This is a standard HTML character that was meant to go between name elements, like between "Sofia" and "Coppola," so the name won't break. It still serves this function, but more often, site designers use it to hold table cells open and to produce horizontal white space.

Note that   is relative to the size of the viewer's text. In this respect, it is often a better tool than the fixed single-pixel GIF, because most typographic measurements are relative, not absolute, and they certainly shouldn't depend on how many pixels per inch the viewer's monitor has.

4.2 Browsers without quality CSS implementations (including Netscape Navigator 4.0 and Internet Explorer 3.0) render <Hn> tags with too much space below. Most headers these days are made as GIF text.

Headings

The Framers of the Web imagined that people would simply use <H1> – <H6> tags to denote headings hierarchically. It was up to the browser to render headings appropriately and represent this logical hierarchy visually. Apart from the total lack of designer's control in this scenario, all major browsers render <Hn> elements (along with most other "orthodox" HTML) with too much space below – to say nothing of further typographic refinement. For example, trained typographers have always chosen specially made (usually lighter) fonts for headings. Times Roman set larger than 14 point is one of the footprints of an amateur typographer.

Third-generation designers often make headlines as GIF text [4.2]. It lets us choose a typeface that most people won't have on their system and integrate the letters into the overall theme or metaphor of the site. Headers are usually part of the branding and identity of the site (see Chapter 5, "Rendering Type").

Subheads

Subheads are any minor heading. I recommend two ways of achieving subheads: either make them bold with no blank line after them, or make them as GIF text and add a tiny amount of white space below them [4.3]. Because most people don't want to bother making subheads as GIFs (it's hard enough making all those headings!), the best solution is to use bold with no following vertical space. When CSS implementations stabilize, we'll be able to add a small amount of vertical white space for a good, clean look. The hallmarks of third-generation typography are subheads tied visually to their children, indents (rather than gratuitous blank lines) separating paragraphs, ample margins, and narrow column measures.

While there are provisions in HTML for up to six levels of subheads, I rarely use more than one. This book has two levels of subheads, which tie the subhead-sections into larger logical groups. On a web page, you might use this two-level strategy when instructing people in a particular procedure that you want to break down into finer and finer steps. But in general, you can usually go to another page before you need a second level of subhead.

Forcing Vertical Space

I've stopped using the structural `<P>` tag to produce a blank line. Now I always make sure to use `<BR>`. The `<P>` tag indicates a paragraph, and that's all it should do. Only use a `<P>` tag to denote a paragraph if you are marking up for a CSS-capable browser or if you don't care how the browser displays your text. In the future (I hope), a `<P>` will more often result in an indent than a blank line.

The most reliable means of forcing a line break is to use the presentational `<BR>` tag. The most reliable means of producing a single blank line is the string `<BR> <BR>`. You can get multiple blank lines with `<BR> <BR> <BR> <BR>`,

and so on. The non-breaking spaces comprise the "lines" that the `<BR>`s break – they produce no vertical space themselves.

Suppose you want to break out a list, a quote, or an image from the rest of the text. Rather than using bullets or frame borders, you may want to use vertical white space to make things more clear. In that case, use multiple blank lines, as described above. Use as many as you need to get the distinction necessary to set it off from its neighbors. Each level in the hierarchy should be visually distinct and consistent throughout an entire site [4.4].

4.3 Because of poor typographic support in most browsers, companies resort to making even subheadings as GIF text to get the control they need.

4.4 Third-generation typography makes sure each unit of vertical space is distinctive and functional.

4.5 A small collection of the Web's ugliest horizontal rules.

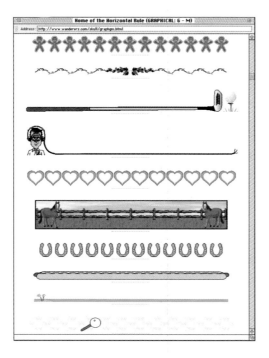

If you need to space down a bit, use several non-breaking spaces in a row, separated by `<BR>` tags. If you need finer control, either rethink the design, build an image to do the work, or resort to the single-pixel GIF trick (explained at the end of this chapter).

Careful vertical spacing is especially useful in the design of forms, which are too often just scattered white boxes with no grouping or hierarchy to help the user through the process (*see Chapter 8, "A Storefront"*).

One of the great things about hypertext is that major sections can be broken into separate pages of different size, rather than fixed-length sheets. I limit my column length to what I consider readable in about a minute. I put in hyperlinks to things that are not germane to the flow of my message. In a nonlinear world, I can lay out all the possibilities, but I also try to guide them through the center of the stream. If they want to visit the side streams, that's fine, but I try to bring them back to the main story. I use sections, subsections, and pages to take readers on a journey and guide them as they go.

Intra-Paragraph Vertical Space

Space between lines is called *leading*, because in the old days, when typographers set metal type by hand, they'd put a thin strip of lead between the lines to increase interline spacing.

Back in the old days (1995 and 1996), we used a cheap trick to get leading: we'd put a single-pixel GIF every few words and adjust it to create "poor man's" leading. That was such a ridiculous hack that only a few people bothered to do it. We've found other ways to get leading, but they're not worth doing. The Web just isn't ready for interline space yet. If you have a large GIF image with a few lines of text, feel free to add a bit of space between them to enhance the design. Until CSS implementations get better, designers will have to do without leading.

Banish Horizontal Rules!

Horizontal rules – lines across pages – are used as separators on millions of web pages [4.5]. Horizontal rules became a prevalent part of web culture because people wanted more white space in their pages. When they typed a string of <P> tags in a row, they didn't get more vertical space – the tags all collapsed into one single blank line. To get more space, they had to put *something* in between the <P> tags, so they typed <HR> and – lo! – they were given more space! Whenever they wanted more space, they added the <P><HR><P> triplet, and thus the Web became littered with horizontal rules. That's my take on it, anyway.

The people who programmed the first browsers didn't provide a way to indent paragraphs. They figured a blank line between paragraphs was probably the best choice, since people could be viewing the Web with character-based terminals. So they forced a blank line between paragraphs.

As separators, horizontal rules and blank lines are visual junk floating in cyberspace. They disrupt the reader's visual path down the page. Look at well-designed books; they don't have

horizontal rules. Well-designed sites don't either. Book designers sometimes use a delicate printer's mark, an ornament to separate sections of text, giving the reader a short pause without blocking the path onward. On the Web, we can use new pages instead.

Vertical white space, indents, and new pages are the proper tools of separation because they are part of the hierarchy of white space that gives the text more meaning.

Horizontal White Space

Horizontal white space can make or break the established visual hierarchy on a page. Using invisible table cells and characters, margins and indents can turn even the most poorly written propaganda into readable columns of poorly written propaganda [4.6].

Creating Margins

Web sites are different from traditional printed books in many ways, but not when it comes to presenting text. Nothing beats margins to help the reader

4.6 The hierarchy of horizontal white space: margins and indents.

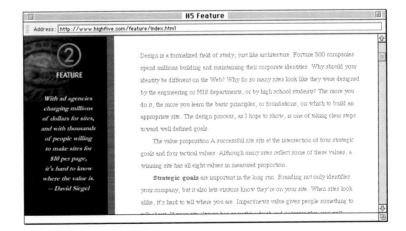

4.7 Using a table to make a fixed-width left margin.

4.8 Creating a left margin with HTML.

```
<TABLE>
  <TR>
    <!-- this cell establishes the margin -->
    <TD WIDTH="180"> </TD>
    <TD><!-- content goes in this cell --></TD>
  </TR>
</TABLE>
```

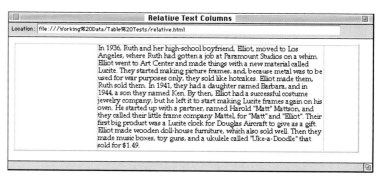

4.9 Relative text columns help guarantee a right margin. The proportions shown are 25%, 65%, and 10% of the overall page width. This preserves both margins under all circumstances but will lead to a narrow column if the window is made smaller.

have a pleasant reading experience. A margin separates the text from all the noise on screen, making it easy for the reader's eye to pick up the next line as it moves down the page. The broader the margin, the more the text column stands out. When the type goes all the way to the edge, it's easier for the eye to go back to the current line or skip ahead two lines.

If you read Chapter 12, you'll see why web designers will be pouring text into tables to create margins for quite some time. For that, you need the invisible-table trick. The idea behind the invisible-table trick is simple: use table code to get white space, but turn off the borders so no one knows you're using them.

To set a left margin, make a table with two columns. Leave the left cell empty, specify its width, and place your text in the second cell [4.7]. When the borders are turned off, the empty left cell acts as a margin. It's not a precise science, because tables weren't designed to be text containers for page layout. (*You'll find good examples of how wide to make margins in the example chapters in Part II of this book*).

The best way to set the width of the margin cell is to designate the cell width either in absolute numbers or using percentages. Then, simply toss a non-breaking space into the empty table cell to make sure it stays open [4.8].

An *absolute margin* will be the same size no matter how wide or skinny the viewer's browser window is. In many cases, it's best to use a

relative margin of between 10% and 20% of the window width. Another good rule is that the left margin should be *at least* one fifth the width of a column of text, and preferably one fourth. It depends on the assumptions you can make about your audience and their viewing conditions.

Centered text. I wouldn't normally center a column of text. I like to make sure I have a good relationship between a column of text and its left margin. Centering text is only for certain effects, usually used on short documents like invitations.

To set a right margin, you can't simply add a column to the right of the text. It won't matter at all if you have a column to the right of a fixed-size text column. There's no way to ensure a right margin unless you make your text column relative (percentage-based).

Relative-width text columns can work in certain situations, especially if you don't mind them being narrow. Narrow columns are easier to read than wide ones. The big problem occurs when people open their browser windows wide – you don't want a column of text that exceeds about 12 words (*see "Line Length" on the next page*). If you find yourself using a relative column width to guarantee a right margin, you might want to start with cell widths that are 25%, 65%, and 10% of the overall page width, respectively [4.9]. The tradeoff on right-hand margins is that if you make your text column relative, you'll see it get wider and narrower as the window is resized. This can be good up to a point, but it's also possible to go beyond the bounds of easy reading – another reason to leave tables behind as soon as we have a better way of setting text.

Line Length

Many people who use computers are accustomed to long lines of text that fill the page and make the reader feel like he's watching a tennis match. But good typography is easy on the reader, not a challenge. Long lines of text make it harder for the eye to get back to the left margin and pick up the next line. Ideally, each paragraph should have 10-12 words on a line for normal reading. Ideally, a typographer sets the line length (also called the *measure*) and sets the relationship of the leading to the line length. Longer lines usually have more leading.

On the Web, these things are beyond a designer's control. Because we don't know the web surfer's font size, we have no idea how many words are on a line.

Macintosh designers: make sure to look at your designs on Windows machines, as Windows font sizes are quite different.

Setting line length is a function of your audience's viewing conditions, which you can't know. Therefore, you can either set text with no margins, use relative-width columns, or you can guess what measure (in pixels) would be best for your viewers. If you have supporting fixed-width graphics (navigation bars, illustrations, callouts, and so on.), you may want to use a fixed-width text cell. I often use text cells that are 380 pixels wide. Anything over 450 pixels is too wide for easy reading, unless you know your audience uses high-resolution displays.

Relative text-column widths are probably best for text-only pages, though you must still guess what the proportions should be. After you take your best guess, test your pages on people in your target audience group and see what their systems do.

For a relative-width column of text, use a four-cell approach. One cell has an absolute measurement (the minimum), and the next three are relative [4.10 A-C]. This gives you a column of text that looks good under normal circumstances, compresses if the window is really narrow, yet won't extend the text too wide if the window is opened up. It takes a few more lines of HTML, but once you get it working you can use it over and over [4.11].

For fixed-width columns, eliminate the fourth empty table cell and specify a number for the width of your text column, which will have the same two table cells to its left. There are other ways to get effects like this – experiment and see what works best for your material (*see "Working with Tables" later in this chapter*).

Multiple Columns

Several sites use a multiple column approach to laying out text. It's not hard to see where they got the idea, but it can be hard to understand why they would try this on a web site. Because some people have small monitors and

A

4.10 A-C This four-column table uses one hard and one soft column to make a left margin with a relative-width text cell. When viewed normally (A), it keeps the given column width, but if made narrow, it will shrink the column appropriately (B), and if the window is opened wide (C), it won't follow the window edge. (*See Chapter 9 for a three-column alternative.*)

B

C

4.11 HTML for a four-column table.

```
<TABLE WIDTH=100% BORDER=1 CELLPADDING=0 CELLSPACING=0>
  <TR>
    <!-- ABSOLUTE BLANK CELL -->
    <TD WIDTH=60> </TD>
    <!-- RELATIVE BLANK CELL -->
    <TD WIDTH="10%"> </TD>
    <!-- BEGIN TEXT CELL -->
    <TD WIDTH="70%"><FONT SIZE="+1"
COLOR="#9999FF"><CENTER><B>Center this! </B>
</CENTER></FONT><BR>Your text here! </TD>
    <!-- ABSOLUTE BLANK CELL -->
    <TD WIDTH="10%"> </TD>
  </TR>
</TABLE>
```

73

4.12 Multiple column text works better on short subject material containing links (LEFT) than it does on longer text that needs scrolling (RIGHT).

big fonts, you can easily cause them to scroll back up to continue reading, and that's a misdemeanor, if not a felony. If your columns contain short-subject material, say, each with a link to more details, the two-column approach can give a newspaper look and feel to the page [4.12]. As long as people can zigzag across columns, this approach can work. I strongly recommend not using a vertical bar between columns (even if you're clever enough to figure out how to make one that stretches to accommodate the length of the text). Instead, use enough white space to make it hard for the reader's eye to accidentally jump across to the next column. This is called a *gutter*, and it serves simultaneously as a left and right margin.

Indents

Indents do not start paragraphs. Contrary to what you see sporadically in *The New York Times*, indents come *between* paragraphs. Since the first edition of this book came out, many people have decided to make web pages with both blank lines and indents before every paragraph. For this, they are in violation of the Geneva convention – cruel and unusual punishment of viewers.

Use three to five non-breaking spaces to make indents for any paragraph that has a paragraph right above it. Do not indent the first paragraph of a section or one with white space above it. I tend to use the smallest amount of space that is positively discernable and won't be skipped. Edward R. Tufte refers to this design principle as "the least effective difference." Typographers often add an *em-quad* of indent, where the *em* is defined as the size of the type. Thus, indents are often the same width as the distance from one line of type to the next, assuming the text has no lead. There are times when you might want a bigger indent for style reasons, but they are rare.

Unfortunately, before complete CSS implementations are the norm, there is no reliable way to specify an em-quad. Instead, we put non-breaking spaces at the beginning of our paragraphs.

Indented Lists

In my humble opinion, browsers so far have done a poor job of rendering lists. That's why I don't use the HTML markup tags to denote ordered or unordered lists. I build them visually instead, to be sure they're seen the way I want them to look.

Simply indent your lists the same as you would indent a paragraph. This flush style looks good and puts the information first [4.13]. Rather than using bullets, which are useless pieces of junk browsers use to render lists, separate list items with vertical white space and use bold to list items for differentiation.

Like horizontal rules, bullets make up for unavailable space when putting a certain number of list elements on a fixed-size page. Bullets come from the paper world, where pages end and people try to pack as much on one page as possible.

Space Between Sentences

Putting two spaces after a period is an old secretaries' myth, propagated by old secretaries who become typing teachers. Because browsers ignore consecutive spaces, it won't affect your web pages (unless you use the <PRE> tag). But it makes your email and word-processor documents harder to read.

A period is an excellent signal that a sentence has come to an end. The period itself has quite a bit of white space above it – enough to distinguish it and the following word space from a regular word space. You don't add extra space between sentences in your handwriting, we never do it in books and newspapers, and so far no one's complained. Why should it be right for your word processor or your email? It isn't. More space makes the sentences float apart, making life difficult for the reader, no matter what your typing teacher taught you.

4.13 Indented lists look much better than bulleted lists.

75

4.14 Here is a web page as it's normally presented (LEFT) and after a small touch-up – removing bullets and changing the default background color (RIGHT). You decide which communicates more clearly.

Bullets are a last-resort approach to lists. They are ugly, identical, and convey little meaning. My rule on bullets is to design around them in all cases [4.14]. Designers can use different colors or shapes of bullets to denote the status of a line item, but that's only for presenting search results and other tabular material. Custom rotating 3-D bullets have gotten out of hand.

Space Between Words

An inter-word space should not be too big. One of the first things you learn in a good typography class is that a word space should be roughly the width of the letter "i." More space breaks the natural rhythm of the sentences. Justifying text (aligning the two margins, as in the typesetting of a novel) usually stretches the spaces between words. On the screen, this is much harder to read because it breaks the reader's

natural reading rhythm (the eye scans along in regular jerks called saccades).

Justified text works in novels and long-material publishing, but you must use it with finesse, and the Web is not the place. For starters, web browsers don't hyphenate, and the subtle algorithms behind line layout are much more serious than any browser is capable of today. (The text of this book isn't justified, and I'm willing to bet it hasn't bothered you. Flush left is best.)

Space Between Letters

The great typographer Jan Tschichold said: "Good typesetting is tight." Type designers put narrow sidespaces on lowercase characters for a tight fit. Words should clump together, forming recognizable shapes. Don't add space between lowercase letters unless you want to make them harder to read.

76

There's a lot of lowercase spacing going around these days. It has become trendy to add space between letters. If you do it for a logo, that's one thing. Don't do it for any GIF text other than a logo. Try letterspaced caps instead. *(See Chapter 5, "Rendering Type.")*

Offsets and Alignment

Way back in 1995, I wanted to make my foreground images align perfectly with my background images. I tried, but they kept moving around when people visited my pages with different browsers. This is the dreaded *browser offset* problem.

To see my dilemma on your screen, make an HTML file [4.15] with a square image in the upper left corner. (Alternatively, visit the Book Site to see a live demonstration page that shows what your offset is.)

The square won't be exactly in the upper left corner. It will be offset from the background by a certain number of pixels, both vertically and horizontally. The number of pixels depends on your browser [4.16].

Lately, Netscape has been fairly consistent in making browsers with 8 pixels of horizontal offset and 8 pixels of vertical offset, even though designers have been begging for zero offsets for over two years. Apparently, the people at Netscape feel that 8 pixels is just fine for us and we should live with it. With Netscape's browser line, misalignment of the foreground and background is virtually guaranteed, and they don't think we should put foreground images right at the edge of the window.

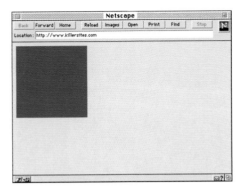

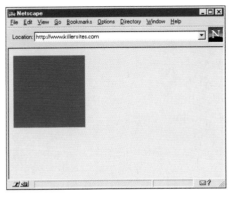

4.16 Virtually all browsers have different default offsets on different platforms. Note the difference between Mac (LEFT) and Windows (BOTTOM). All Netscape browsers have offsets. Don't make your design depend on a particular offset, whether 0, 8, or 13 pixels.

```
<HTML>
  <HEAD>
  </HEAD>
  <BODY BGCOLOR="#CCCCFF">
    <IMG SRC="square.gif">
  </BODY>
</HTML>
```

4.15 A good way to determine your browser's automatic offsets.

Microsoft's Internet Explorer team was the first to recognize a need for precise alignment. They introduced two attributes for the `<body>` element: `LEFTMARGIN` and `TOPMARGIN`. They aren't set to zero by default (for backward compatibility), but they go where Netscape's tags do not: to the edges of the browser window.

I can only imagine that the Netscape browser team thought they shouldn't honor an intelligent attribute like this because that would legitimize it and possibly threaten their market share. As a result, there are no good ways to get full-bleed graphics or precise alignment between foreground and background [4.17].

Some people (including yours truly) have gotten around the offset problem by putting their HTML page into a single large frame that's 100% wide and 100% tall. At first, we were excited by this discovery. Then came the news that Netscape browsers misalign frame contents about 20% of the time, forcing visitors to reload to get the intended effect. It looks cool but is not reliable *(see "Frame Liabilities," later in this chapter)*. The end result is that pixel-accurate background alignment is not practical.

Working with Tables

Because we'll be pouring text into tables for a while, it's good to know what you can and can't do with tables. The Framers of the Web had in mind a syntax for displaying tabular data [4.18]. Tables can be very difficult to build and adjust, so they made tables "smart." Tables attempt to balance the contents, spreading columns judiciously across the page. It would be great if we could turn these smarts off for presenting text, but we can't, so we use trial and error to format our pages.

By forgetting about the 2.0 browsers, we can use simpler means of controlling our tables. As the 4.0 browsers dominate and 5.0 implementations arrive, I'm sure there will be other issues to contend with. Here is what we at Verso Labs have been able to ascertain (many otherwise productive hours have been lost to bring you this information).

Turn Off Table Borders

Many site designers leave their table borders turned on. Why? I have no

4.17 Verso's home page uses a frame for a full-bleed effect. It works most of the time.

idea. I always turn off table borders using the `BORDER="0"` attribute on the table tag. So do most of the High Five award winners. It's pretty easy to do.

There's even a web site – www.borderequalszero.com – dedicated to showing people what can be done with borders turned off!

According to Todd Fahrner, design technologist at Verso, "Visible boxes and grids are for forms that *solicit* information in certain places, rather than *present* it." In general, use boxes only in areas where you want someone to type something. Otherwise, use white space to present information.

A well-designed annual report presents the data clearly, using shading and good typography, not a bunch of heavy lines with numbers in boxes. A good table presents information as cleanly as possible. Whether presenting straightforward text or numeric information, try to show only a minimum of what Edward R. Tufte calls chartjunk – extra embellishments that take attention away from the data. Table borders are chartjunk [**4.19**]. (Next time you print a spreadsheet, turn off the grid lines, use bold for the headings and totals, and see whether you like that better.)

Table Cells As Text Containers

Unconstrained tables try to create the best layout with whatever you put into them. As an experiment, try making a table that has five columns. Put images and text, in different sizes

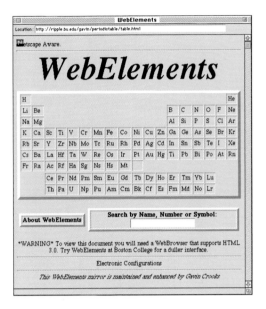

4.18 Tables were intended for illustrations and, well, tabular material.

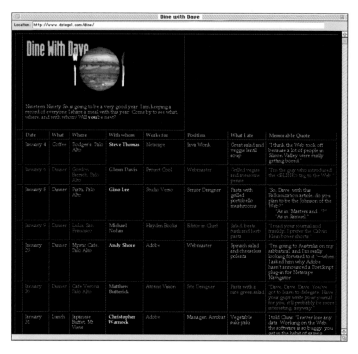

4.19 Turning off borders reduces chartjunk.

and amounts, into the tables. Overload some cells with too much text or a huge image. Use the "nowrap" attribute of table cells (`<TD NOWRAP>`) and watch what happens. Change the width of your browser window from wide open to very skinny. In case you don't have your browser in front of you, the point is that table cells tend to be elastic.

To control the width of your table cells, use either relative or absolute widths [4.20]. To specify relative cell widths, use `<TD WIDTH="x%">`, where x is the percentage of the width of the table containing the cell. (This isn't valid HTML, but both major browsers support relative table specifications.) *Relative cell widths* give you flexible tables that resize when the window size changes. *Absolute cell widths* specify the width in pixels. This cell does not change size when the window does. Make the following table with both relative and absolute numbers [4.21], then adjust the browser window width. (You can see this on the Book Site, but it's more instructive to make your own.)

While relative widths can be acceptable for setting a single column of text, third-generation sites often have graphics that depend on preserving certain dimensions. To constrain tables, set the widths of individual columns using `<TD WIDTH="x">`, where x is the number of pixels you want the column to be. (It would be nice to be able to specify this number in a measurement, like centimeters, or in some way tie it to the font size, but let's get back to reality.) Although I can set the width of a table, I usually specify the width of

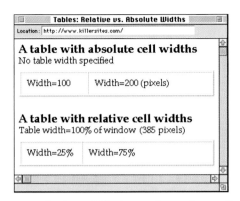
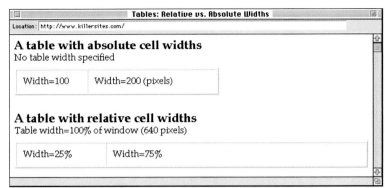

4.20 Absolute widths keep columns from collapsing, while relative widths move with the browser window.

```
<TABLE BORDER="2">
  <TR>
    <TD WIDTH="100">Width=100</TD>
    <TD WIDTH="200">Width=200
    (pixels)</TD>
  </TR>
```

```
<TABLE BORDER="2">
  <TR>
    <TD WIDTH="25%">Width=25%</TD>
    <TD WIDTH="75%">Width=75%</TD>
  </TR>
</TABLE>
```

4.21 HTML for absolute (LEFT) and relative (RIGHT) column widths.

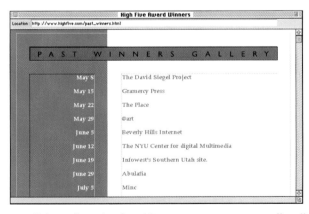

4.22 Using cellspacing for white space assures a non-collapsible gutter. (Visit the page yourself and view the Document Source to see the HTML.)

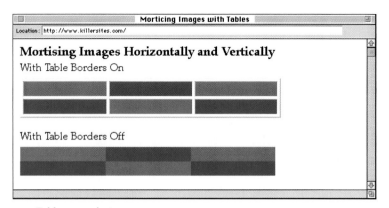

Mortising Images Horizontally and Vertically

With Table Borders On

With Table Borders Off

4.23 Table rows abut right on top of each other.

each table cell and let the browser determine how wide to make the table: simply the sum of the column widths.

I rarely set the *height* of a table or table cell. Like web pages, tables have infinite bottoms. For better or worse, tables grow and shrink to accommodate their contents. If you specify <TD VALIGN="BOTTOM">, the contents of that cell sink to the bottom.

In general, use relative cell widths inside a table that is specified relative to the size of the screen. Use absolute cell widths in tables containing items that aren't flexible.

Use CELLSPACING and CELLPADDING to Guarantee White Space

Cellpadding describes the distance between the contents of a cell and its walls. *Cellspacing* describes the amount of space surrounding each cell. These tags apply to horizontal and vertical distances to all sides of a table cell simultaneously. I often use cellspacing to create a gutter where I want to separate two columns by a given

amount [4.22]. This is especially useful when designing forms (*see Chapter 8, "A Storefront"*).

Use Table Cells to Mortise Images

If you put two images next to each other with no carriage return between the <IMG> tags, they will join together with space between them. If you insert a carriage return, you'll see a row of pixels separating the two images (hey, I don't write the browsers, I just report what they do, okay?). If you want your two images to stay glued together (let's say one's an animated GIF and one isn't), it's best to put them in neighboring table cells and turn off the borders [4.23].

Now for the vertical splice. Stacked tables always have a bit of white space between them. Rows in the same table do not. If you want images to mortise together, put them in neighboring cells and neighboring columns with borders turned off [4.24A]. And remove all the hard carriage returns from your code, as specified in the next section.

Eliminate Hard Carriage Returns When Mortising Table Cells

Now for the bad news. Netscape Navigator 3.0 and Communicator 4.0 are even more picky about getting table cells to abut than 2.0 was. They require that you remove carriage returns to get this effect. I know what I'm about to say sounds ridiculous, but these days, to be sure your table cells mortise together, **you must not have any hard carriage returns within any table cell**. In other words, remove all carriage returns between `<TD>` and `</TD>`. That's right. Each table cell, no matter how much is in it, should really be on one single line in the source file [**4.24B**]. You may be able to get around this in certain situations, but you'll save yourself a lot of detective work if you adopt this standard.

When we build sites by hand these days, we put all our tables on one single line. You're probably wondering how we keep our sanity. We use a power tool. A program called BBEdit on the Macintosh has an auto-format feature that will collapse code (remove carriage returns) automatically. It can also reformat the code so that you can read it, make sense of it, make changes, and so on. With BBEdit, you can keep your code readable, yet minimize the size of the files you ship. On a large, table-laden page, the carriage returns and formatting characters can account for up to 20% of the size of the file. Removing them can actually give you measurable file size reduction. We've seen pages lose 10K just in the HTML by collapsing the code this way.

Note: HTML in this book contains carriage returns for easy viewing, the way BBEdit formats HTML. With a single click, we collapse it and ship it.

```
<TABLE BORDER="0" CELLSPACING="0"
CELLPADDING="0" WIDTH="450">
  <TR>
    <TD><IMG SRC="./resources/dot_red.gif"
    ALIGN=LEFT WIDTH="150" HEIGHT="50"
    BORDER="0"></TD>
    <TD><IMG SRC="./resources/dot_blue.gif"
    ALIGN=LEFT WIDTH="150" HEIGHT="50"
    BORDER="0"></TD>
    <TD><IMG SRC="./resources/dot_red.gif"
    ALIGN=LEFT WIDTH="150" HEIGHT="50"
    BORDER="0"></TD>
  </TR>
  <TR>
    <TD><IMG SRC="./resources/dot_blue.gif"
    ALIGN=LEFT WIDTH="150" HEIGHT="50"
    BORDER="0"></TD>
    <TD><IMG SRC="./resources/dot_red.gif"
    ALIGN=LEFT WIDTH="150" HEIGHT="50"
    BORDER="0"></TD>
    <TD><IMG SRC="./resources/dot_blue.gif"
    ALIGN=LEFT WIDTH="150" HEIGHT="50"
    BORDER="0"></TD>
  </TR>
</TABLE>
```

4.24A This code generates the table at the bottom of illustration 4.23, but only after the code is collapsed. If you try this exact example, it won't work properly in some Netscape browsers.

```
<TABLE BORDER="0" CELLSPACING="0" CELLPADDING="0" WIDTH="450"><TR><TD><IMG
SRC="./resources/dot_red.gif" ALIGN=LEFT WIDTH="150" HEIGHT="50" BORDER="0"></
TD><TD><IMG SRC="./resources/dot_blue.gif" ALIGN=LEFT WIDTH="150" HEIGHT="50"
BORDER="0"></TD><TD><IMG SRC="./resources/dot_red.gif" ALIGN=LEFT WIDTH="150"
HEIGHT="50" BORDER="0"></TD></TR><TR><TD><IMG SRC="./resources/dot_blue.gif"
ALIGN=LEFT WIDTH="150" HEIGHT="50" BORDER="0"></TD><TD><IMG SRC="./resources/
dot_red.gif" ALIGN=LEFT WIDTH="150" HEIGHT="50" BORDER="0"></TD><TD><IMG
SRC="./resources/dot_blue.gif" ALIGN=LEFT WIDTH="150" HEIGHT="50" BOR-
DER="0"></TD></TR></TABLE>
```

4.24B This code is identical to that in 4.24A, but all the hard returns have been removed.

Writing code by hand, collapsing it, and debugging it is about as much fun as overhauling your lawn mower. It's times like these when you want to make entire web pages as one large GIF image. The best solution is to use a sophisticated tool (BBEdit for hand coding or Fusion for layout) or don't try to do these kinds of table tricks. If your table cells won't go together, remove the carriage returns and see if that fixes the problem.

Use Alignment for Flush-Right Text

As any basic manual on HTML will show, alignment works for both text and images. I use alignment mostly to align things to the right edge of a table cell when I'm going for a special typographic effect like a gutter or a form. (*See various uses of alignment throughout the later chapters.*)

Although flush-right text is harder to read, it can be effective in certain situations. There are times when you

4.25 Flush-right text can be effective if used sparingly.

may want to put some text in a margin or simply alternate alignment of paragraphs down the page. Experiment with flush-right text and see what you can create [4.25].

Nest Tables Only When Necessary

Realize that a table often will not display until its entire contents have downloaded. Therefore, long tables with lots of text or tables with other tables in them will be blank for as long as it takes to get everything to the user's machine. I put tables inside of tables only if necessary. I use nested tables most often to make larger containers into which several tables fit. This can be a good alternative to frames, but it doesn't do the job of frames. Each situation is different. Nested tables are difficult to debug, but they can help in complicated situations [4.26].

Use Colored Table Cells to Present Tabular Data

There's no need to use table borders when presenting tabular information. Colored text, bold and regular weights, and pastel-colored backgrounds can all help a third-generation-site designer convey information. It's best not to reverse type out of a dark background, except perhaps for headings, but the following examples should give you good ideas for presenting information using colored table cells and good typography [4.27].

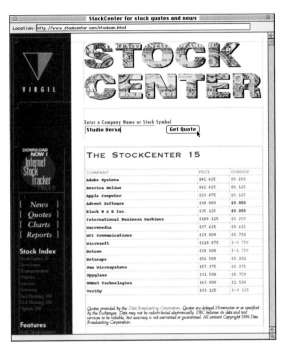

4.26 Use nested tables to divide your page into smaller areas, or put everything into one table if you can (borders turned on for illustration).

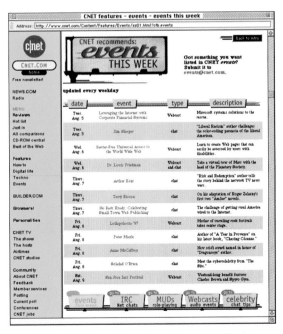

4.27 Colored table cells can be much more effective than cells with borders.

The Single-Pixel GIF Trick

When I first started designing third-generation sites, the single-pixel GIF played an important role as the official duct tape of the Web. It upset a lot of people, and it made a lot of people very happy. I've moved it to the end of this chapter to show that it's on its way out, and the sooner the better. Use the single-pixel GIF if you need to position something where a table or a non-breaking space won't do the trick. Throw it away when new technologies arrive to help us do real layout.

I'm not trying to take a tool away from third-generation site designers, but the more you work with single-pixel GIFs, the more you yearn for real control. Single-pixel GIFs have their drawbacks. They sometimes fail to load. When you put your mouse over them, Internet Explorer (and some versions of Netscape's browser) tries to show you the ALT text. They also make a mess out of the underlying HTML. Although it was the breakthrough that made a number of killer web sites possible, it's now time to see if we can get along without it.

Single-Pixel GIFs Explained

Because some people bought this book to learn about the single-pixel GIF trick,

I'll explain it here, with the caveat that it is a last-resort maneuver.

While you can scale or add space to any image, the trick is to do it with a single-pixel GIF that is transparent and use it to move elements around on a page. Scaled, the single-pixel GIF will stretch to become x pixels wide and y pixels tall. With space added, it will "fend off" other page elements.

This might seem complicated, but a few experiments will demystify the process [4.28 A–C]. Change the numbers, save the file, and reload the page. In practice, I usually use HSPACE or VSPACE, because they can be used independently. They are also safer to use – should the browser fail to render the transparency, only a single pixel will be colored.

There are many examples of single-pixel GIFs at the book site, and some of them are still valid.

See Chapter 12, "Transitional Strategies," for more ideas of alternatives for using single-pixel GIFs.

Here's one way to position an image without resorting to the use of a single-pixel GIF. To add space around any image, you can include HSPACE="X" or VSPACE="Y" arguments in the <IMG> tag. If you use HSPACE="X", the browser will display X pixels of space on all four sides of the image, causing it to fend off other elements by that many pixels in all directions [4.29 A–C]. In this way, you can position graphics and tables in two-pixel increments without a single-pixel GIF. You may specify either of these arguments independently.

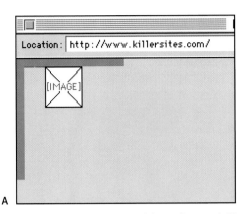

A

```
<IMG SRC="./resource/dot_clear.gif"
HSPACE="10">
```

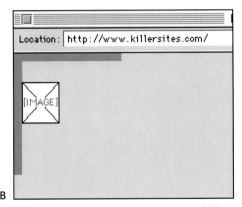

B

```
<IMG SRC="resource dot_clear.gif"
WIDTH="1" HEIGHT="21">
```

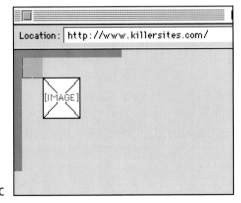

C

```
<IMG SRC="resource dot_clear.gif"
VSPACE="10" HSPACE="10">
```

4.28 A-C (LEFT) Use HTML's `<img>` tag attributes with a single-pixel image to move other things around on a page. Used with HSPACE (or VSPACE) (A), the single-pixel image (shown in light blue) has space on both sides that fend off neighboring images. Using the HEIGHT (or WIDTH) attribute (B), the single-pixel image itself stretches to move neighboring images. Using both WIDTH and HEIGHT (c) moves the image in two dimensions.

4.29 A-C (RIGHT) HSPACE and VSPACE can be used to create empty space around an image, setting it off from other objects on the page. Note that in this case, the HEIGHT and WIDTH tags denote the actual size of the target image and should not be changed for positioning purposes.

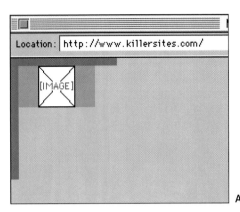

A

```
<IMG SRC="./images/xfile.gif"
HSPACE="20" HEIGHT="40
WIDTH="40">
```

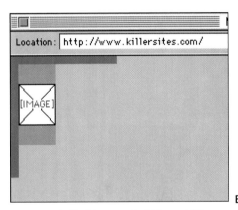

B

```
<IMG SRC="./images/xfile.gif"
VSPACE="20" HEIGHT="40
WIDTH="40">
```

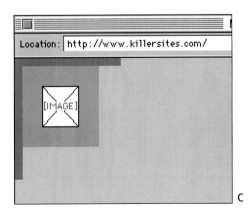

C

```
<IMG SRC="./images/xfile.gif"
HSPACE="20" VSPACE="20"
HEIGHT="40 WIDTH="40">
```

87

Always add both HEIGHT and WIDTH tags to all images, including single-pixel GIFS.

About Scrolling

Scrolling is a traditional user-interface no-no. The way it's done today, it

Table Liabilities

If you're using a table to present a long list, the table machinery evaluates everything in the list before deciding how wide to make the table. Be careful not to put too many elements on a page, and be careful not to put too many elements into a single table. It's best to break your tables up, so people can see the first screenful or so quickly, and continue with separate tables that come in as the page arrives. Many small tables stacked on top of each other are better than one big table.

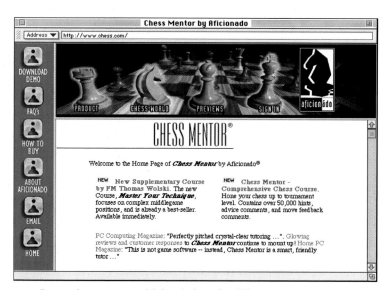

4.30 Frames let you use multiple windows for different purposes. A typical site has a title frame, a directory frame, and a target frame.

should be. Scrolling is not inherently bad, however. Given better ways to scroll, surfers will scroll web pages as easily as they do word processor documents. As Alan Cooper points out in his excellent book *About Face: The Essentials of User-Interface Design*, scroll bars should have their arrows grouped together, not separated by an "elevator shaft."

Instead of the normal scrolling mechanism, I'd like to suggest a rocker plate (a two-dimensional variant of the rocker switch) located in the lower-right corner of the window. The plate would be on a virtual hinge right at the center, so it responds to small mouse movements. The more you drag it up, the faster it would scroll, and if you drag it to the center, scrolling stops. Users could start (or stop) autoscrolling by hitting the space bar and speed up or slow down the scroll rate by moving the mouse over the plate. If the mouse left the plate, scrolling would stop. As companies give their browsers more capability, they will also have to give them more usability.

Microsoft has introduced a mouse with a scrolling wheel built-in. I think we'll see plenty of people scrolling web pages for the foreseeable future.

In practice, I don't mind scrolling a little. I mind scrolling a lot, but if the measure is narrow I find smooth scrolling fairly effective. Sites like Salon (www.salon1999.com) use narrow columns, force scrolling, and don't get many complaints. My general rule is to let people scroll no more than about 4-6 screens before giving them a new page.

For an interesting story on scrolling and user testing at the Discovery.com site, see my other recent book, *Secrets of Successful Web Sites*.

Frames and Framesets

Frames are a power feature, introduced by Netscape, that take the Web to a new level. Frames let you display several URLs on one page. Unfortunately, power tools can kill. Frames are the subject of much controversy. Now that designers can turn frame borders to zero, I find they have their uses.

Frames are a *meta-document format* – they display multiple HTML documents simultaneously [4.30]. To make a frame, you describe a *frameset*, which contains a number of frames, or windows containing HTML documents. You can specify relative or absolute sizes of the windows. You can also include some default HTML in case the surfer arrives with a browser that can't see frames. You can name windows and use them as targets for hotlinks – when a visitor clicks on a link, the resulting URL displays in another frame.

Frames can be manipulated with a scripting language like JavaScript. If you are technically inclined, you can have one click affect two different frames (for example, updating a status bar while showing another document in the main window). The main advantage of frames is *persistence* – what you see in one frame doesn't go away when you scroll down or visit another page in another frame.

Deadly Sin Number One

Blank-Line Typography

In second-generation typography, site designers let the browser's default style sheet add a blank line of space between paragraphs properly marked with <P> tags. In third-generation typography, site designers use indents, no matter what it takes to make them.

When you use blank lines as paragraph separators, the meaning of a blank line goes away. It turns into punctuation. In third-generation typography, indents separate paragraphs, and the right amount of vertical white space – maybe a blank line, maybe a bit more – separates sections, clumping paragraphs into logical groups for better reading. Without this effective tool, blank lines escalate the situation, so you need something louder (say, a horizontal rule), to indicate a major break in the flow of text. This kind of unsubtle typography escalates until we see web pages that are full of nothing more than separators.

Of indents, typographer Jan Tschichold said, "So far, no device more economical or even equally good has been found to designate a group of sentences. There have been no shortage of attempts, though, to replace an old habit with a new one."

4.31 Used well, frames can aid navigation through complicated spaces.

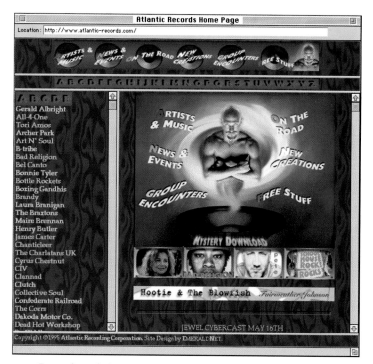

4.32 Frame-based sites can present navigation problems. In this example, there are no fewer than five primary clickable zones.

Frames can't solve all your problems. They invite several pages to load, which can slow surfing. Site designers often use them to compensate for bad design or lack of an overall concept. Good designers are starting to use frames in sensible ways.

There are four main reasons people use frames: for fun, for layout, for hierarchies, and for indexes into flat data spaces. Make sure you know which category you're in before you reach for the <FRAMESET> tag. A *hotlist* is a bad use of frames, but a *directory* is a good use of frames.

Frames for fun. Frames are often just another techno-feature people use to make their pages "cool." Bad design magnified.

Frames for layout. Because you can turn off frame borders in 3.0+ browsers, you can set up vertical margins as frames, rather than using tables. As I've mentioned, you can't bet on precise alignment from one frame to the next. Nevertheless, some intrepid designers have used frames successfully. It is worth considering making a frame-based third-generation site, but realize that the degree of difficulty goes up considerably when you do. Very few of the top-50 most visited sites of the Web use frames for anything [4.31].

Frames for hierarchies. Many people use frames to present hierarchies. I think the concept of frames is good, but they take us into very deep water from a user-interface point of view, and they haven't been implemented as well as they should have been. Many sites that were frame-based have taken their frames down.

It is possible to construct an entirely frame-based site, as I have at www.highfive.com, but I don't recommend it as a front end to a hierarchy of documents.

Frames for indexes. I use frames as indexes into larger, flat data spaces that would otherwise be awkward in HTML, because it would take too many pages. Suppose you have a yo-yo catalog that offers 200 different kinds of yo-yos. Putting up a regular HTML index, even if you group them carefully, still means having to go through a lot of pages to browse the yo-yos. In these situations, use frames as windows into flat databases (*see Chapter 8, "A Storefront"*).

The yo-yo catalog is a good example of a flat database, where you have many items with similar-sized descriptions. (If each item broke down into many descriptive entries, that would be an even more difficult problem, possibly beyond the ability of frames to present well.) Frames are especially good for catalog pages, so you can flip back and forth between items to compare them.

The High Five site and the Navitel site are both examples of frame-based sites. These sites have only a single-level hierarchy – their site maps are relatively flat. This kind of application works quite well, especially if you keep it simple and don't try to scale it into something much bigger [4.33].

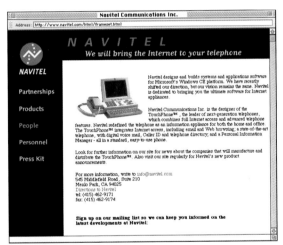

4.33 These sites are relatively flat. Any new information pops up in a new window.

Frame Liabilities

All Netscape browsers – even 4.0 versions – have about a 20% chance of misaligning the foreground material in any frame. Many frame-based sites aren't built so that you see this effect, but if you try to align foreground and background in any frame, there's a reasonable chance that frame won't display properly. Perhaps this will be fixed after a few more releases, but don't hold your breath.

4.34 Frames can be useful when you want to compare several items.

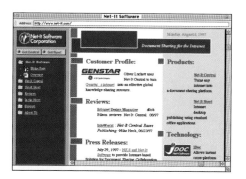

4.35 This site, from *Secrets of Successful Web Sites*, uses a "poor man's JavaScript" trick to activate an indicator. See it at www.secretsites.com.

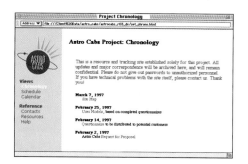

Frame Magic

If you make a frame-based page, use it for indexed material. Always make it a "dead end" area of your site, not the home page. Never put links inside your target frame, unless those links use special target names (or JavaScripts). The following "Magic Target Names" will help keep you out of trouble:

TARGET="_top" blows away all frames and takes you to the intended URL in a clean browser window.

TARGET="_blank" opens a clean new browser window that appears in front of the previous one.

TARGET="_self" makes the link load in its own window.

TARGET="_parent" makes the link load in the full body of the window, even if it is being viewed through some other frame. Using this tag blows away any frames through which people might be seeing your pages.

Frame Navigation

Always make frame-based sites or pages into a destination, or a *dead end*. On the yo-yo site, the catalog page would use frames, where visitors can click on the index frame, see things in the target frame, and that's it. When the visitors are done, they either hit the Back button or use a link that has the TARGET="_top" designator to lose the frames and go back to a standard HTML document. Careful use of frames in this way will make your database extendable and make it easy to compare items in the target window. Try to keep the list of links in the index window uncluttered and hierarchical (use vertical white space!) without growing too big [4.34].

Many people building frame-based sites have found themselves recreating all the navigation features of the browser, because they find that the "Back" button doesn't do what people want in all situations. So they use JavaScript and other techniques to set up their own "chrome," which they keep on every page to aid navigation [4.36]. Some sites even use a separate navigation window to control what you see in the main windows.

Another use of frames is for extranets and intranets. (See a good example of an extranet site using frames at www.secretsites.com. The book *Secrets of Successful Web Sites*, details a "poor man's JavaScript" solution for displaying status information in one frame while showing new content in another

[4.35].) Functional sites that can control their own navigation are good candidates for frames with their borders turned off.

The rule on frames is never to provide a through-frame link. That is, don't ever let anyone click on a link in a frame and have the page in that frame replaced by another page. Always control the links from a separate navigation page, and provide links to entirely new windows that pop up automatically to display deeper information.

Summary

The appropriate reaction to a chapter like this is to roll your eyeballs in their sockets and say, "I can't believe designers have to go through this stuff to lay out pages!" While it isn't pretty underneath, most of these tricks get the job done most of the way most of the time. Let's not call it proper typography, but let's say it's better than what we would get by letting the browser do the formatting for us.

The differentiating factor between second-generation and third-generation typography is the degree of control site designers have over their pages. They reduce non-data pixels and present data-pixels with utmost care. They put text into tables until style sheets let them do better. They use tables to align the elements of their pages. They use frames to present large flat databases and relatively flat web sites. And above all, they keep all the borders turned off!

Read This Book!

If you only read one book as a result of this chapter, it should be *The Form of the Book* by Jan Tschichold (Hartley and Marks Publishers, 1991). Pronounced "Yan Chickold," Jan Tschichold was one of the most influential typographic designers of this century. It is easily one of the most important books on typography and typographic principles ever written. This linear, non-hyper, high-resolution resource is a treasure of typographic tips.

4.36 Many good frame-based sites have had to invent their own script-based navigation scheme to properly handle frame-based browsing.

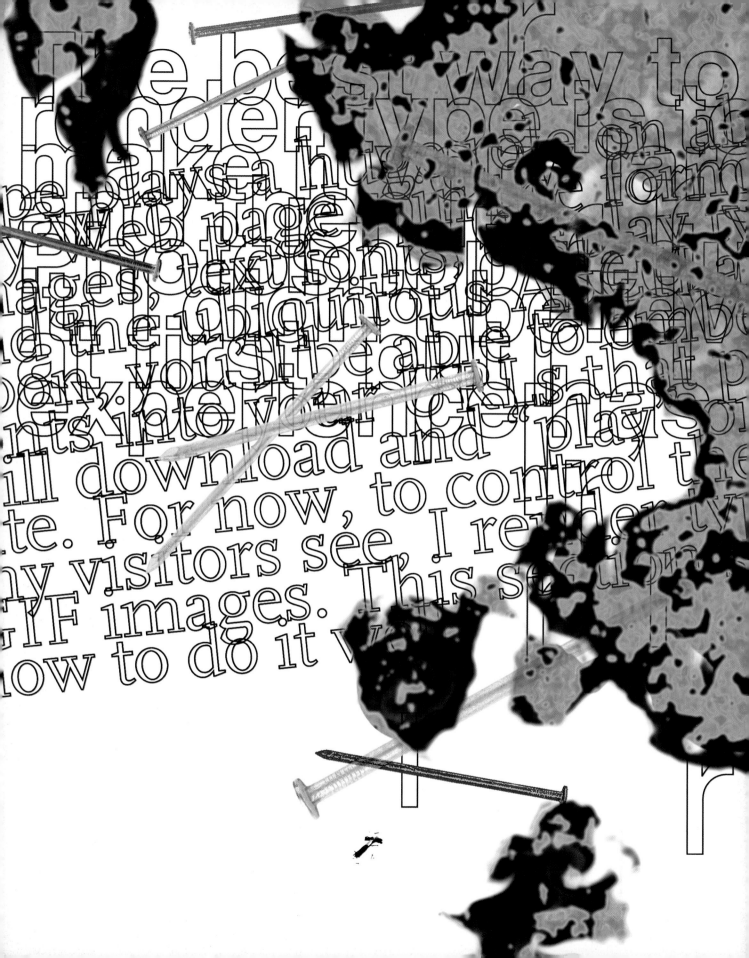

The Balkanization of the Web: Overview

Location: http://www.dsiegel.com/balkanization/intro.html

THE BALKANIZATION OF THE WEB
by David Siegel

> Just as water, gas, and electricity are brought
> into our houses from far off to satisfy our
> needs in response to a minimal effort, so we
> shall be supplied with visual or auditory images,
> which will appear and disappear at a simple
> movement of the hand, hardly more than a sign.
>
> —Paul Valery, Aesthetics.

THIS ESSAY IS ABOUT HTML and the underpinnings of the Web. It is about foundations. The web is not a single structure. Because the Web has now "crossed the chasm," from its technical roots to the colorful world of consumers, it can't be extended by any single group or any single philosophy. Marshall McLuhan envisioned a "Global Village," sort of a big tent that included everyone. I claim the tent has already established three main rings: Information, Exchange, and Entertainment. Each needs its own appropriate infrastructure, built on a common foundation. (A quick detour will take you to my motivations for writing this essay. It is not

BERINGER VINEYARDS

Location: http://www.beringer.com/index.html

Beringer.Vineyards

FINE VARIETAL WINES

5.1 How not to do it: poorly rendered type.

1:1   BICUBIC REDUCTION

VERSO 48PT **VERSO**

VERSO 36PT **VERSO**

VERSO 24PT **VERSO**

VERSO 18PT **VERSO**

VERSO 12PT **VERSO**

VERSO 9PT **VERSO**

VERSO 7PT VERSO

5.2 Especially at smaller sizes, reduce large type images in Photoshop to fit rather than set it directly to size; the final result will be smoother. Make sure you use bicubic interpolation *(see Interpolation sidebar for more details)* for this operation.

TYPE PLAYS AN IMPORTANT ROLE on almost any web page. You see it in images, text, headlines, captions, logos, branding, navigation, and the ubiquitous ASCII art.

Compared to other kinds of graphics, type is an inexpensive source of raw material that can be used over and over to great effect. You don't have to hire an illustrator, take photographs, or create custom illustrations. Simply use type to give your pages depth and a unique look and feel.

Ideally, designers would be able to send an entire suite of typefaces along with a site, the transmission time would be minimal, and the site would use those fonts as text that could be combined, layered, rotated, and transformed in interesting ways – all on the browser. In addition, the fonts would be protected from misuse and unauthorized copying.

While we all look forward to the perfect type solution, we continue to use GIF images of type, make the files as small as possible, and glue them into our sites using the <IMG> tag. And that – the brute – force method of rendering type – is what this chapter covers. It may not be elegant, but it works on all graphical browsers.

Reduce Type in Photoshop

Without anti-aliasing, type looks cheap and uneven **[5.1]**. If you want to render type below about 20-point, make it large first and let Photoshop reduce it using bicubic interpolation **[5.2]**.

High-quality fonts contain *hints* to help render the characters consistently and appropriately on screen at small

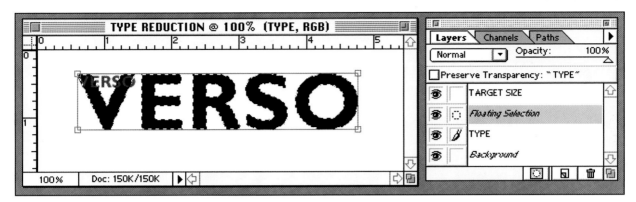

5.3 Scale your type down to the target size in Photoshop.

sizes. Photoshop doesn't use these hints. Render a line of small m's in Photoshop – they won't all look the same. As the technology improves, rendering will improve. For now, to create type smaller than 20 point, first generate the type at around 80 point, then scale it down to the target size [5.3].

Photoshop offers no numerical control in the Image>Effects>Scale command. You can work around this by creating a layer in Photoshop containing type in the target size as a guide, then scaling the larger type down on its own layer to match. When the layers match, delete the guide layer.

Do It Last

If you've ever watched a good carpenter framing a house, you'll see she leaves all the nails sticking out a bit until the structure is finished. When everything is in place and working, she takes a minute to "set" all the nails at once. It's easier to make adjustments before the nails are embedded into the wood. The same applies to web sites, especially if they have many type-laden images.

Preserving Character Shapes

If you use Adobe Type Manager (ATM) to render your Type 1 fonts, make sure to open the ATM control panel and choose "Preserve Character Shapes." If you don't, the descenders of your characters may be cut off.

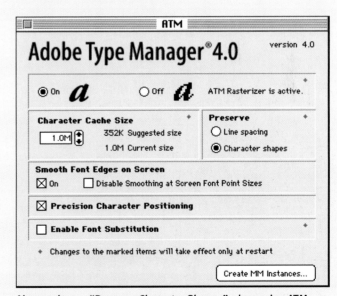

Always choose "Preserve Character Shapes" when using ATM.

Rendering type as GIFs is tedious work. Because changes usually come at the last minute, I wait for final copy before making final production images. As you'll see, the strategies for making final images depend on how many there are, how much flexibility you need in making more on demand, the degree of automation required, and the skill of the person in charge of cranking out these images.

Do It All at Once

Whenever possible, generate all the type images for an entire site from a single master file. This way, all sizes, colors, weights, and intermediate colors (used for anti-aliasing) will be consistent.

1. Reduce (index) the colors of the master file to the lowest acceptable number.

2. Look at the palette of the indexed image. Note that with Photoshop, when you reduce to index mode using the adaptive method, Photoshop will shift the originally specified RGB values so that you are most likely no longer working within the color cube. You'll have to hand-correct the palette, or the key values in the palette, to conform to your original color cube values. (*See "Photoshop Liabilities" in Chapter 3, "Preparing Images."*) DeBabelizer does not shift the RGB values. (*See Appendix 3, "Image Optimization for the Web," for an automated method using DeBabelizer.*) Alternatively, try reducing colors using only the color cube, and see if you get acceptable results.

3. Select and cut each individual type element carefully, and include any necessary white space to help position the image on the page. Don't forget to take into account that some words will have ascenders or descenders and some won't.

4. Export GIFs from the new files using an exact palette, assigning meaningful file names.

5. Enter the dimensions, pathnames, and the A L T attribute texts of the GIFs into your <I M G> tags.

For large projects, I usually modify step 3 and use a standard fixed-size rectangle for all the elements. This makes step 5 easier, because all the images will have the same dimensions. Otherwise, if the images vary in size and if your HTML editor doesn't keep track automatically, make a list noting the names and pixel dimensions of the GIF files as you save them; you'll need these when coding the HTML. If you use the "Automated Type Pipeline" described in the sidebar in this chapter, you can batch-print a catalog of all of the images created through this process, including the file name and image dimensions. If possible, limit image dimensions to a few standard sets to keep the HTML clean and simple.

For Large Jobs, Keep a Record

Photoshop doesn't retain the text you type as you work. I like to keep all my text in a word processor. I grab what

Playing with Type

These examples show how you can play with type in Photoshop to build fun, interesting typographic images that take the place of other graphics. One exception: under no circumstances should you take your logo, emboss it, and put it into the background of your site.

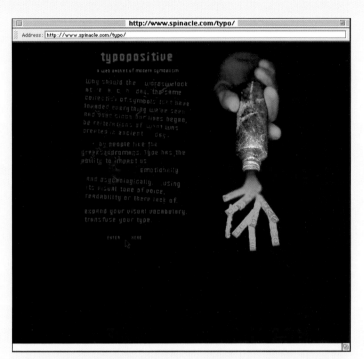

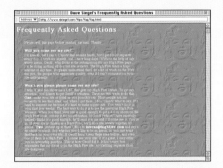

Never do this: embossed backgrounds make the content harder to read.

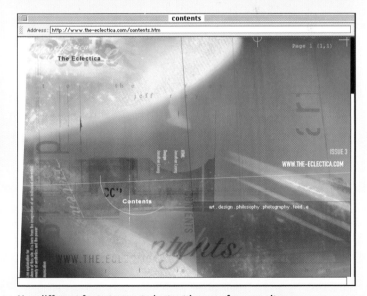

Use different fonts to create instant images for your sites.

5.4 A-D One image reduced to 5 (A), 6 (B), 7 (C), and 8 (D) colors. Follow the Golden Rule to get the smallest file: Start out too low and work up to the minimum acceptable set of colors.

Height and Width Tags

Always use HEIGHT and WIDTH tags for all images. This improves page loading speed, because the text can flow into final position before the images arrive. Some HTML editor tools, like BBEdit for the Mac, put the dimensions in for you automatically.

I need from this file and paste it into Photoshop's Type Tool dialog box. In the word processor, I can spell-check and concentrate on getting the words right. I can save old versions and choose fonts faster than in Photoshop. I can also make notes of the steps for rendering a job's type right along with the text. Having a record like this makes the inevitable revisions a snap.

Some designers make all their type in Illustrator (or FreeHand), create large outlines, then copy and paste the outlines into Photoshop for reduction. This method involves an extra step, because making large type directly in Photoshop and pasting it in from outlines is equivalent. If you want to set type on a curve or apply some other special effect to the outlines, however, you must first create the effect using a program like Illustrator and then import the outlines into Photoshop.

Reduce Colors, Increase Runs

Type looks best without jaggies, but anti-aliasing introduces many intermediate colors along the edges (see "Anti-Aliasing" in Chapter 3). Intermediate colors reduce the compressibility of the image by shortening the runs of any single color. Always try to keep the number of transition colors to a minimum while preserving the visual smoothing effect of anti-aliasing.

When setting type on a flat background, you almost never need more than six intermediate colors. In fact, three or four intermediate colors ually do the trick. If you count the o main colors, this means you can always reduce type to between 2 and 3 bits deep [5.4 A-D].

Occasionally, you can do without anti-aliasing entirely. If you have a large area of type and need to get the file size down, or if your type is very small (say, below 8 points), or if you're going for a hard-edged look, try setting type without anti-aliasing.

When setting small type without anti-aliasing, you can avoid Photoshop's irregular word- and letter spacing by importing and editing a screen capture of text in a word processor.

The Poor Man's Bold

What to do when bold is too dark and regular is too light? Using Adobe Multiple Master fonts, you can interpolate the stem weight to make the font you need. Alternatively, you can use this

Interpolation

Interpolation means filling in between two known extremes. When you resize an image in Photoshop, the program adds or subtracts information to get the final size. When reducing an image, interpolation helps you throw information away by blending two or more pixels into one. Internally, Photoshop anti-aliases type by making a large 1-bit (aliased) image of your letters, then it uses its own scaling capability to reduce the image. This gives you an anti-aliased image, but it doesn't do anything special to preserve the important visual characteristics of the letters.

There are two methods of interpolation in Photoshop: bicubic and bilinear. Bicubic, more complicated and thorough, is the higher quality method, and is the Photoshop 4.0.1 default setting. Bilinear is lower quality and is usually chosen only for speed reasons.

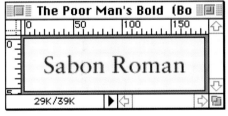

A

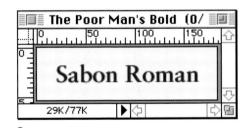

B

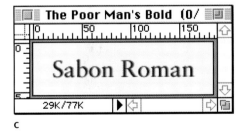

C

D

5.5 The regular weight (A), copied and shifted right one pixel (B), 50% transparency applied to the copy (C), and at 25% transparency (D).

Dither on the Client

Properly reduced type gets its main colors from the color cube, is anti-aliased, and is reduced to the fewest number of intermediate colors necessary. Large areas of color that are not from the cube will dither on low-end systems [5.6 A, B]. However, you don't need to index *every* color in your type image to the color cube. If all your main areas of color come from the color cube, but the intermediate shades are too subtle, they will dither when displayed in only 256 colors.

That's okay! You can often let these colors dither. If you let the client (in this case, the browser program) do the dithering (which it does automatically to colors outside the cube), visitors who can see more than 256 colors will benefit, and the low-end visitors won't know the difference [5.7 A1-C2]. The file size doesn't change. This may not be significant in many situations, but if you have subtle shades in between main colors, people who can see thousands of colors will get a better experience. *(Chapter 10 provides a good example of this effect.)*

In Photoshop 4.0, the Free Transform always uses bilinear interpolation to scale type, even if you specify bicubic interpolation as the default. This problem was fixed in version 4.0.1, which makes that Photoshop update especially worthwhile for people who care about the quality of their type. The update, which is good for other things as well, is available free at www.adobe.com.

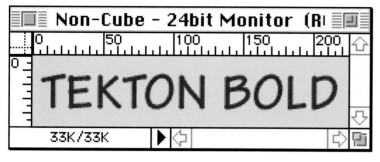

A

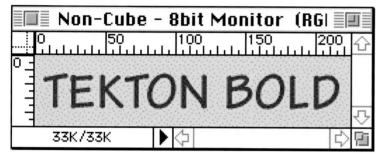

B

5.6 A, B This is how non-color-cube type will appear on monitors set to thousands of colors (A) and 256 colors (B).

trick to get an intermediate weight: render the characters you want, then copy and paste this image right back on top of itself, in exactly the same position. Photoshop's transparency feature will darken the intermediate colors slightly, leaving the central colors the same. You can adjust the transparency of the copied layer to change the weight of the letters.

For even more weight, copy the type and paste it as I just described, but shift the new copy right or left by a single pixel (the result is the same in either direction) [5.5 A-D]. This often helps when a regular is too light and a bold is too heavy or unavailable.

A.1

A.2

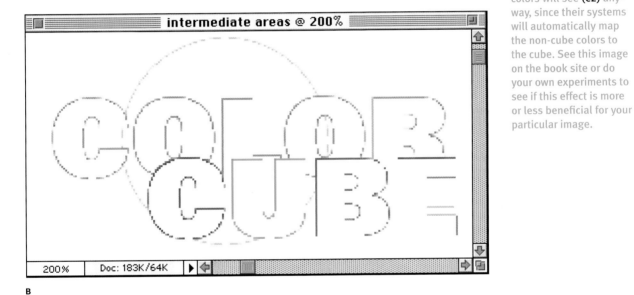

B

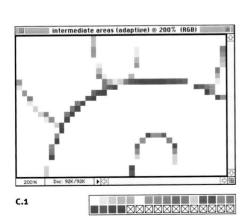

C.1

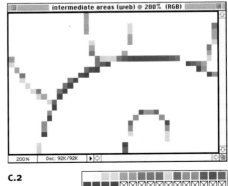

C.2

5.7 Solid areas should come from the color cube (**A1**). Intermediate areas (**B**) will be interpolations of the main colors. Using an adaptive palette (**A1, C1**) results in a natural set of intermediate colors. Reducing colors using the color cube as an exact palette results in a less desirable set of intermediate colors (**A2, C2**). Viewers looking at (**C1**) on a system with 256 colors will see (**C2**) anyway, since their systems will automatically map the non-cube colors to the cube. See this image on the book site or do your own experiments to see if this effect is more or less beneficial for your particular image.

Hand Retouching

Sometimes you have to use the pencil tool to fix type after you've reduced colors. When you can't reduce the number of colors any further, a few artifacts often remain in the image. I zoom in and look for uneven areas of color, like sawteeth in the vertical edges, and fix them by hand [5.8]. I fix, fill, and round up stray pixels.

I sometimes get caught up in anti-aliasing a curve by hand. Straight lines are one thing; be prepared to put in long hours once you start fiddling with curves. It's also tempting to want to strengthen or clean up letter stems with intermediate colors at their edges, but don't do it. If you clean too much, you'll change the weight of your letters for the worse.

Develop your eye. Experiment until you can recognize when hand retouching is worth your time.

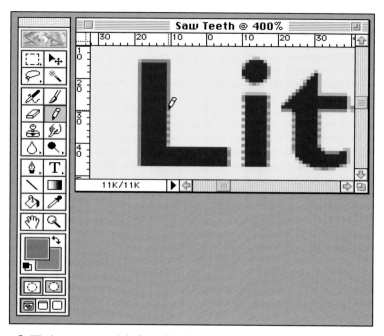

5.8 Eliminate saw teeth before shipping.

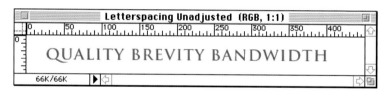

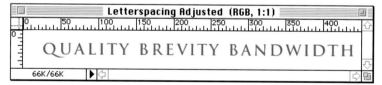

5.9 Letterspacing, before (ABOVE) and after (BELOW).

Keep Type in Layers

Always keep type on a separate layer in Photoshop. Since Photoshop anti-aliases layers automatically, you'll be able to change type and background colors at any time. If you set type into the background, you will lose this flexibility.

Fine Points of Spacing

Fine typography has always included hand spacing of capital letters and special character pairs. Words set in caps should generally be *letterspaced* – fit loose, rather than tight. Words set in upper- and lowercase should be spaced tightly, so whole words appear as units. Good fonts provide many built-in *kerning pairs* to make certain letter combinations look good together in software like PageMaker. Photoshop by itself can't take advantage of this built-in intelligence. You have to make fine spacing adjustments by hand [5.9].

An especially good introduction to a broad range of typographic design issues is *Stop Stealing Sheep*, by Erik Spiekermann and E. M. Ginger (Adobe Press, 1993). See the Book Site for a list of good books on typography and pointers to online bookstores that carry them.

Drop Shadows

Drop shadows are misunderstood and overused. The most common reasons to use drop shadows are to help differentiate the type against the background, to make a "cool" 3-D effect, and to "jazz up the page a bit." The first is the most important.

The best drop shadows help enhance edges. When the type and background contain similar colors, a drop shadow gives a hard edge to bring out the character shapes **[5.10]**. Most print magazine covers use this trick. In these situations, you don't need much shadow.

Drop shadows are occasionally useful as true shadows for 3-D effects, but these instances should be rare. Second-generation sites often sport headlines floating three inches off the background, next to flying extruded logos. Third-generation sites don't rely on 3-D lettering to make a splash.

To make a drop shadow, I copy the object into its own layer by dragging it onto the new-layer icon. By reducing the brightness and contrast, I turn the new layer very dark. Then I place it underneath the object layer, moving it until the shadow appears one pixel down. After hiding the marquee, I use the arrow keys to move the shadow layer left and right, to see which is better.

Shadows

If you're making one shadow for many shapes on several layers in your document, you can create it on one layer automatically. View the desired foreground layers only (hiding the background layer), then merge the layers into a new layer that contains the separate elements on it, which you can then darken.

Keep in mind that shadows aren't just black; they actually *darken the tonal value* of the surfaces they fall on.

5.10 Drop shadows can give your pages a new dimension. Make sure not to add too many dimensions at once.

Automated Type Pipeline

For large-scale jobs at Verso, we've developed an automated type rendering, color correction, cropping, and file-naming process. This Macintosh-based process uses Quark or PageMaker, Adobe Screen Ready (available only on the Macintosh at this writing), DeBabelizer, and AppleScript. Newcomers to web design and production will want to follow the manual Photoshop method described in this chapter first, to master the fundamental concepts.

If you face a tight deadline, have limited patience for manual tweaking in Photoshop, and need consistency and quality in a large-scale job, you'll find this automated process a real time saver.

Here's how it works, using the production of a large number of header elements as an example.

1. In the page layout program of your choice – Quark or PageMaker generally – define a page size that represents the final crop size of the header elements. If all of the headers in your page design are to occupy a 380 x 96 pixel space, define a 380 x 96 point page. Don't worry if you can't get the page small enough – you can fix it later.

2. Paste or type all of your headers, delimited by page breaks or character breaks or hard returns, into a text box in the page layout program. If you put in 1,000 headers, they will flow to create a 1,000-page document.

3. Select all, and style the headers as a batch using a style sheet or whatever styling tools are available in the page layout program – font family, weight, size, color, etc. This is much more powerful than Photoshop's text-handling features.

4. This file becomes the master text file. Note that if you use PageMaker, you can specify RGB values for the color of the type, and those values will be preserved throughout this process. Quark 3.x will always constrain the values to the CMYK gamut upon export, which makes it complicated when going through DeBabelizer –you can correct it in DeBabelizer, but it wouldn't be necessary if Quark let you export RGB colors in EPS files.

5. Once you have your big page layout document with all the headers styled the way you want, export these pages as ".eps" files. PageMaker lets you do this natively by printing to a file and specifying EPS; since EPS doesn't support multiple pages, PageMaker will spit out 1,000 individual files into a directory. With Quark, you can either do it manually or use an AppleScript, available free on the Internet, to export all pages as EPS files. (See www.quark.com for a library of helper scripts.)

6. Use Adobe Screen Ready to convert the EPS files into high quality anti-

Automated Type Pipeline (continued)

aliased PICT images, named and numbered in a separate directory.

7. Using DeBabelizer, convert the PICTS as a batch into color-corrected GIFs by using DeBabelizer's palette reduction and correction scripting facilities, trimming to size if necessary. This is where you make sure the main colors come from the cube. One way is to use one image to pre-build and optimize a palette, then use that exact palette for the rest of the images.

8. The result: a directory of 1,000 nicely cropped and color-corrected GIFs with a numbering scheme. The process takes only minutes and provides quality and consistency you can't get otherwise. It may take some time to set up, but you can make another 1,000 images any time, without the hassle of turning the crank by hand.

9. Print a catalog of your images from DeBabelizer to correlate image content with file names and sizes.

If necessary, I go down two pixels, then (reluctantly) three, but rarely more. I add a small amount of Gaussian blur to the shadow if it's more than two pixels away.

Once you've made a shadow choice, be careful to give the same look to all shadows on the same page. If one shadow falls down and to the left, all shadows should fall down and to the left. Don't bother trying to match the drop shadows built into the Mac and Windows operating systems. If you are trying to achieve the effect of multiple light sources, you should probably rethink the design – drop shadows rarely work effectively in such situations.

If you're making one shadow for many shapes on several layers in your document, you can create it on one layer (use the "Merge Layers" command) or keep them on separate layers. I try to keep them on separate layers, each

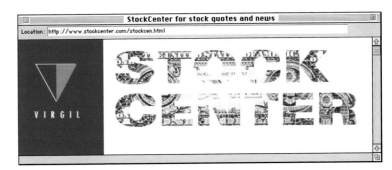

5.11 Without the drop shadow, type fades into the background (ABOVE). Adding a black drop shadow (BELOW) emphasizes the type.

Invest in Good Quality Fonts

How many web pages have large banners rendered as GIFs in Times Roman? Try something else! As font prices have gone down, so has the quality of type in general. Buy only fonts made for the graphic design market, not those that come packaged on a CD-ROM of 2,000 fonts. Cheap fonts are inferior and will make your pages look uneven. Some fonts I use:

Sans Serif: Avenir, Rotis, Officina, Univers, Gill Sans, Myriad, Stone Sans, Futura, Syntax, Frutiger, OCRB, Copperplate, Verdana, Meta.

Serif: Sabon, Galliard, Bauer Bodoni, Walbaum, Stone Serif, Rotis semi-serif, Melior, Serifa.

Scripts: Kunstler, Snell Roundhand, Isadora, Mistral.

I also like Adobe's Tekton and Graphite, and AGFA's Eaglefeather, but then I designed them. If purchased from a large, well-known vendor, all these fonts will render correctly. Multiple Master fonts like Myriad are particularly handy, giving you unlimited weights and widths. There are hundreds of other good fonts to choose from and thousands of bad ones.

There are also several good type foundries online, offering fonts from Grunge and Goudy to Ragged and Rigatoni. These days, deconstructed and distressed type is all the rage. Use these fonts sparingly, perhaps for branding, rather than for navigation. Designers often get carried away with a particular funky font, making their sites hard to read.

below its own element, then link each element layer to its shadow layer. That way, when I move the element, the shadow goes with it.

Keep in mind that shadows aren't just black; they actually darken the tonal value of the surfaces they fall on. Thus, if your background is yellow, your shadow should be brown, not black. Use Photoshop's transparency setting for that layer to get a good shadow color against the proper background color below. Shadows need the same anti-aliased edges their foreground elements have.

Initial Caps

Believe it or not, studies show that people more often read text with an initial cap than without. Initial caps mark a first paragraph as special, attracting reader attention. Initial caps need not be huge or fancy. A little bigger, a little bolder, and nicely balanced does the trick. Invest in some good display typefaces or special initial-caps fonts and make elegant first paragraphs.

The two types of initial caps are bounded [5.12] and unbounded [5.13]. An *unbounded initial cap* has a transparent background. *Bounded caps* sit in boxes, with or without borders. Bounded caps should always be inset (dropped, as in *drop cap*) in the paragraph, with the text aligned to the top. Add extra space around the box so that the text doesn't crowd it. Display faces work best.

Unbounded initial caps can be inset (dropped), standing, or hanging out in the margin (probably in a different table cell). Cut the right edge very close to the character. A "J" makes a good unbounded cap. An "F" is more problematic, because it will be too far away from its neighboring characters. If your character has space on the right side ("F," "T," "P," and so on), keep it small to avoid a large gap. If it's an initial "T," hang the left edge out in the margin a little bit, so it doesn't look indented. Unbounded, same-color drop caps are a subtle way to start new pages. You don't know how large a visitor's fonts are, so if your drop cap offsets three lines of text on your screen, there could be a gap on someone else's screen. Add some white space at the bottom so that text lines aren't jammed up against the bottom of your character as they wrap around underneath.

A good rule: no more than one initial cap per page.

Captions

Add captions to your photos and illustrations. There's no need to struggle with HTML to create captions – the wording isn't likely to change, and you can always include the text in the **A L T** attribute. A small caption below each image in an article adds very little to the size of the file, guarantees the right relationship of caption and image, and frees you from having to worry about it later. Because you don't know what size text people are using, at least you know your captions will stay under control.

Make sure to bring captions right underneath (or next to) your images. Too much white space causes them to float away visually. Add just a few pixels between an illustration and its

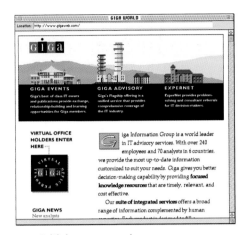

5.12 Initial caps can make a page look sophisticated.

5.13 An unbounded initial cap standing on the baseline.

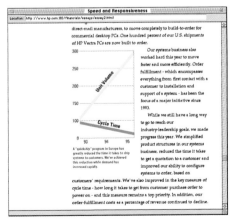

5.14 Captions under images look sharp and don't get lost.

5.15 Small caps can be effective if used sparingly.

caption. Make them bold or use a contrasting color, but avoid italics, since they don't look as good at small sizes on computer screens [**5.14**]. Don't worry about adding extra colors to your image; just make sure they compress well by eliminating extra intermediate colors.

One word of warning: do not add caption text to a JPEG image. Either make a separate GIF caption or use a table cell with text.

Small Caps

True small caps are the mark of an advanced typographer. Beginning a new chapter (or web magazine article) with a few words in small caps draws attention, inviting the reader to pick up the line and continue reading. Use them when you want a formal voice: titles, names, stationery, invitations (web

invitations with secret URLs are even more fun than printed ones), important documents, and more [**5.15**].

Small caps are usually just a little taller than a lowercase x (the *x-height*), and they are often slightly wider than regular caps. There are three ways to put them into your web pages:

1. In your HTML, use a size difference (`<FONT SIZE=-1>`) to make small caps directly in the text. It won't look perfect, because the smaller characters will look too light, but it will load quickly. It's a bit of a hack, though – good typographers cringe when they see such unevenly weighted characters together.

2. You can also manufacture small caps in a GIF image. If you don't have a font with small caps, you can make your own. Don't just reduce the size of the caps. Reduced caps will be lighter than their associated real caps and the line will look uneven [**5.16**]. Instead, use a font with a slightly heavier version – usually a demibold or a book weight – and add the regular caps to the slightly bolder caps set in a smaller size to get a "poor man's small caps" [**5.17**].

3. The best way to get small caps is to buy a set. Type designers go out of their way to make small caps work well with regular caps. I often use the small caps of a beautiful typeface called Sabon (designed by Jan Tschichold). Eaglefeather's small caps are also quite distinctive [**5.18**].

Screen Resolutions

At the intersection of the browser wars and the platform wars, we have screen resolution. The more you know about this subject, the flatter your forehead becomes. It would take an entire chapter to go into all the details, but here is the essential picture: Macintoshes use a fixed measure of 1 pixel = 1 printer's point. Hence, 12-point type is always 12 pixels tall. If a Macintosh monitor has more than 72 dots per inch, 12-point type is smaller than it should be. On the Mac, a square 72 pixels high and a character in 72-point type are the same height (relative to the monitor's resolution).

Windows machines are a bit more complicated. Windows treats type and resolution separately, so a 72-pixel square will be whatever size it is (depending on the resolution of the screen), but 72-point type will be 72 points (one inch) tall when actual monitor resolution is 96 DPI. Windows drivers usually let users define the relation of points to pixels, which is a good thing for users and frustrating for designers who must balance sizes of images and live text.

While that is fairly easy to understand, it's not exactly true. Windows users can specify the number of pixels per inch via a control panel.

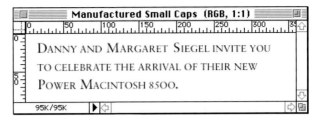

5.16 Manufactured small caps look uneven.

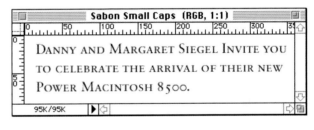

5.17 Use a slightly heavier weight to get a "poor-man's small caps."

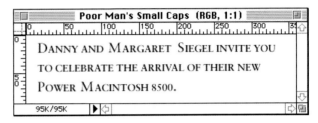

5.18 Both Sabon's and Eaglefeather's small caps are designed to work well with the caps.

Better Browsing Fonts

Whether you have a Macintosh or a Windows machine, you'll be glad to know that Microsoft has collaborated with world-famous type designer Matthew Carter and Monotype's Tom Rickner to produce two excellent fonts designed for on-screen applications. Verdana and Georgia are available for both platforms, absolutely free, from Microsoft's Typography site.

These are specially made TrueType fonts that should replace Times Roman and Helvetica (Arial) as your own personal browsing fonts. You should encourage people to download them and use them on their browsers, and you can even call them by name in your HTML. Specifying `<FONT FACE="Verdana, Arial, Helvetica">` says your first choice is Verdana, but if they don't have that, they should try the other fonts, in order. You can also simply say `<FONT FACE="Verdana">` and let the client deal with substitutions on its own.

Get these two well made fonts from www.microsoft.com/truetype, in the core fonts section of that site, and watch for new developments from Microsoft and Adobe.

Verdana and Georgia are free, and they're great for browsing.

Furthermore, multi-sync monitors can make pixels larger or smaller without the system knowing. What conclusion can we draw from this? The Macintosh operating system and Windows handle type differently, based on different units of measurements, and, because of multi-sync monitors, you never ever know what your audience really sees.

Therefore, web designers must make an important assumption. We must assume that viewers will set their default font size and resolution the way they like them, even though we know that most viewers never change their default settings (or even know they can). When we specify type in our web pages, we always assume that the "normal" size (`<font size="3">`) is just right, and we always increase or decrease font sizes by specifying *relative* size changes. That is, we use `<font size="+1">` rather than `<font size="4">`.

Summary

Choose your fonts with care, anti-alias them well, make them compressible yet smooth, and stick with the GIF format until something better takes over. Your type will still be fuzzy, but it's the best we can do until screens have higher resolutions.

Very soon, browsers will be able to see fonts embedded in an HTML document (*see Chapter 12: "Transitional Strategies"*).

Part II

CHAPTER 6

A Page Makeover

What you'll learn in this chapter:

Page structure

Browser offsets

Anti-aliasing

Control of vertical space

Tiling backgrounds

Sharon Stargazer's Home Page

Location: http://www.killersites.com/

SHARON STARGAZER

Hey! What are you doing looking at your computer? You should be out looking at the stars. This month, look for Mars near the horizon just after sunset. It's the big red one!

News Flash
I am having an astronomy party! Come as your favorite constellation! Read my digital invitation to see if you're invited! (hint: if you're in the Milky Way, you're invited.)

About Me
Everything you ever wanted to know about me and my life looking at the stars. You'll find some of my favorite **people** here, too. You'll also see work by other researchers, including Dan Mills, Stacy Rosenblatt, Tatjana Keller, Rebecca Shulman, and Richard Powers. Check them out!

Space: The Final Frontier
Some day I will find my own Comet and name it **Comet Stargazer**. Until then, you can read some of my papers on interstellar gravity waves.

Space Poetry
Images of space come in several flavors. I have a large collection of space poetry that grows every day. Submit your own poem for my collection!

I hope you'll come back for more space goodies soon!

Ciao,

Sharon Stargazer

Sharon Stargazer's Home Page

Location: | http://www.killersites.com/ |

WELCOME TO SHARON STARGAZER'S HOME PAGE

Hey, what are you doing looking at your computer? You should be looking at the stars. Although I work at a small startup, I spend most of my free time at the Griffith Park observatory cataloging star clusters and measuring nebulae. It's really cool. There's a photo of the observatory here, and some neat star pictures here, and a shot of the 50,000 volt Tesla coil here. If you really need to, you can also click here. Thanks.

NEWS FLASH!

- Get your fresh news items here!
- Old news is archived at this link.

ABOUT ME

- My mom says I should get a life and stop surfing the web so much. I told her it's a great way to meet people. If you want to, you can click this link and learn everything you ever wanted to know about me, including my cat, Kepler, and a lot of links to friends pages and more.

SPACE: THE FINAL FRONTIER

- Some day I will find my own Comet and name it **Comet Keller**. Until then, you can read some of my papers on intrastellar gravity waves.
- Click here for my paper on gravity waves as they affect solar radiation.
- Click here for my paper on perambulating gravity waves.
- Click here for my paper on gravity waves and their influence on the expansion of the universe.
- Click here for my paper on gravity waves and quasars.
- I have a bunch more papers on gravity waves, and they are here.
- I also have some cool space poetry. Check it out!

SPACE LINKS GALORE!

- NASA Ames research
- Hubble Telescope shots
- Russian space links
- Quasar home pages
- Randy's really cool moons
- Big images of satellite photographs of the Sahara - not very good, but they take a long time to download.
- Another cool link

I hope you'll come back for more goodies soon!

Ciao,

SHARON

6.1 A typical first-generation site.

GREAT SITES are built one page at a time. To illustrate several methods and principles presented in previous chapters, I'll go through a web page makeover from start to finish. This should give you a starting point for doing projects in a more precise, layout-oriented way. Rather than making an entire site (front door, entry, and so on), I'll make a simple, elegant personal home page.

The purpose of this chapter is to present third-generation working methods, bringing many of the concepts from earlier chapters into a real-world example. Follow along and see how much control you can get over the page.

For most first-generation home pages, a makeover is like shooting fish in a barrel. Almost anything you do will improve the look **[6.1]**.

This scroll-down page is a "table of contents" with very little content. It shows neither Sharon's enthusiasm for astronomy nor much of her personality. Black type is hard to read on a gray background, and the textured background makes things worse. There's precious little information on what to expect behind the text links, the colors aren't intuitive, and the edge-to-edge typography gets worse as you open the window. The horizontal rules add insult to injury. Furthermore, the list of links takes your attention away from what she has to offer. Sharon is ready for a third-generation page.

Strategy

Rather than edit the existing HTML, I'll start with a fresh "sheet of paper" and build it up from scratch. I want to use a background image that combines stars for theme and white as a background for text. I'll get there in steps, starting with a dark blue bar down the left side and modifying it later. Then I'll put everything into a table and set up a simple layout with no bullets, rules, or HTML "junk." Finally, I'll discuss some possible additions.

Note: This chapter has been rewritten from the first edition. The single-pixel GIFs have been removed, and I've used Photoshop 4.0 to create the images.

The Redesign

First I'll make a background image. Then I'll position a foreground image on top of the background and add the text. Once the page is in good shape, I'll add a few finishing touches. As an encore, I'll get myself out of a mess caused by inconsistent browser offsets.

A Clean, Tiling Background

Most tiling background images add texture to a page. Many backgrounds try to create a 3-D effect, which interferes with the text, causing it to float above the page. But background images can also give a page structure. In this case, a blue bar down the left side provides a strong contrast with the white area, setting it apart from the noisy clutter of the desktop. I start by making a very wide, short image that tiles (repeats) vertically in the browser window.

In Photoshop, I open a new file, 25 pixels high by 1200 wide. Why 25 pixels high? It only needs to be one

pixel tall to tile, but if you try it with a 1 x 1200 file, you'll see that it takes far too long for the browser to replicate this file over and over – it "rolls down" very slowly. It works, but it puts too much demand on the client computer. In my experiments, I've found that 25-pixel-high images download and un-roll faster than other heights, though the difference between 25 and, say, 20 pixels is small. More than 25 makes for too long a download, and GIF inflation can become a problem on large background images (*see "Image Inflation" in Chapter 3*).

The width of 1200 pixels prevents the background from tiling horizontally in most browser windows. If you make it, say, 600 pixels wide, it might look fine on your machine, but in a larger window, a second blue column will appear to the right of the text. I can make this image large, yet keep the file size small, because solid areas compress well [**6.2**]. For the sake of maximum contrast and readability, I would never make the right side anything but white.

On a new layer, I make a rectangle 120 pixels wide and fill it with blue. This color should come from the color cube. I choose an RGB value of 0, 0, 51, which in hex (`"#000033"`) is simply the darkest blue you can get (*if this isn't clear, see "The Color Cube," in Chapter 3, before continuing*).

I export the file as a GIF. I turn interlacing and transparency off. Even though it is quite wide, this 1-bit image compresses down to a mere 374 bytes.

Now for the HTML. I type the following code into a new file, open it in the browser, and voilà! [**6.3**].

Layer Management

Always leave the background layer of a Photoshop document a single color. Everything else goes into separate layers for easy anti-aliasing and flexibility.

Many tools anti-alias by default, which can either be beneficial or horrific. I make sure I'm in RGB mode, because CMYK isn't for display screens, and I always use pixels, rather than inches, as my standard unit of measurement.

```
<HTML>
  <HEAD>
    <TITLE>
      Sharon's Home Page
    </TITLE>
  </HEAD>
  <BODY BGCOLOR="#FFFFFF"
  TEXT="#000000"
  LINK="990000"
  ALINK="#FFFFFF"
  VLINK="#666666"
  BACKGROUND="./spine.gif">
  </BODY>
</HTML>
```

6.2 The blue area on the left tiles down to become the vertical bar. Make the file 1200 pixels wide overall, so it doesn't tile again to the right.

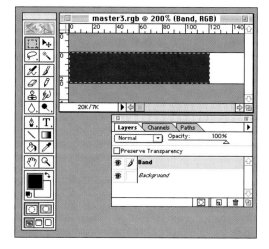

A Third-Generation Banner

I'd like to put a red circle in the foreground, centered on the border between blue and white. This breaks the plane of the blue bar, causing the circle to stand out above all other elements. Visually, it will become the front-most image, drawing the eye like a lit match. I am going to put Sharon's name over it, so you know right away whose page it is. (To me, this is more consistent with the overall astronomy theme than the <H1> HTML heading, but that's just my opinion.) I'll start with a circle 80 pixels in diameter – two-thirds the width of the blue band. This should give me a balanced look: not too scrawny, yet not overpowering. I open a new Photoshop document, 120 x 120 pixels – a bit larger than the circle. On a new layer, using the ellipse tool, I draw a red circle, which is anti-aliased by default. Anti-aliasing makes the edges of the circle look smooth [6.4].

6.3 The tiling background as it looks in the browser.

I save the circle as a GIF, designating pure white as the transparent color. I view this GIF at various positions, using

120

6.4 A circle, aliased (LEFT) and anti-aliased (RIGHT).

```
<HTML>
  <HEAD>
    <TITLE>
      Sharon Stargazer's Home Page
    </TITLE>
  </HEAD>
  <!-- Page Parameters -->
  <BODY BGCOLOR="#FFFFFF" BACKGROUND="spine.gif">
    <!-- Begin Red Circle Placement -->
    <IMG VSPACE=15 HSPACE=20 WIDTH=80 HEIGHT=80
    SRC="./redcircle.gif">
    <BR>
    <IMG VSPACE=15 HSPACE=80 WIDTH=80 HEIGHT=80
      SRC="./redcircle.gif">
    <BR>
    <IMG VSPACE=15 HSPACE=140 WIDTH=80 HEIGHT=80
      SRC="./redcircle.gif">
    <!-- End Red Circle Placement -->
  </BODY>
</HTML>
```

6.5 Note the use of HSPACE to control the horizontal position of the circle.

the image's **HSPACE** and **VSPACE** arguments for spacing [**6.5, 6.6**].

What's going on? Because GIF supports only one level of transparency, all the near-white pixels (which are actually shades of pink) make the shape look good against white, but not against blue. I anti-aliased the circle against a background of solid white, but half the background is blue [**6.7**]. I'm in trouble.

To anti-alias the GIF properly, I add a new layer, draw a blue rectangle, and position the circle against it [**6.8**].

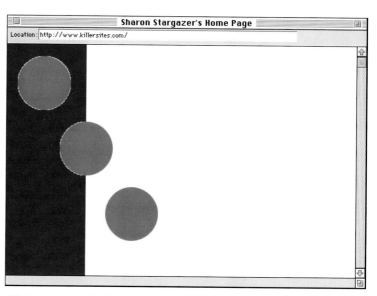

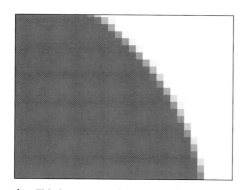

6.7 This image contains many colors to make the edge look smooth.

6.6 The use of anti-aliased foreground images requires precise alignment over backgrounds with major color changes.

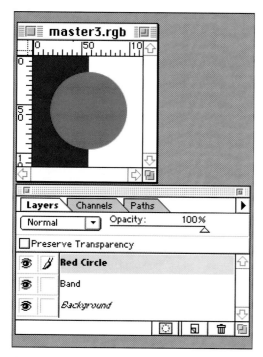

6.8 Create a layer for each image, positioning the circle precisely.

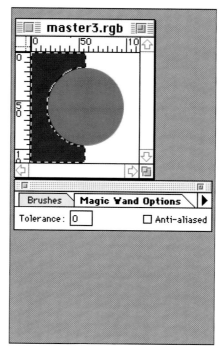

6.9 Flatten the image, then select the blue area with the magic wand. Delete it.

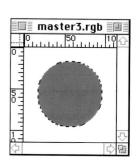

6.10 Select everything *but* the circle. Invert the selection.

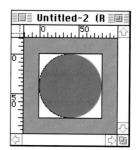

6.11 Place the copied selection into a new file.

Note: These anti-aliasing problems wouldn't happen if we had 256 levels (8 bits) of transparency, but with GIFs, we can designate only one color (1 level) as transparent.

I flatten the image. Now I want to get rid of the large blue and white areas, so I can take the anti-aliased circle over to my other file. This is a three-step process. First, I select the blue area using the magic wand *with no anti-aliasing* and a tolerance of zero **[6.9]**.

Second, I add the white area to the selection by shift-clicking the magic wand on the white area **[6.10]**. I invert the selection, giving me a circle that contains the entire anti-aliased image.

Third, I simply copy the circle and paste it into a new file, which will be just big enough to accommodate the copied image **[6.11]**. No sense shipping extra invisible bits.

I reduce this image to eight colors using Photoshop 4.0's built-in web palette, which is the same as the color cube (*see "Reducing File Size" in Chapter 3*). This automatically reduces to seven colors: black, white, red, and four intermediates from the cube. That is all the shades of red I need to make the anti-aliasing work. Then I export the image as a GIF, designating pure white to be transparent **[6.12]**.

I replace the existing circle image with the new one (using the same file name to avoid the hassle of changing the HTML) to see how it looks **[6.13]**.

Unfortunately, anti-aliasing a foreground image is not always this simple. In fact, things will get more complicated. Now, I want to add Sharon's name in front of the circle. I return to the Photoshop file and expand the canvas size by a few hundred pixels on the right side to make room.

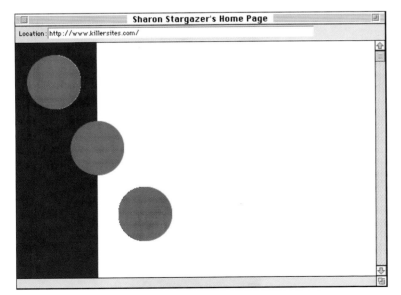

6.13 The right placement makes all the difference.

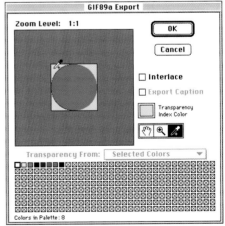

6.12 With Photoshop's GIF89a export plug-in, you can designate a single color as transparent.

6.14 Sans-serif type-faces generally read better on screen.

To complement the clean look of the page, I experiment with a few sans-serif typefaces, with the name both in upper-and lower-case. Gill Sans bold caps loosely spaced is one of my favorites [**6.14**]. Sans-serifs are usually a good choice, because many serifed fonts have features that become blurry when anti-aliased (*see Chapter 5, "Rendering Type," for more information*).

The Text

Now for the table work. This page will use two main tables, one to position the header and one to position the rest of the text. They are both quite similar, with the header table's left cell specified as 70 pixels wide, and the text table's left cell 135 pixels wide. Rather than using single-pixel GIFs, I've managed to use non-breaking spaces both to space these tables and between the bold subheads.

Look carefully at the code [**6.15**]. You'll see how I use vertical space to lay out the page, replacing bullets with good typography. If you build a page like this, you can adjust the width of their left-hand cells and watch the page change accordingly. It's clean and easy to modify.

Finally, I make a GIF with Sharon's name in a favorite script typeface called Shelley (*see "Hand Retouching" in Chapter 5*) and add it to the page. This is a nice touch that doesn't take long to make. Another possibility would have been to scan Sharon's actual signature, but Sharon, alas, does not exist.

124

6.15 The table for this page is straightforward. The left margin is 135 pixels wide (see image 6.16).

```
<HTML>
  <HEAD>
    <TITLE>
      Sharon Stargazer's Home Page
    </TITLE>
  </HEAD>
  <BODY LEFTMARGIN=0 TOPMARGIN=0 BGCOLOR="#FFFFFF"
  TEXT="#666666" LINK="#CC0000" ALINK="#FF3300"
  VLINK="#330099" BACKGROUND="./images/spine.gif">
     
    <BR>
     
    <BR>
    <TABLE BORDER="0" CELLPADDING="0" CELLSPACING="0"
    WIDTH="431">
      <TR>
        <TD WIDTH="70">
           
        </TD>
        <TD ALIGN=LEFT WIDTH="361">
          <IMG SRC="./images/header.gif" ALIGN=TOP
          WIDTH="361" HEIGHT="86" BORDER="0" VSPACE="5">
        </TD>
      </TR>
    </TABLE>
    <BR>
    <!-- Begin the table -->
    <TABLE BORDER=0 CELLPADDING=0 CELLSPACING=0 WIDTH=485>
      <TR>
        <TD WIDTH=135>
           
          <BR>
        </TD>
        <!-- This "blank" cell uses the br as filler -->
        <TD WIDTH=350>
          Hey! What are you doing looking at your computer?
          You should be out looking at the stars. This
          month, look for Mars near the horizon just after
          sunset. It's the big red one!
          <BR>
           
          <BR>
           
          <BR>
          <B>
            News Flash
          </B>
          <BR>
           
          <BR>
          I am having an astronomy party! Come as your
          favorite constellation! Read my
            <A HREF="./me/invite.html">
```

125

```
     digital invitation</A>
to see if you're invited! (hint: if you're in
the Milky Way, you're invited.)
<BR>
 
<BR>
 
<BR>
<B>
     <A HREF="./me/index.html">
     About Me</A>
</B>
<BR>
 
<BR>
Everything you ever wanted to know about me and
my life looking at the stars. You'll find some of
my favorite
<B>
     <A HREF="./me/people.html">
     people</A>
</B>
here, too. You'll also see work by other
researchers,
   <A HREF="./me/mills.html">
   Dan Mills</A>
,
   <A HREF="./rosenblatt/index.html">
   Stacy Rosenblatt</A>
,
   <A HREF="./keller/index.html">
   Tatjana Keller</A>
,
   <A HREF="./shulman/index.html">
   Rebecca Shulman</A>
, and
   <A HREF="./powers/index.html">
   Richard Powers</A>
. Check them out!
<BR>
 
<BR>
 
<BR>
<B>
     <A HREF="./space/index.html">
     Space: The Final Frontier</A>
</B>
<BR>
 
<BR>
Some day I will find my own Comet and name it
<B>
```

```
        Comet Stargazer
</B>
. Until then, you can read some of my papers on
  <A HREF="./waves/index.html">
  interstellar gravity waves.</A>
<BR>
 
<BR>
 
<BR>
<B>
      <A HREF="./poems/index.html">
      Space Poetry</A>
</B>
<BR>
 
<BR>
Images of space come in several flavors. I have a
large collection of
  <A HREF="./poems/index.html">
  space poetry</A>
that grows every day. Submit your own poem for my
collection!
<BR>
 
<BR>
 
<BR>
I hope you'll come back for more space goodies
soon!
<P>
Ciao,
<BR>
 
<BR>
<IMG SRC="./images/signature.gif" ALIGN=TOP
WIDTH="213" HEIGHT="38" BORDER="0">
    </TD>
  </TR>
</TABLE>
</BODY>
</HTML>
```

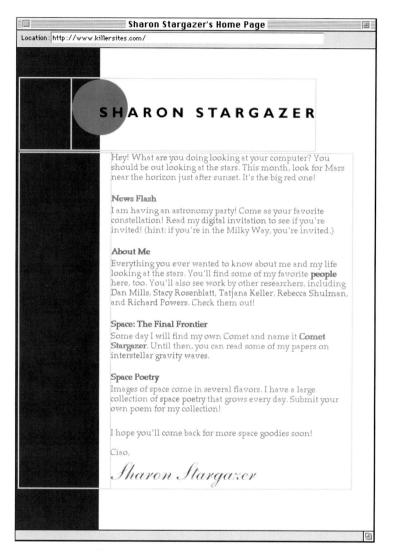

6.16 Now it's really coming together!

Sharon Stargazer's Home Page
Location: http://www.killersites.com/

Pushing the Envelope

Now that I've built a page [6.16], I'm ready to make it better. I like the look I've established, but it's not very astronomical. I go to NASA's site for inspiration and find a familiar, impressive shot of the earth [6.17].

NASA's reproduction guidelines say I can use this image for Sharon's page (as a taxpayer, I've already paid for it). I want to substitute the earth for the red circle and make the blue band represent space with the help of a few stars.

Here's a tricky part: getting the earth separated from its background so I can anti-alias it properly. When "cutting" an image out of a photograph like this, I use the marquee tool rather than the magic wand. The magic wand rarely works well for this kind of operation, because there are usually too many subtle and irregular color gradations in a photograph.

I feather the circular selection by one pixel [6.18], cut, paste into a new file, and reduce the earth to the size of the red circle: 80 pixels across [6.19].

6.17 Many copyright-free images are available at US Government sites like NASA. But make sure you read their guidelines first. Be aware that copyright issues on the Internet are complex and not to be trifled with.

I bring the earth into my master (RGB) Photoshop document. I paste the image in, and Photoshop 4.0 automatically creates a new layer. (When I re-index the image, Photoshop will flatten the document, so I will lose whatever other layers I had.) I save my master file, then I hide the red circle, flatten the image, index, and export it as a new document. Because I feathered the Earth image, it will automatically pick up the dark blue anti-aliasing on the left and the white anti-aliasing on the right [6.20]. Bring the type back, and whoops! [6.21]

Now the type doesn't work. It needs a new color. Here's a neat trick: I make a new layer by dragging the current layer's name onto the New Layer icon, which duplicates the layer. In this new layer, I select the image only. Then I choose a nice ochre from the color cube (*conveniently stored in my color picker; see "The Color Cube" in Chapter 3 for details*) and fill the selection. The type changes color. I turn off the black layer and look at it [6.22].

Can you see the problem? There isn't enough contrast with the background. I tried some other colors, but the real solution is to add a drop shadow to set the name off from the background. When I do a drop shadow on type, I often cast the shadow down and to the left, because that makes the leading edges, stems, and feet of the characters stand out strongly against the shadows [6.23]. On the other hand, most drop shadows go down and to the *right*, indicating a virtual light source high and left. The choice is yours.

With the earth and type looking good, I flatten the layers and cut and

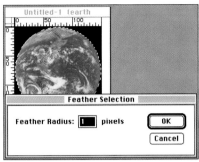

6.18 Feather selection for a soft edge.

6.19 Replacement for the circle.

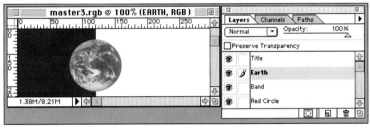

6.20 The earth goes on its own layer.

6.21 The type is placed over the earth.

6.22 The ochre text is better than bold, but...

6.23 A drop shadow helps make the text more legible.

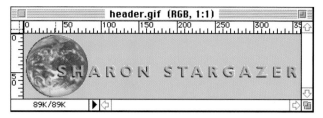

6.24 Bright green is the chroma-key color for this image. Note the halos around the earth and type.

6.25 The top image in final form.

paste it into a new file. Unlike the red circle I made earlier, this time I can't safely pick white as my transparent color when exporting the GIF. Why? Chances are, at least a few pixels in the clouds will be white like the background, especially after I reduce the number of colors in the image to lengthen the runs and improve compression (*see "Reducing File Size" in Chapter 3*). If I designated white as the color to make transparent, the clouds could get "holes" in them. Instead, I have to choose a chroma-key color that will become transparent. A chroma-key color is one that doesn't occur anywhere in the image (*see "The GIF Format" in Chapter 3*). Because my image is already indexed, and all the colors in the image are in the palette and are already being used, I return to my RGB version and use the magic wand (tolerance=0, anti-aliasing off) to select both the blue and white background areas by hand with the magic wand, making sure to shift-select the *counters* (blank spaces in the letter shapes) of the letters, and replace the blue and white with bright green [**6.24**]. This is the chroma-key color.

I make the GIF as usual, choose green rather than white as the transparent color, save the image again, reload in the browser window, and voilà – the green is gone, and the earth shines brightly [**6.25**]

The Finishing Touch

To complete the original idea, I make a star pattern in the blue background area. This turns out to be pretty difficult. Stars aren't white. They're all

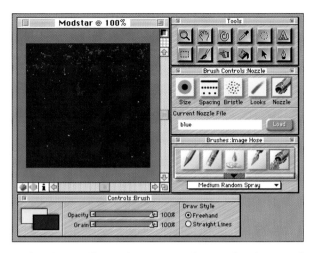

6.26 Painter's tiling and Image Hose features lay the ground for my star field. It's a powerful tool: don't get carried away!

6.28 The earth moved! Different browsers currently have different offsets: This is the same page viewed with Internet Explorer.

6.27 The final page, ready to go – almost.

Anti-Aliased Layers

To select everything on a layer in Photoshop while preserving transparency and anti-aliased edges, simply select all, then wiggle the arrow keys back and forth (one pixel left, one pixel right). This will select everything, ready to fill.

A different but equally good Mac method is to click the Preserve Transparency box, then simply option-delete the entire layer to fill. See which method you prefer.

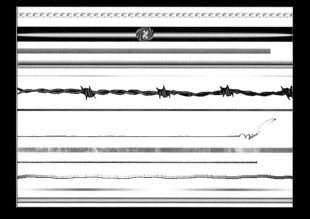

Deadly Sin Number Two

Horizontal Rules

Horizontal rules are a weak substitute for proper hierarchy and organization of vertical space on web pages.

There are millions of horizontal rules on the Web, doing nothing but taking up space and breaking the natural flow of pages. Horizontal rules are not spacers; they are barriers.

The only time they are useful is in very crowded newspaper front pages, where space is so tight that the proper amount of white space is too "expensive." Newspapers need to resort to these kinds of compromises; web pages don't.

different colors. If the pattern of stars is too regular, or if your background strip is too short, repetition will be obvious. Too tall and it will take a long time to load. Getting a reasonable pattern only 25 pixels high is easier if you have the right tool for the job.

With tiling backgrounds, you must watch the edges closely to get a smooth transition. Fortunately, Fractal Design Painter has a tiling feature that helps do it automatically. Using the "image hose," loaded with single-pixel "stars" and with tiling turned on, I get a good start on the star field [6.26].

Painter does most of the work; making it perfect takes some manual editing. Of course, now that I've done it, you can just take mine right off the book site and use or modify it rather than start from scratch.

Look at the final page and compare it to the original gray site [6.27]. (*You can probably tell, since the chapter doesn't end here, that the story isn't over.*)

Background Registration

Now for the fun part: a cross-platform browser check [6.28].

This is a big disappointment. All of my careful image placement and background correction turns to garbage unless I can register the background and foreground images precisely, at least in the horizontal direction. Most browsers currently have different offsets, both horizontally and vertically (*see "Offsets" in Chapter 4*). That completely trashes my work. There are three solutions:

1. Change the background to eliminate the color transition.

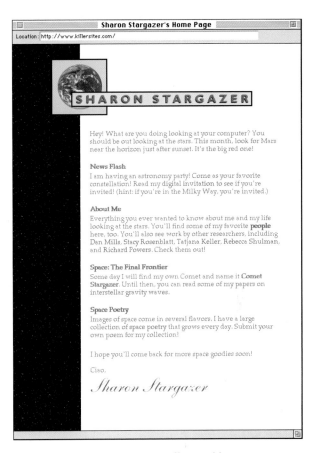

6.29 Sharon might like this, but it's not for me. (Note that I had to re-anti-alias the signature against black to make this illustration.)

6.30 No anti-aliasing means no offset problems.

Because of browser offsets, you really can't put an anti-aliased image over a background that has two or more prominent areas of color. If you put the earth entirely over the dark blue star pattern, or make the star pattern wider, you can get away with anti-aliasing only to the dark blue color, because the stars are too small to cause noticeable anti-aliasing problems. In fact, Sharon herself might be quite pleased with this version **[6.29]**.

Personally, I resist these kinds of pages, unless they are mostly thematic and don't have much text. Yes, it looks "cool," but it is hard to read. The only reason it works at all is that the dark blue dominates, the bright pixels are few, and the vertical hierarchy pulls its weight. If you have only a little text on your home page, this could be your solution. I prefer dark text on a light background.

2. Don't anti-alias foreground images that appear over major color transitions.

6.31 Internet Explorer was the first browser to give us zero offsets. Here is the final page, with borders visible (left), and as seen through Internet Explorer (right). Netscape still refuses to honor LEFTMARGIN="0".

Instead, use an image that doesn't require anti-aliasing. My solution is to make the top banner into an image that doesn't anti-alias **[6.30]** *(See "Anti-Aliasing" in Chapter 3 for details)*. This banner can move all over the place and it won't matter.

I have resisted the urge to make a big fat rectangle and fill it. Big rectangular banners are an easy way to make sites but not to engage your audience. After some trial and error with the color cube, I find some colors that

work together. The bordered banner approach is a success. It's not as nice as the original, but it works.

3. Set offsets to zero for 3.0 and 4.0 browsers.

Internet Explorer version 2.0 and later gives me the ability to set the offsets to zero. Netscape Navigator 3.0 does not. Internet Explorer can read two important tags: LEFTMARGIN and TOPMARGIN, which I set to zero immediately and rearrange some of the HTML. Viewed through Internet Explorer, the page finally renders as it should **[6.31]**.

```
<BODY LEFTMARGIN="0"
TOPMARGIN="0" BGCOLOR="#FFFFFF"
TEXT="#666666" LINK="CC0000"
ALINK="#FF3300" VLINK="330099"
BACKGROUND="./images/
spine.gif">
```

I'd like to design every page I make with no offsets (true typographic margins are not the same as browser-window offsets), but not all browsers will let me. Because of this, I must throw in the towel and use a solution that doesn't rely on perfect registration between background and foreground.

The lesson: If a foreground image has any anti-aliasing on the edges, it must register perfectly unless the background is a solid color. Images that don't have anti-aliasing don't need registration. Background registration is practically impossible until more surfers can see zero offsets.

Summary

Believe it or not, this entire page weighs less than 13K. This is not a full site, but it is a third-generation home page. Notice how little HTML there is. Most of the work is in Photoshop, struggling with anti-aliasing and transparency issues. The page is easy to update and keep alive, the graphics look great, and surfers will love it.

To aid navigation throughout, add a small version of the earth to all the pages of the site and link it back to the front page.

Application

It is a good idea to add current content to a page like this. To keep going, I might put "the astronomy site of the week" or the "astronomy fact of the week" at the top of the page, to draw people to the site regularly. If enough people come to this page to see the current information, undoubtedly many will also cruise the rest of the site. Any other urgent news items should go right at the top of the page, below the title.

If I really wanted to impress people, I'd make an animated GIF of the world spinning behind Sharon's name (*see "The GIF Format" in Chapter 3*). Then I could use a downscaled version around the site as a navigation device. If visitors clicked on the little spinning globe, they would go back to the front page.

To go *all* the way, I'd include an animated background GIF on the front page that, very subtly, would make the stars twinkle. There's only one problem with that plan: At the time I write this, no browser can see animated background GIFs. Maybe, for the sake of surfers in general, it's just as well.

Netscape's 4.0 browser now supports animated background GIFs. I'm afraid this will lead to even less legible pages, so I'm not showing or encouraging widespread use of this feature, which is the 4.0 equivalent of the original <BLINK> tag.

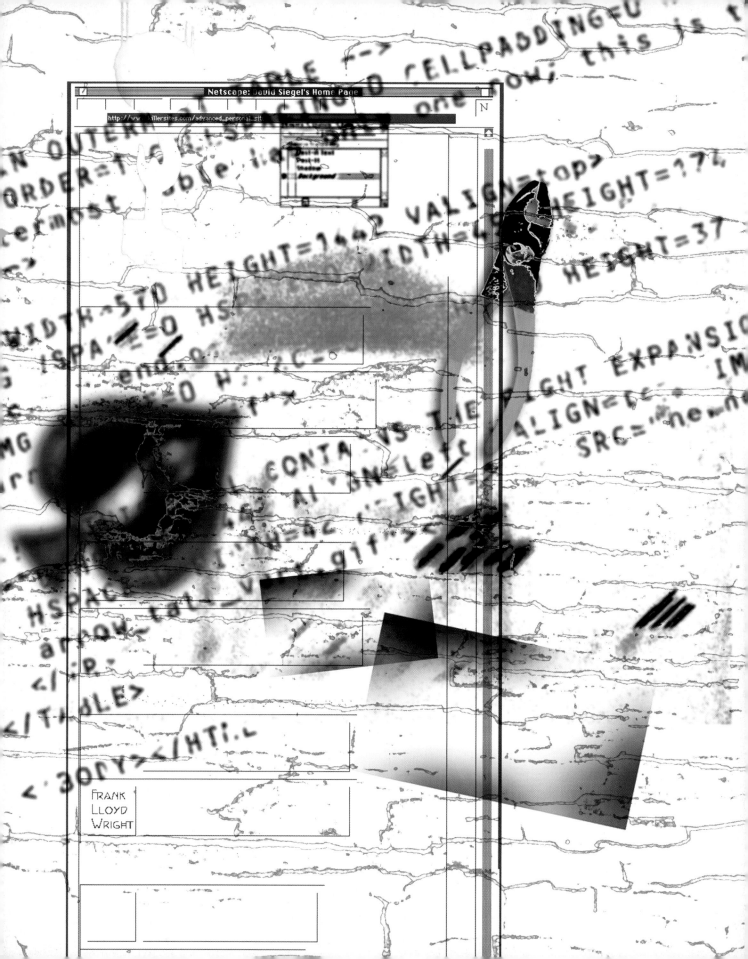

CHAPTER 7

A Personal Site

What you'll learn in this chapter:

How to render type

Breaking the page into sections

How to split and mortise images

Nesting tables

Creating a simple metaphor

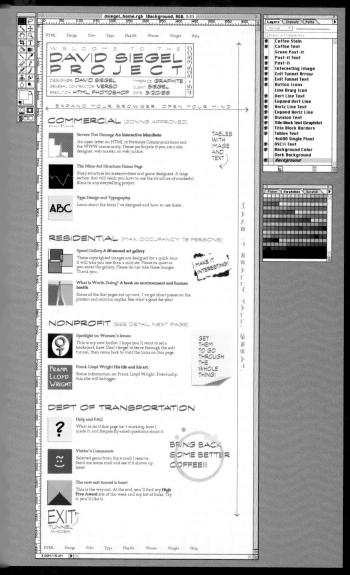

.1 Make your mistakes in Photoshop, not HTML. Creating a layer for each element keeps things flexible.

THIS CHAPTER explains how I made the core page of my first personal site and added a nice entrance. I have always had a strong interest in architecture, and I've designed a number of typefaces based on the distinctive handwriting of architects. I wanted a blueprint metaphor to give the feeling of looking at a plan for my site.

The plan has the title block on top, telling visitors what's going on as soon as the page starts to load. There are four main sections: professional, personal, nonprofit, and various pages about my site (leading to my list of links). Once a page has more than about six choices, use a hierarchical grouping to prevent showing a long vertical list of equally weighted links. I use the opportunity to bring out the metaphor by labeling these sections with catchy phrases and dropping a surprise graphic into each area. Breaking the page into areas this way makes scrolling an adventure.

Strategy

The page should play with the "sheet of paper" metaphor as the visitor scrolls down. The two intersecting arrows that span the height and width of the page reinforce a sense of space and boundedness just like paper. They illustrate the main trick of this chapter: splitting the arrows into two separate GIFs and mortising them back together with a table.

I could make a huge background image with these arrows, but a background GIF with the blue elements would inflate too much for many surfers' systems (*see "The GIF Format" in*

Chapter 3). I also wanted a set of text links to appear at the top of the page, for those who have been there before and want to go right to a particular page.

Photoshop

I prototype just about everything in Photoshop, so I can make all the design decisions before any HTML work begins. In Photoshop 4.0, each item automatically gets its own layer – I use many more layers than elements, because several layers are experiments [**7.1**]. For example, I tried the "Make it really tall" graphic turned bottom-to-top (as an architect would do it), but I think it reads better top-to-bottom (as the page scrolls).

The Blueprint Metaphor

I want to use a light-blue background the color of a faded blueprint [**7.2 A-C**]. By changing the color of the background layer in Photoshop, I get a feel for how this will play on the Web (remember that colors tend to appear darker on PCs than on Macs).

Because the metaphor depends on it, I would like to use the light blue color, even though it's not in the color cube. What will visitors with 8-bit displays see? A quick test in Netscape and Internet Explorer with 256 colors shows they will see white. If they saw a dark cross-hatching pattern, that would be bad. Alternatively, I could use a blended background image [**D-F**], but it would involve adding another image to the load. I finally decide on bgcolor="#EDEDFF".

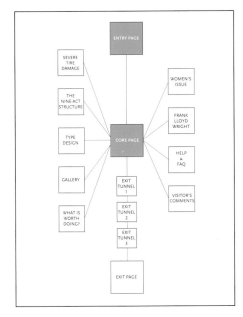

Simplified site plan.

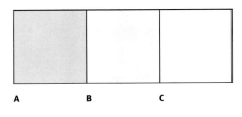

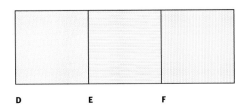

7.2 Background colors: The lightest color-cube blue (**A**) is too dark, while the non-color-cube blue (**B**) performs acceptably on high-end systems. (**B**) shows up as white on 256-color systems (**C**), because background images are mapped to the color cube without dithering (to save time in rendering). The cross-hatch (**D**) and interlaced patterns (**E, F**) are worth considering, too. The cross-hatched version is most effective.

A R204 G204 B255
HEX #CCCCFF
Lightest color-cube blue

B R237 G237 B255
HEX #EDEDFF
As seen with
thousands of colors

C R237 G237 B255
HEX #EDEDFF
As seen with 256 colors

D R204 G204 B255
HEX #CCCCFF
Crosshatched with
R255 G255 B255
HEX #FFFFFF

E R204 G204 B255
HEX #CCCCFF
Horizontally interlaced with
R255 G255 B255
HEX #FFFFFF

F R204 G204 B255
HEX #CCCCFF
Vertically interlaced with
R255 G255 B255
HEX #FFFFFF

139

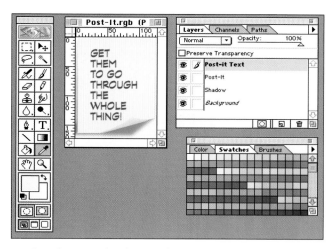

7.3 I use layers and paths to make a convincing sticky note.

7.5 Measure twice, cut once: With complicated table work, I like to tape a marked-up image to my monitor.

7.4 Scans great, with half the caffeine of doing it by hand.

I make the title block and all the hand lettering using my Graphite font, which is an Adobe Multiple-Master typeface. With ATM's Font Creator, I make special wide and narrow versions of Graphite. For example, the section dividers are the real workhorses of the page, so I make them with an extra-bold, extra-wide version of Graphite. For the color, I choose a dark blue (`"#000033"`) from the color cube. Who needs black text on every page? Because type is made of so much white space, light-colored text doesn't work very well – darker is better.

Special Effects

I make my own yellow sticky note in Photoshop, along with a realistic coffee stain. I use three layers to make the sticky note. The yellow layer with the type wasn't difficult, but the shadow was.

The best way to make a shadow like this is to use Photoshop's *paths* feature. Get your shadow path just right, then fill the path using a feather of 4 pixels. I keep adjusting the path shape until the real shadow appears **[7.3]**.

The coffee stain was straightforward. I used a coffee cup to stain a piece of paper, scanned the paper (is this cheating?), and adjusted the color, transparency, and contrast **[7.4]**. Once you get good at this, you can design logos for Fortune 500 companies.

Finally, I make the buttons for each section, pointing to the branches of my site. I decide on a 74 x 74-pixel square, with a one-pixel bevel that raises them just off the page. (One pixel of beveling is about all I can stand – knee-jerk beveling has reached epidemic proportions on the Web.) Bevels are essentially a shadow effect. I want the shadows to go down and to the left also. Note that the one-pixel bevel edges of the buttons are lightened and darkened, rather than painted over, for a good shading effect [7.8 C].

Reduce Colors, Lengthen Runs

I'm ready to make the elements that will compose the page. The first thing I do is print out the Photoshop page and draw boxes on it with a ruler to decide where the table cells will be [7.5]. I have split the horizontal arrow, so the cross-over point is part of the vertical arrow image.

Now that I know the individual images needed, I make the GIFs in two passes. I can index all the images made out of blue and white together, for a consistent look. Then I can go back and index the others. First, I hide all the layers containing any colors other than blue [7.6]. I flatten this entire page and use adaptive color reduction with no dithering.

Remember that anti-aliasing one solid color to another takes only four or five intermediate colors *(see "Anti-Aliasing" in Chapter 3)*. I reduce this image to a 3-bit palette (8 colors): white, blue, and six intermediates [7.7 A]. That's plenty. I export the GIFs without interlacing, because in this situation it's not worth the (admittedly small) price [7.7 B]. In this case, it's okay to use the web palette as an exact palette to map to, because from dark blue to white, the web palette actually has all the intermediate blues I need.

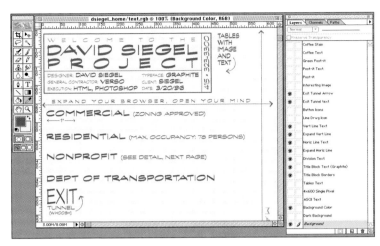

7.6 Anti-alias all same-color images together.

7.7 A Three bits is all you need for anti-aliased type with a solid background *(see "Anti-Aliasing" in Chapter 3)*.

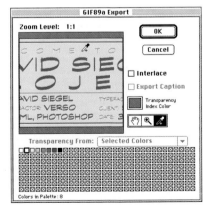

7.7 B When exporting, I designate the light blue background to be the transparent color.

7.8 A-C Start with a small number of colors and work up when indexing to an adaptive color palette.

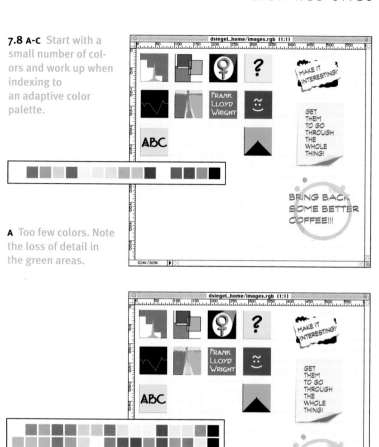

A Too few colors. Note the loss of detail in the green areas.

B This is better, but still not very good.

C Finally, all details show up properly.

The quick Photoshop solution is to reduce using the web palette, letting Photoshop eliminate unused colors from the color table automatically.

Now I tackle the rest of the images. I can index these images together or separately, but doing them together is faster and really doesn't hurt. Remember, palettes are small things; compressibility is what counts. I hide all the layers with blue lettering on them and reveal the rest. In this case, the adaptive-palette approach is more favorable than using the color cube as an exact palette [**7.8 A-C**]. As always, I start with a low number (16 is good) and work up to find the lowest acceptable number (which turns out to be 44 colors). Fewer colors means longer runs for a more compressible image.

In the sticky note, there are some jaggies along the yellow-gray border. I want the shadow to look good, but I don't want to add more colors. I'll occasionally settle for a few jaggies if I can't get a file small enough [**7.9**]. Keep in mind that I use DeBabelizer for these adaptive-palette reductions, because Photoshop doesn't reduce colors accurately.

HTML

I've already sketched the tables by hand; now all I have to do is create them in HTML. This kind of work is easy if you take a systematic approach, commenting your code carefully so you don't get lost and making sure everything works as you take each step.

7.9 Experiment with various bit depths to find one that's just right.

The Zen of Drop Shadows

Drop shadows are generally misunderstood and overused. They are helpful for lifting things slightly off the page, as in the sticky note above, but their enduring place in the designer's palette is as a means of enhancing edges. Dark type on a light background generally needs no such enhancement.

Drop shadows help distinguish foreground from background when there's not much contrast between them. Most drop shadows fall down and to the right, including those of the Mac and Windows operating systems. With type in particular, however, the left side of a character is more important, because the eye seeks these leading edges as it scans a line from left to right.

For this reason, I often drop shadows down and to the left. Each situation has a best solution – have a good reason for your choice. And once you choose, be consistent!

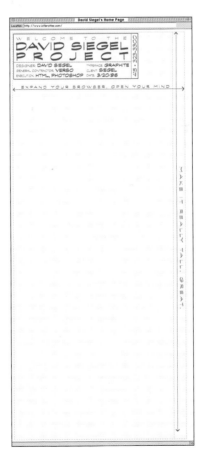

7.10 Start a complicated page by nailing its outside tables into place *(see HTML on the following page).*

7.11 Comments will help keep the code organized as the page expands. Always use HEIGHT and WIDTH tags for your images.

```
<!-- PAGE PARAMETERS -->
<HTML>
   <HEAD>
      <TITLE>
         David Siegel's Home Page
      </TITLE>
   </HEAD>
   <BODY BGCOLOR="#EDEDFF" TEXT="#000055" LINK="#CC0000"
ALINK="#FF3300" VLINK="#005522">

      <!-- BEGIN OUTERMOST TABLE -->
      <TABLE BORDER=1 CELLSPACING=0 CELLPADDING=0
      HEIGHT=1442>

         <!-- Outermost table has only one row; this is the
         left side -->
         <TR>
            <TD WIDTH=570 HEIGHT=1442 VALIGN=TOP><IMG VSPACE=0
            HSPACE=0 WIDTH=455 HEIGHT=174
            SRC="./newhome/back_legend.gif"><IMG VSPACE=0
            HSPACE=0 WIDTH=570 HEIGHT=37
            SRC="./newhome/arrow_horiz.gif"></TD>

            <!-- THIS CELL CONTAINS THE RIGHT EXPANSION ARROW
            -->
            <TD ALIGN=LEFT VALIGN=TOP><IMG VSPACE=0 HSPACE=0
            WIDTH=42 HEIGHT=1418
            SRC="./newhome/arrow_tall_vert.gif"></TD>

         </TR>
      </TABLE>
   </BODY>
</HTML>
```

I like to avoid nested tables whenever possible. Nested tables take longer to render and are difficult to debug. Nested tables are also difficult to maintain, especially in situations with tables nested three or four deep – that's looking for trouble. In this situation, the nested table solution is very simple and straightforward, and the comments make my coding and future maintenance job easier.

The Outer Table

I take an outside-in approach to constructing nested tables. The entire page sits in one large table whose only job is to make sure the large arrow graphics lock together and stay locked. Once I get the outer table set up, the rest of the job looks easier [7.10, 7.11].

Getting the arrow to line up perfectly isn't very difficult, because I cut the

7.12 This basic unit of code plugs into the page's main table.

image up and now I'm just putting it back together. Note the `ALIGN=LEFT` for the tall arrow. That mortises the two images. Without it, there would be a crack, giving away my trick.

The Inner Tables

As the page takes shape, I plug in the cell contents one at a time. Once I splice the arrows back together, I can see the light at the end of the table. Right after that comes the "Commercial Section" image. For the body of each section, I make several two-cell tables for each featured area of the site **[7.12]**.

I plug these in, repeat for the other sections, and the page takes shape **[7.13]**.

I add the four right-margin elements at the ends of my inner tables. The modular table approach lets me

7.13 Note the use of CELLPADDING and the single-pixel GIF to control white space.

Deadly Sin Number Three

Background Images That Interfere

Backgrounds on the Web have reached epidemic proportions. Wallpaper is nice, but reading the handwriting on the wall can cause damage to the retina.

People use background images because they add a "theme" to the page, or because they "fill up all that unused space." It's the kitchen-sink school of page design, which often escalates to homicidal (not killer) site design. Backgrounds do more damage to web pages than almost anything else.

Thoughtless designers get carried away, the pixels fly, and surfers get hurt. The only good background is a solid or nearly solid color: gift wrap makes bad stationery.

adjust each right margin to fit its image individually. These little tables make it easy to copy and paste as individual units when I want to add new items to my page **[7.14]**. (*You can view the source* HTML *at the Book Site.*)

That's all there is to it. I add some text links at top and bottom, and I'm ready for visitors.

This page is not as flexible as I'd like, of course. As I add new features, the right-hand vertical arrow must be remade (In fact, I have lengthened that darn arrow seven or eight times now).

Finally, the text links at top and bottom are separated by non-breaking spaces (` `) to achieve horizontal white space. Notice I do not use vertical separator bars! They are as bad as horizontal rules. In the past, these separators had a function. They separated entries like this when displayed on a search engine. If a search engine picks up my page and displays the top line or two, the entry will be something like "HTML DESIGN FILM TYPE HEALTH WOMEN WRIGHT HELP". If I use vertical separators, it will be "HTML | DESIGN | FILM | TYPE | HEALTH | WOMEN | WRIGHT | HELP."

I admit the second one is better, but there's a better way around the problem. In the next chapter, I'll show how to add special code to your page that only the search engines can see. You can put whatever you want there without affecting the design of the page.

I have actually used single-pixel GIFs here, but only in one small place: between the subheads for each subsection and their associated text. I want a

7.14 Now that I'm pleased with the way the site looks, I can turn off my borders and upload the files to my server.

small amount of white space between these elements, so I use a single-pixel GIF to insert two pixels of vertical white space. You can't get a small space like this without resorting to GIF text. I think it's worth the hassle and the small download to make this page typo-graphically perfect.

A Business Card Welcome

The main page is a good anchor, but it's pretty big for a destination URL. I'd like to put out a welcome mat to give people a feel for what they are about to encounter. My personal site has a complex entryway, but for this chapter I'll suggest a simple, elegant approach that can work for any personal site: a business card, scanned (or made from scratch in Photoshop), all by itself on a page [7.15]. Click the card to enter.

The exit from my site, linked from the bottom of the core page, leads surf-

7.15 A nicely designed business card can make a good entry to your site.

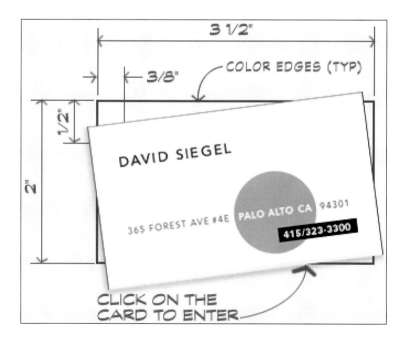

ers back into the currents of the Web with a list of links. (*See Chapter 10, "Creative Design Solutions," for the particulars of my exit tunnel.*)

Summary

This entire page weighs under 60K. The blueprint metaphor takes you out of the Web and into a different, yet familiar world. I achieved it by splitting images and locking them into tables. The page loads quickly, yet feels expansive. Splitting images can help get around the limitations of tables when mixing text and image.

Notice I don't have a "news" section. Because the table takes some seconds to load, I usually put in some items of interest right at the top of the page, so people have something to read as it loads. Although I haven't shown it, this is an effective way to tell people what's new while they are waiting and you have their attention. As the saying goes: "Content is king!"

Application

One of Matthew Butterick's designs for his online 'zine, *Dex,* is a great application of the main technique explained in this chapter: how to cut a large image up to make a killer home page [**7.16**]. Matthew gives the scrolling visitor a visual treat by creating the illusion of a seamless display of playing cards. Visit the site and you'll see how effective it is.

7.16 Table borders turned on: *Dex's* magic secrets revealed at last!

CHAPTER 8

A Storefront

What you'll learn in this chapter:

Making templates

Client-side image maps

GIF versus JPEG

Frames

Influencing a histogram

Forms

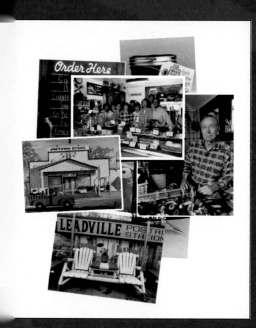

3.1 Familiar materials, endless possibilities.

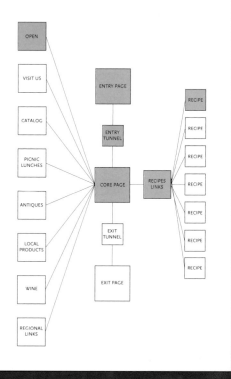

Site Diagram

JIMTOWN STORE is a mom-and-pop country store in California's scenic Alexander Valley. Great food, local products, wine-country color, and an interesting history make it a cultural and epicurean landmark. The Web offers Jimtown Store a way to position itself squarely on the itinerary of visitors to Sonoma County and a chance to build a mailing list for its growing catalog business. It gives the owners, John Werner and Carrie Brown, a way to get going on the Web, gauge demand, and spread awareness among out-of-towners.

In addition to illustrating the development of a third-generation site, this chapter also shows how I work with clients (in this chapter, the word "client" refers to the store owners, not the browser). After my first meeting with John and Carrie, I take away a pile of photos, brochures, napkin scribbles, some good insight into their needs, and ideas. (*Note: Consider this an exercise in building the original prototype. The actual site has since gone through several revisions by the owners.*)

This chapter has been updated for the second edition, and the HTML changed to reflect the capabilities of 3.0 browsers. Non-breaking spaces now replace the single-pixel GIFs, and the frames have lost their borders.

Strategy

Jimtown Store has already built a strong visual identity in its landmark gas station storefront and homemade look, extending to its products, packag-

8.2 The Jimtown color palette.

8.3 This painting captures the homey charm of Jimtown better than any glossy photo.

ing, and print materials. I'll bring these assets to the Web using scanned photographs, brochures, and maps as starting points. This strategy is appropriate and within reach of small businesses, most of which have a sizeable investment in paper brochures and flyers [8.1].

Modem-Friendly Design

Optimizing printed material for use on the Web is challenging enough technically, but the more important challenge is conceptual – integrating the images into a cohesive metaphor. In second-generation site design, images are often merely decorative, or at best, illustrative. In third-generation

design, images become structural elements of a site. Because these images are so important, I have to make sure they don't tax visitors' systems too much. I will spend a lot of time making a few key images look great, rather than including too many. I will also use frames to make an expandable page of recipes. Though I rarely use frames – mostly because they can make navigation too complicated – they can be quite helpful if you expect to make a large, growing list of something like products or recipes.

Jimtown Store's single most distinctive asset is the storefront itself, painted in sunny yellow with green trim. These colors occur throughout Jimtown's print materials and are

8.4 The final RGB version of the painting. Note the enlarged entry area.

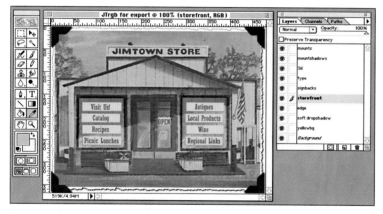

8.5 I make the signboards using rectangles and adding shadows.

8.6 The edge and photo mounts call for a light background like yellow.

a natural choice for the site's color palette. The red and blue of the store's interior make nice accents **[8.2]**.

The Metaphor

My first idea for an entrance was to have a place where all the Jims on the Web could register and form a kind of "Jim Club." It would have been good for the Jims, but not for business. Instead, I decide to make something that places Jimtown on the map. I play with several metaphors by doodling on paper. Then I notice the old-fashioned deckle-edge cards inset with photo mounts in their brochure, and that gives me an idea: simply present the store through a series of postcards. The postcard ratio of 4:3 happens to work well for browser windows.

Phase 1: Photoshop

This site will need a lot of work in Photoshop. I must make a series of postcards that look great together and download quickly. The photos and cards I'm given are less than ideal – especially the existing colors, which I adjust to emphasize the Jimtown palette.

Building the Anchor Image

Several of the store images were photo-graphic, but one was a folk-art painting on a board **[8.3]**. I chose the painting over the photographs because I had to change it significantly to make it work in the postcard format, and it's a lot easier to edit a painting than a photo-graph.

The store windows actually have hanging yellow signboards, which the owners move around to emphasize various specials and delicacies. This gives me an idea for a navigation scheme: I'll make clickable signs in the windows.

After extended surgery in Photoshop – enlarging the entryway, doors, and windows to make room for the signs, towing the truck and replacing it with porch material, and generally touching up – the store image is ready for business **[8.4]**.

In the windows, I draw simple rectangular signboards and fill them with the Jimtown palette's yellow. Using a red from the Jimtown palette, I set the text in a typeface called Rockwell Condensed, with a Western look that seems to fit Jimtown's feel **[8.5]**.

I trim the storefront image in a 4:3 ratio to approximately 470 pixels horizontally, so that with a few pixels of border treatment, it will fit snugly in many browsers' default window width. This will be my postcard size. On a new layer in Photoshop, I draw a deckle edge by hand and reproduce it for the other three sides. This looks a bit flat, so on new layers I make a drop shadow for the card and some old-fashioned photo mounts in the dark blue accent color I picked out earlier. While I'm thinking color, I pour the Jimtown palette's yellow into the background **[8.6]**.

When rendering type, I stick with color-cube colors for both back- and foreground colors (*see "Dither on the Client" in Chapter 5*).

Deadly Sin Number Four

The Slow Load

Conversations among friends can survive long silent pauses, but few web pages can afford to take long to load.

A good rule is that most pages in a site should be under 30K, a few can be 30-50K, and perhaps one or two can weigh in at 70K. Pages larger than that should either belong to 800-pound gorillas or be put on a diet.

If you want to force your visitors to go out to lunch while your page loads, fill it full of 8-bit dithered GIFs in the foreground, and don't forget an enormous high-quality JPEG in the background.

Spread out heavier loads by reusing elements cleverly; once loaded, they are cached and therefore load again almost instantly.

8.7 Without dithering, this image looks patchy.

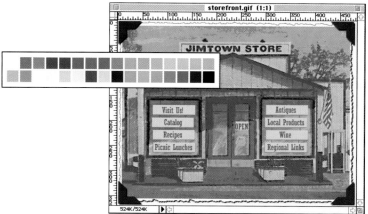

8.8 Photoshop uses any area selected before indexing to build the histogram (ABOVE), thus influencing the resulting palette and image (BELOW).

Reducing the File Size

The painterly gradations of this image will surely suffer with substantial color reduction. This makes for a good image-compression exercise. If I can't find an acceptable balance between image size and quality, I might have to go back to the drawing board for this image, and possibly for the metaphor as well. That's why I carry this image to completion before working on the rest of the site.

When indexing images and exporting GIFS, I always save a backup copy of the file to protect me from myself. You can't imagine how much time I have lost after inadvertently overwriting my layered RGB Photoshop files with indexed images. (I have a theory that when you die and go to heaven, the workstation they give you has all the files you ever lost on its hard disk.)

I index the image to a 5-bit adaptive palette with no dithering and export a GIF as a trial [8.7].

Two problems: the image quality is poor, and the file is a fat 50k. With this few colors, dithering would improve the quality, but it would also shorten the runs and make the image file larger. A larger palette would do the same. Both dithering and larger palettes make files less compressible as GIFS. What I need is a *better palette* – one that will cause less important areas like the sky to clump into even longer runs but will preserve the look of more important areas, like the storefront. I can get it by influencing the histogram (*see "Reducing File Size" in Chapter 3*).

To influence the histogram, I revert to RGB mode and shift-select the areas

156

heavy in the key colors: yellow and green, red, and dark blue. I select the deckle edge and image mounts, too, because it's important that they have accurate color. I re-index (5-bit, adaptive, no dither) and export as another GIF [8.8].

Rats. This has shaved only 4K from the first attempt, and the image quality is only marginally better. The image isn't compressing very well because the runs are still too short. Further palette reduction (to, say, 25 colors) will ruin its painterly quality.

See "Choosing JPEG and GIF Tools" in Chapter 3 for some power tools I could have used to squeeze this image down even more when I first built this site.

Images like this are good candidates for the JPEG compression scheme. I revert to my last-saved RGB copy and save as a JPEG image. By saving several JPEGS, I decide to keep the one whose Q-factor is 25% of the original, which basically amounts to choosing low image quality (high compression) [8.9].

This yields a more dramatic savings over GIF: the image is now 33K. Most of the image looks great far better than the GIF versions. The only downside is that the type has become blurry and looks bad. Hard edges and type are the first casualties of JPEG compression (*see "The JPEG Format" in Chapter 3*).

Which image to use? It's a judgment call, but I'm leaning toward the JPEG, because the 33K file size is awfully appealing. If the blurriness of the type is objectionable to the client, I can probably save again with improved quality (sacrificing some compression)

8.9 A low-quality JPEG yields substantial file size reduction.

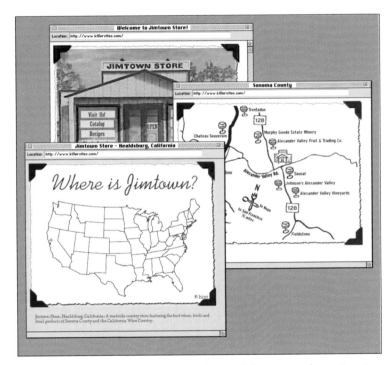

8.10 Image map links will take people from each hot spot to the next postcard.

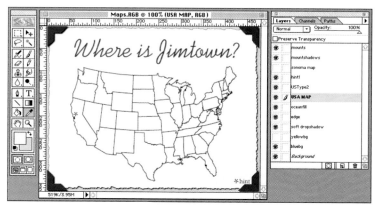

8.11 Note the layers I use to help myself choose among alternate possibilities.

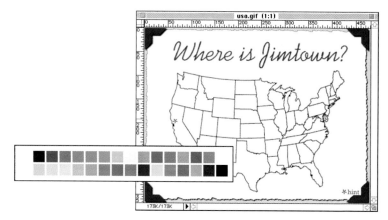

8.12 A good splash screen must weigh in under 25K. At 23K, this image is a keeper.

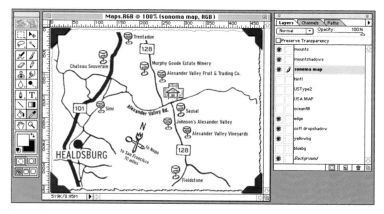

8.13 There's not enough room to show Jimtown in relation to San Francisco.

and still come out better overall than the 46K GIF. It would be nice to combine the best of both methods, but there really is no way to do that without z-axis layering *(see Chapter 13, "Looking Forward")*. Now that I am confident this core image will work, I'll turn to the postcard images for the entryway.

I made that image last year, before the HVS tools were available to help reduce JPEGS even further. See Chapter 3 for more on HVS color reduction.

Where is Jimtown?

The entryway is a simple sequence of two postcard-maps that places the store geographically, builds anticipation, and brands the Jimtown name, logo, and location on the way in. If nothing else, surfers will remember the name and location of Jimtown after visiting this site [**8.10**].

Making the U.S. Map

I return to my master Photoshop document and hide all layers except the postcard edge treatment, the photo mounts, and the page background. I find a stock EPS image of the U.S. and use a two-step process to paste it into Photoshop as pixels from Illustrator. First, I open the map in Illustrator and save it. Then I eliminate all but the outermost boundaries of the continental U.S. and increase the line width a bit. I select and copy this object and paste it into Photoshop *without* the anti-alias option checked. I can fill this with white and it forms the underlying color of my image. Returning to Illustrator, I revert to the saved image and grab all the state lines. This time, I paste into a new layer, check the anti-alias box, and position them over the white background, and I can now color these lines a nice dark Jimtown blue [8.11]. These two layers together give me the map I want.

The type is Kaufmann Script, a popular face reminiscent of the hand-lettered signs in the store. I want to establish green-on-yellow as fore- and background colors for the type on the card. For the page background itself I choose a light color-cube blue, because yellow here wouldn't provide enough contrast with the mostly yellow card. Adding a big hint on the map in red spoils the "Where is Jimtown?" game but draws people into the site.

Indexed to a 5-bit adaptive palette with no dithering, this full-screen image reduces to a lean 19K [8.12]. With interlacing (worth a few extra kilobytes for large-area images like this), the page goes to 23K. An animated GIF with a little delay before the red hint comes on would be a nice touch, but it would make the page too large for an entry. A rollover would be clever but too frustrating for some surfers. Even cutting it into several areas would push it past 20K. Smaller is better. I leave it as is, with interlacing, at 23K.

Making the Sonoma Map

The second map begins life as a photocopy of a brochure. I scan it, then reconstruct each element manually in Illustrator, redoing the type, introducing wine-glass icons from yet another Jimtown brochure, and building a

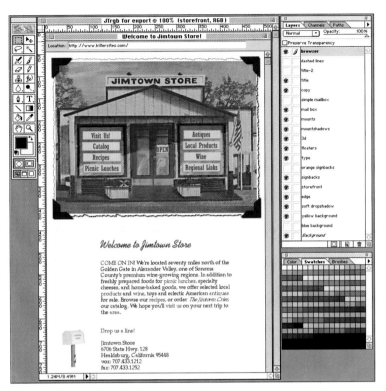

8.14 Mocking up sites in Photoshop is the best way to present initial work to a client.

compass rose from fork and spoon. I make sure people are oriented by referring to San Francisco, because there's no room to show it on this map. The storefront logo, in red like the hint on the preceding page, foreshadows the next page and beckons them on through this short entry tunnel [8.13]. This entire page comes in under 20k.

The Final Mock-Up

Now that these three images are working, it's time to flesh out the core page. I modify some copy from the Jimtown brochure and render a heading in green Kaufmann Script below the card area all in Photoshop. This serves as a

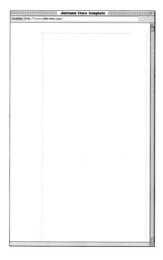

```
<HTML>
  <HEAD>
      <TITLE>
          Jimtown Store template
      </TITLE>
  </HEAD>
  <!-- Page Parameters -->
  <BODY BGCOLOR="#FFFFCC" TEXT="#003300"
  LINK="#990000" VLINK="#000033" ALINK="#FFFFCC">
      <!-- Vertical Spacer -->
       
      <BR> 
      <BR> 
      <BR>
      <!-- Begin Table -->
      <TABLE WIDTH=480 BORDER=1 CELLPADDING=0
      CELLSPACING=0>
          <TR>
              <!-- Left blank cell -->
              <TD WIDTH=107>
                   
              </TD>
              <!-- Begin cell with images and text -->
              <TD WIDTH=320>
              </TD>
              <!-- End cell with images and text -->
              <!-- Right Blank Cell -->
              <TD WIDTH=53>
                   
              </TD>
          </TR>
      </TABLE>
      <!-- End Table -->
      <!-- Vertical Spacer -->
      <BR> 
      <BR> 
      <BR> 
      <BR> 
      <BR> 
      <BR>
  </BODY>
</HTML>
```

8.15 The basic HTML template for the Jimtown site (ABOVE), and as it appears in the browser window (TOP LEFT).

160

model for the section headers. I lift a mailbox from a photo of the storefront and place it, free-floating, at the foot of the page **[8.14]**.

To prepare all this for my client meeting, I even use aliased text type and mock up the browser window in Photoshop, making all three full pages look like I made them in HTML. Because several layers still have some elements I decided not to use, I can show John the process by which I made my decisions.

Phase 2: HTML

This site doesn't need any single-pixel GIFS. I can build the entire site using tables and non-breaking spaces, with frames only for the recipe page.

Because tables can be difficult to work with, it pays to set up one good template that reflects a grid structure appropriate to many of the pages you're creating. This way, once you've made a few pages, you've made the rest. Careful planning, consistency, and clean execution will save the day – maybe even a few. (See *Secrets of Successful Web Sites* for more on planning and project management.)

The postcards are 480 pixels wide, so this will be the absolute width of my layout. I divide 480 into 9 parts: 2 units for a left margin, 6 for a central text area, and 1 for a right margin. This translates to table columns of 107, 320, and 53 pixels, respectively. This division of a 9-unit grid is one of the formulas advocated by the great typographer Jan Tschichold, though he had books with facing pages in mind.

The Template

The HTML for this table becomes the basic template for this site **[8.15]**. All my table measurements are absolute (pixels, rather than percentages). I want the text to have a fixed relationship to the images; both are part of the composition. Colorwise, the header of the template expresses the Jimtown palette on every page:

```
<BODY BGCOLOR="#FFFFCC"
TEXT="#003300" LINK="#990000"
VLINK="#000033"
ALINK="#FFFFCC">
```

The text is dark green, the links are dark red, and visited links are the same dark blue as the photo mounts. Red is always a good link color, and visited links should be discernible without jumping off the page the way unvisited links should. The active link color is the yellow of the background, providing visual feedback without adding another color.

The Core Page

I begin with the core page, because this will have the most complex layout and navigation features **[8.16]**. The template table was built around the width of the postcard – 480 pixels – so I don't need to build the card into the table. It sits in the upper left-hand corner of the page, and the 3-column table falls neatly below it **[8.17]**.

Placing the mailbox is a matter of specifying a new row, centering the image in the margin cell, and aligning it to the top.

8.16 The core page. Welcome to Jimtown Store.

I want some space between the text and the company-contact information. This is where you might be tempted to add a horizontal rule, but I manage to resist the urge. Instead, I simply add some white space before beginning the next table row. There are many different ways to make vertical white space. I add a few `<BR>`s separated with non-breaking spaces (` `) to space down a few lines. The non-breaking spaces keep the `<BR>`s from collapsing in some browsers.

I asked John and Carrie for a paragraph that has each of the nine areas of the site worked into it, so each key word becomes a text link to an inner page. This serves as a verbal introduction and a backup in case visitors don't understand the clickable window signs, or their browsers don't yet support client-side image maps.

Building a Client-Side Image Map

This simple site does not need complicated navigation. The storefront serves as the central map. This image has nine hot zones, each a bit larger than the associated signs on the painting [8.18]. An image with clickable areas like this is called an *image map*. A thorough discussion of image maps is beyond the scope of this book. The most important thing is to make *client-side image maps* [8.19]. A client-side image map puts the coordinate information into the HTML of the page, so the visitor's browser (the client) knows which file to get as soon as the surfer clicks her mouse. In contrast, old-style *server-side image maps* depend on a trip to the server to make sense of the surfer's click. This makes them

8.17 The 2:6:1 ratio is embodied in the `<TD>` parameters of this table.

```
<HTML>
  <HEAD>
    <TITLE>
      Welcome to Jimtown Store!
    </TITLE>
  </HEAD>
  <!--Page Parameters-->
  <BODY BGCOLOR="#FFFFCC" TEXT="#003300" LINK="#990000"
  VLINK="#000033" ALINK="#FFFFCC">
    <IMG SRC="./storefront.jpg" ALT="Image of Jimtown
    Store, with links to other points in the site"
    WIDTH="480" HEIGHT="368" BORDER="0">
    <BR>
    <!-- Vertical Spacer -->
     
    <BR>
     
    <BR>
     
    <BR>
    <!--Begin text table-->
    <TABLE WIDTH=480 BORDER=1 CELLPADDING=0
    CELLSPACING=0>
      <TR>
        <!--Blank Cell-->
        <TD WIDTH=107>
        </TD>
        <!--Text Cell-->
        <TD WIDTH=320>
          <IMG SRC="./welcome.gif" ALT="Welcome to
          Jimtown Store!" WIDTH="320" HEIGHT="28"
          BORDER="0">
          <BR>
           
          <BR>
          <A HREF="./open.html">
            <FONT SIZE=-1>
              COME ON IN
            </FONT></A>
            ! We're located seventy miles north of the
            Golden Gate in Alexander Valley, one of
            Sonoma County's premium wine-growing
            regions. In addition to freshly prepared
            foods for
          <A HREF="./picnic.html">
            picnic lunches</A>
            , specialty cheeses, and home-baked goods,
            we offer selected
          <A HREF="./local.html">
            local products</A>
            and
          <A HREF="./wine.html">
            wine</A>
            , toys and eclectic American
```

```
                    <A HREF="./antiques.html">
                      antiques</A>
                    for sale. Browse our
                    <A HREF="./recipes.html">
                      recipes</A>
                    , or order
                    <A HREF="./catalog.html">
                      <I>
                        The Jimtown Crier
                      </I></A>
                    , our catalog. We hope you'll
                    <A HREF="./visit.html">
                      visit us</A>
                    on your next trip to the
                    <A HREF="./regional.html">
                      area</A>
                    .
                    <BR>
                     
                    <BR>
                  </TD>
                  <!--Blank Cell-->
                  <TD WIDTH=53>
                     
                  </TD>
                </TR>
                <TR>
                  <!--Mailbox Image-->
                  <TD WIDTH=107 VALIGN=TOP ALIGN=CENTER >
                    <A HREF="mailto:jw@jimtown.com">
                      <IMG SRC="./mailbox.gif" ALT="mailbox icon"
                      WIDTH="54" HEIGHT="87" BORDER="0"></A>
                  </TD>
                  <TD WIDTH=320>
                    <A HREF="mailto:jw@jimtown.com">
                      Drop us a line!</A>
                    <BR>
                    <BR>
                    Jimtown Store
                    <BR>
                    p 145:
                    <FONT SIZE=-1>
                      6706 State Hwy. 128
                      <BR>
                      Healdsburg, California 95448
                      <BR>
                      vox: 707.433.1212
                      <BR>
                      fax: 707.433.1252
                    </FONT>
                    <BR>
                  </TD>
                  <!--Blank Cell-->
                  <TD WIDTH=53>
```

```
             
          </TD>
        </TR>
      </TABLE>
      <!--End text table-->
      <BR>
       
      <BR>
       
      <BR>
    </BODY>
  </HTML>
```

```
      <!-- image map -->
      <IMG SRC="./storefront.jpg" ALT="Image of Jimtown Store, with links to
      other points in the site" WIDTH="480" HEIGHT="368" BORDER="0"
      USEMAP="#storemap" ISMAP>
      <!-- Begin client-side image map -->
      <MAP NAME="storemap">
        <AREA SHAPE=RECT COORDS="298,241,384,262" HREF="./regional.html">
        <AREA SHAPE=RECT COORDS="300,217,386,237" HREF="./wine.html">
        <AREA SHAPE=RECT COORDS="298,192,385,211" HREF="./local.html">
        <AREA SHAPE=RECT COORDS="300,167,386,187" HREF="./antiques.html">
        <AREA SHAPE=RECT COORDS="181,156,278,292" HREF="./open.html">
        <AREA SHAPE=RECT COORDS="71,242,157,263" HREF="./picnic.html">
        <AREA SHAPE=RECT COORDS="70,217,157,238" HREF="./recipes.html">
        <AREA SHAPE=RECT COORDS="69,193,154,213" HREF="./catalog.html">
        <AREA SHAPE=RECT COORDS="70,168,157,188" HREF="./visit.html">
      </MAP>
      <!--End client-side image map-->
```

8.19 The client-side image map is part of the core page.

165

8.18 Make your hot zones oversized to accommodate inaccurate pointing.

slow, and they can't be tested or demonstrated off-line.

Most image map tools assume you're using GIFS as your map images, so they will read only GIFS. In this case, the storefront image is a JPEG. Here's a trick: I save a copy as a GIF, open it with an image-map program, make the map, then throw away the GIF. The browser doesn't care what kind of image I use for the image map.

With the core page finished, I lay out the site by copying the template many times and giving the files the names I used in the map file.

The Interior Pages

All the images for the interior pages are 320 x 240 pixels, to match the width of the text column and to preserve the aspect ratio of the postcards [8.20]. I can include either landscape or portrait images in this format. By sticking with consistent dimensions, I make site construction and maintenance easier.

Home-Style Navigation

For most of the pages in the site, I don't want random-access navigation. Random access means you can get to any page from any other. In this case, it's necessary on the core page, but too imposing for the interior pages. Instead, I encourage frequent return trips to the core page. These round trips aren't tedious, because the core page will stay in the browser's memory.

This is called caching (pronounced cashing); cached images reload very quickly.

The little red Jimtown icon at the foot of the interior pages makes a perfect homing beacon [8.21]. Anything else would be too complex. How does a visitor get back to the entrance, the "Where's Jimtown?" card? She can either go Back in her browser's "Go" menu or re-enter the URL. I am much more interested in people bookmarking the home page than getting back to the entrance.

I look for opportunities in the text to link intrasite pages. Intrasite links refer to another part of the store. Anything that links outside the site goes into the Regional Links exit page, so people won't leave the site prematurely.

Making Headlines

The best way to make the type for a site like this is to know every single headline beforehand. I get consistent results by putting all the type together on a single page, reducing the colors, and making the GIF images from that master page. (*For details on these procedures, and to learn about an automated process we've developed at Verso to do this for large-scale site production, see Chapter 5, "Rendering Type."*)

The headline GIFs are all 24-point Kaufmann Script. It's big enough that I can type it without having to reduce from a larger size. I tried the regular and the bold, but I wanted something in between. After typing all the headlines, using the Move tool I select the entire image, hold the option key

8.20 A model interior page for the Jimtown site.

8.21 The Jimtown logo makes a perfect homing device.

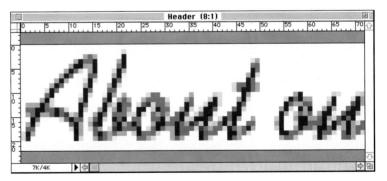
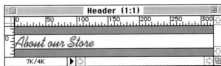

8.22 I need seven colors to render the type: green, yellow, and five intermediate shades (ABOVE). All my headers are 320 pixels wide (BELOW).

8.23 Always start with another form and modify it.

```
<HTML>
  <HEAD>
    <TITLE>
      Jimtown Store Catalog
    </TITLE>
  </HEAD>
  <!-- Page Parameters -->
  <BODY BGCOLOR="#FFFFCC" TEXT="#003300" LINK="#990000"
  VLINK="#000033" ALINK="#FFFFCC">
    <!-- Vertical Spacer -->
     
    <BR>
     
    <BR>
     
    <BR>
    <!-- Begin Form -->
    <FORM METHOD="POST" ACTION="http://foo.bar.com/
    cgi-bin/scripts/form">
      <!-- Begin Table -->
      <TABLE BORDER=1 CELLSPACING=6 CELLPADDING=0
      WIDTH=480>
        <!-- 1st Row -->
        <TR>
          <TD WIDTH=107>
             
          </TD>
          <!-- Descriptive Text -->
          <TD WIDTH=320>
            <IMG SRC="./catalog.gif" ALT="Order our
            Catalog" WIDTH="320" HEIGHT="28" BORDER="0">
            <BR>
            <BR>
            <FONT SIZE=-1>
              HERE AT THE STORE
            </FONT>
            we'd like to make it easy for you to get
            more info or actually buy things from our
            catalog,
            <I>
              The Jimtown Crier
            </I>
            . Leave us some of your vitals and we'll
            mail you a copy.
            <BR>
             
            <BR>
             
            <BR>
          </TD>
          <TD WIDTH=53>
             
          </TD>
        </TR>
```

```
<!-- 2nd Row -->
<TR>
  <TD ALIGN=RIGHT>
    Name:
  </TD>
  <TD>
    <INPUT TYPE="text" NAME="namefield"
    SIZE="24" VALUE="">
  </TD>
</TR>
<!-- 3rd Row -->
<TR>
  <TD ALIGN=RIGHT>
    Address:
  </TD>
  <TD>
    <INPUT TYPE="text" NAME="addressfield1"
    SIZE="32">
  </TD>
</TR>
<!-- 4th Row -->
<TR>
  <TD ALIGN=RIGHT>
    Address:
  </TD>
  <TD>
    <INPUT TYPE="text" NAME="addressfield2"
    SIZE="32">
  </TD>
</TR>
<!-- 5th Row -->
<TR>
  <TD ALIGN=RIGHT>
    City:
  </TD>
  <TD>
    <INPUT TYPE="text" NAME="cityfield"
    SIZE="24">
         State:
    <INPUT TYPE="text" NAME="statefield"
    SIZE="4">
  </TD>
</TR>
<!-- 6th Row -->
<TR>
  <TD ALIGN=RIGHT>
    Zip Code:
  </TD>
  <TD>
    <INPUT TYPE="text" NAME="zipfield"
    SIZE="12">
  </TD>
</TR>
```

```
                    <!-- 7th Row -->
                    <TR>
                      <TD ALIGN=RIGHT>
                        Phone:
                      </TD>
                      <TD>
                        <INPUT TYPE="text" NAME="phonefield"
                        SIZE="16">
                      </TD>
                    </TR>
                    <!-- 8th Row -->
                    <TR>
                      <TD ALIGN=RIGHT>
                        Fax:
                      </TD>
                      <TD>
                        <INPUT TYPE="text" NAME="faxfield"
                        SIZE="16">
                      </TD>
                    </TR>
                    <!-- 9th Row -->
                    <TR>
                      <TD ALIGN=RIGHT>
                        Email:
                      </TD>
                      <TD>
                        <INPUT TYPE="text" NAME="emailfield"
                        SIZE="24">
                      </TD>
                    </TR>
                    <!-- 10th Row -->
                    <TR>
                      <TD>
                         
                      </TD>
                      <TD>
                         
                        <BR>
                         
                        <BR>
                        <INPUT TYPE=IMAGE BORDER=0 SRC="submit.gif"
                        VALUE="Send">
                      </TD>
                    </TR>
                  </TABLE>
                </FORM>
                <BR>
                <A HREF="./core.html" NAME="Jimtown Storefront">
                  <IMG SRC="./home.gif" ALT="Return to the Jimtown
              Storefront" WIDTH="74" HEIGHT="60" VSPACE=18 HSPACE=100
              BORDER="0"></A>
```

```
            <!-- Vertical Spacer -->
            <BR>
             
            <BR>
             
            <BR>
             
            <BR>
             
            <BR>
             
            <BR>
             
            <BR>
         </BODY>
      </HTML>
```

down, and hit the down arrow once. This makes a copy of the entire image, shifted down one pixel, giving the type a slightly bolder look.

This curvy script demands more intermediate colors than a sans-serif to render properly. After a few experiments, I end up reducing to seven colors **[8.22]**.

Once the image is indexed, I set a fixed-size rectangle marquee and try to enclose each block of type in the same way: no pixels of yellow to the left, and one or two at most on top. I paste each cut image into a new file and re-index. I try to be consistent. All of my header GIFs are 320 pixels wide, regardless of the length of the text. The reason is mostly convenience, so I can mix and match the headers without having to type in new dimensions every time.

Of course, clients *always* need more headlines after making the initial site. Things change, especially on the Web. To make additional headlines, I type them into the large headline RGB page and re-index, then I cut the new headlines out and export GIFs.

The Order Form

Most forms on the Web are ugly – it's as if the functional requirements of a form somehow make even conscientious designers give up. Because different browsers render user-input fields very differently, layout can indeed be a challenge. By laying out forms in tables, however, and being aware of the cross-platform differences, you can design forms well **[8.23]**.

Don't be afraid of form elements. You can place them as you would anything else. This table follows the same proportions as the other pages: 2:6:1. Instead of white space in the first column, however, I right-align the form-field headers. This alignment scheme reinforces the site's left margin line.

Forms Look Different on Different Machines

Forms really change from browser to browser, platform to platform. In particular, the widths of the user-input fields can vary widely. If you specify too

171

8.24 This table uses CELLSPACING=6 for white space control.

wide an input field, your table might break. Generally speaking, PC browser input fields are wider than Macintosh ones. Because I design on a Mac, I usually end up shortening my fields considerably after viewing them on a PC. Too short is better than too long.

I use cellspacing to get the elements to keep a little distance from one another, as you can see with the borders turned on [8.24].

Mac designers – make sure to look at your forms on Windows machines!

Instead of accepting the ugly generic Submit buttons browsers put up by default, I make my own, usually in a dark color with text knocked out [8.25].

What happens when people submit a form? Forms send user-input data to a program running on a Web server. This needn't be intimidating. Sometimes these programs are complicated, but in this case, the program simply sends the feedback to John Werner's email account.

The form won't work until a program is set up and running on your server to accept form input. It's beyond the scope of this book to explain how to write these programs, but I want to make the point that they are fairly easy

to set up. Many good technical books explain the procedures in detail. Your service provider will either help you get one set up or find someone who can. *Personally, I don't know how to write these server-side programs. There are people in my studio who do, and I gratefully keep them supplied with fresh pizza to keep my forms working.*

The Recipe Page: Frames

My goal is to make the recipes a substantive feature of the site, drawing people from other food and Sonoma sites to the growing list of refined country-style recipes provided by the Jimtown staff. With frames, the recipes will be easy to see and print

8.25 Macs (LEFT) and PCs (RIGHT) render form elements differently.

8.26 Frames are useful in limited situations, like a list of recipes that form a dead end in your site.

```
<HTML>
  <HEAD>
    <TITLE>
      Recipes
    </TITLE>
  </HEAD>
  <FRAMESET ROWS="90,*" FRAMEBORDER="0"
  BORDER="0" FRAMESPACING="0">
    <FRAME SRC="./top_frame.html" BORDER="0"
    MARGINWIDTH="0" MARGINHEIGHT="0">
    <FRAMESET COLS="140,*" FRAMEBORDER="0"
    BORDER="0" FRAMESPACING="0">
      <FRAME SRC="./left_frame.html" BORDER="0"
      MARGINWIDTH="0" MARGINHEIGHT="0">
      <FRAME NAME="RIGHT"
      SRC="./right_frame_01.html" BORDER="0"
      MARGINWIDTH="0" MARGINHEIGHT="0">
    </FRAMESET>
  </FRAMESET>
</HTML>
```

This frameset divides the page into three frames, each with its own HTML file.

8.27 To see or print recipe files on their own, hold the mouse button down on the link and choose New Window With This Link.

on demand. The basic approach is to list the titles in the left frame, which will drive the display of recipes on the right. *(For details, see "Frames and Framesets" in Chapter 4.)* Remember: Framesets don't describe content, they specify the default dimensions of frames, or windows, that point to other HTML documents **[8.26]**.

The frame dimensions relate to the margins I've used throughout the site. I choose the left side as the navigation frame and the right side as the target frame. Any links you click in the navigation frame appear in the target frame. It's a simple matter of setting up the HTML in the links file so the links point to the target file. Use the `<BASE TARGET="RIGHT">` tag in the left file to link to the frame on the right.

174

Each recipe goes in its own file. To accommodate the frames, the recipe files must have a smaller left margin than the other pages [**8.27, 8.28**].

I link the home icon to the core page. The syntax of this button is important, because it dismisses the frames [**8.29**].

The best thing about this frame-based approach is that it's easy to add more recipes, attracting food enthusiasts from all over the Web. It's also a benefit to surfers, who don't have to keep going in and out of recipes to get around. It's much easier to peruse a dozen recipes through frames than with straight HTML. Used this way, frames can be a good design choice.

The Entry Blurbs

To set up the entry page, I add a few things to the front page that help people and search engines know where they are. At the bottom of the front page, I add a short text blurb [**8.30**].

The entry blurb also tells search engines quite a bit about the site, as does the tag at the top of the page. I also add three special "meta" tags for the search engines to pick up: description, keywords, and distribution (*see sidebar, next page*).

Summary

Retail sites can be straightforward if you start with a good plan, don't bite off too much, and go for quality. Once you develop a concept and a few good templates, sites come together quickly. Consistent, distinctive table structures, colors, and typography brand a site,

```
<HTML>
   <HEAD>
     <TITLE>
        Menu
     </TITLE>
   </HEAD>
   <!-- Page Parameters -->
   <BODY BGCOLOR="#FFFFCC" TEXT="#003300"
   LINK="#990000" VLINK="#000033"
   ALINK="#FFFFCC">
     <TABLE BORDER=0 CELLPADDING="0"
     CELLSPACING="0" WIDTH="320">
        <TR>
          <TD WIDTH="20" ROWSPAN="3" NOWRAP>
             
          </TD>
          <TD>
            <IMG SRC="../head_brie.gif"
            ALT="ABOUT OUR STORE" ALIGN=TOP
            WIDTH="267" HEIGHT="28"
            BORDER="0" VSPACE="20">
          </TD>
        </TR>
        <TR>
          <TD WIDTH="267">
            Our most-requested sandwich is
            one good hours after being made.
            The heady, olive-scented oil
            marinates into the bread,
            improving its flavor. (Great
            with greens and seasonal
            tomatoes).
            <BR>
             
            <BR>
            1/3 baguette
            <BR>
            2 Tbls Jimtown's Olive Salad
            <BR>
            3 oz Brie cheese (rind removed)
          </TD>
        </TR>
        <TR>
          <TD>
            <IMG SRC="../spoonfork_2.gif"
            ALT="About our Store" ALIGN=TOP
            WIDTH="70" HEIGHT="72"
            BORDER="0" HSPACE="60"
            VSPACE="20">
            <BR>
          </TD>
        </TR>
     </TABLE>
   </BODY>
</HTML>
```

8.28 A typical recipe.

Search Engines

A new site needs all the help it can get. Search engines send out spider programs that crawl the Web, gathering key words from sites and putting them into huge databases. I like to load a site like this with keywords that will improve its chances of appearing in a database search. In addition to a good description in the tag, which registers on most search engines, there are two general approaches, both of which can help publicize your site (most search engines ignore any words you put in comments).

The visible way is to put a succinct sentence at the bottom of your entry page that sums up your business. This is a good idea unless it really goes against the intended effect of the front page, which may be trying to be more mysterious. When in doubt, I leave a little description like this on the front page for all who happen to come by.

The invisible way uses hidden tags, or "meta" tags, to tell search engines exactly what the page is about. This is great for visual sites that don't want to put a lot of words in HTML on the front page. One invisible way is to put key words in the ALT tag of an image. Some search engines ignore these, others don't. The more reliable way is to use meta tags.

The code for appropriate Jimtown description, keywords, and distribution meta tags is below. Fill in the descriptions for your sites, put the tags at the top of your first page, and check the search engines occasionally to see if they've picked you up. It's always a good idea to put these tags into your pages.

```
<META NAME="DESCRIPTION" CONTENT="A well-bred
crossroads emporium featuring the nest in Sono-
ma cuisine. Local wines, homemade specialties,
cheese, picnic lunches, fresh roasted coffee,
Napa fruit, fresh baked goods, antiques, Wine
Country tour information, and the best olive
salad in Healdsburg, Alexander Valley, or Sonoma
County.">

<META NAME="KEYWORDS" CONTENT="Healdsburg, Napa,
Alexander Valley, Sonoma, tours, food, wine,
country, vineyard, champagne, espresso, emporium,
delicatessen, lunch, dinner, picnic, fruit,
bread, cheese, antiques, olive salad, sandwich">

<META NAME="DISTRIBUTION" CONTENT="global">
```

giving it a memorable signature without relying too heavily on images. Consistency also makes site construction and maintenance relatively easy.

I think it's important for mail-order companies to get onto the Web sooner rather than later. Building net equity is hard; the best way to distinguish yourself from the competition is by offering quality. In my experience, people are quite willing to type a credit card number into a web page to get something they want. List your distributors, put up a Frequently Asked Questions page, solicit feedback, and read and respond to email. I recommend testing the waters with a small, well-presented offering and seeing what happens.

Test your ideas on prospective surfers, both on paper and in Photoshop, before committing to HTML. Because sites take a lot of work to make and can be expensive to maintain, business owners should take small steps by laying a strong foundation and adding features as time goes on.

Application

This general approach works for any storefront. Small business owners like to save money. Here is a way to work existing materials into a compelling site. If you have a quality storefront photo, you can make it into an image map as I've done here. Rather than putting boards in the windows, you can "etch" the words into the glass using Photoshop, or you can make whatever signs are appropriate for the business.

```
<TD>
  <A HREF="./core.html" TARGET="_PARENT">
    <IMG SRC="./home.gif" ALIGN=TOP
    WIDTH="74" HEIGHT="60" BORDER="0"
    VSPACE="2"></A>
</TD>
```

8.29 The return navigation button takes people back to the core page. Note the use of TARGET="_PARENT" to make the frames disappear.

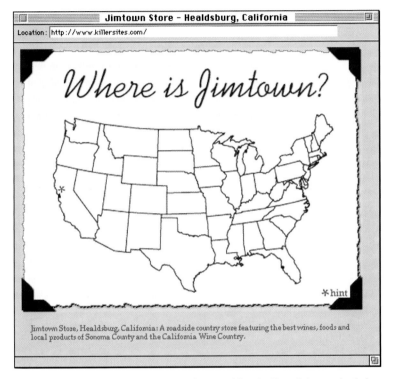

8.30 An entry blurb tells search engines and borderline visitors what's behind the curtain.

Using Quotes

Earlier versions of Netscape were lenient with people who forgot to use quotes around file names and arguments. Recent versions are more strict. Always use quotes on target and file names. This also goes for colors and other tag specifications.

```
ambl  html ><img border=0
ght=    SRC  animations/d1.gif"><    td

ambl  html ><img      der=0
ght=    SRC  animat  s       ></      td

amble html  ><im
ght=5   SRC  an                 .gif"></      td
n -->
mg BORDER=0  id
 dot black                d>

 0 of   able
```

CHAPTER 9

A Gallery

What you'll learn in this chapter:

Putting animated GIFs in tables

Simulated randomness

Directory structure

Preloaded images

Setting expectations

Creating a contact-sheet metaphor

Image processing above the color cube

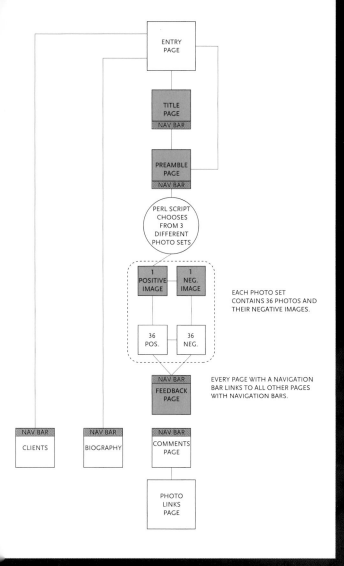

ENTRY
PAGE

TITLE
PAGE
NAV BAR

PREAMBLE
PAGE
NAV BAR

PERL SCRIPT
CHOOSES
FROM 3
DIFFERENT
PHOTO SETS

1
POSITIVE
IMAGE

1
NEG.
IMAGE

EACH PHOTO SET
CONTAINS 36 PHOTOS AND
THEIR NEGATIVE IMAGES.

36
POS.

36
NEG.

NAV BAR
FEEDBACK
PAGE

EVERY PAGE WITH A NAVIGATION
BAR LINKS TO ALL OTHER PAGES
WITH NAVIGATION BARS.

NAV BAR
CLIENTS

NAV BAR
BIOGRAPHY

NAV BAR
COMMENTS
PAGE

PHOTO
LINKS
PAGE

Site diagram

Doug Menuez is one of the country's most versatile and interesting photographers. He was a photojournalist for *Time* and *Newsweek* during the 1970s and 1980s. He's done editorial and documentary work, as well as fashion and advertising photography. For 10 years he's been shooting life on the digital frontier, documenting people in high-tech companies across the globe.

Doug came to my studio in search of a cutting-edge, provocative site that combined words and images to bring his view of the digital revolution to surfers interested in photography and photojournalism. He wanted to show the disparity and similarities between the digital *haves* and *have-nots* – the people who use whiz-bang technological innovations and the people who make them in faraway places. Doug's primary concern was image quality. We decided to optimize this site for visitors with 28.8 kbps modems and systems that display thousands of colors. We specifically decided not to worry about the color cube and web surfers who could see only 256 colors; that would limit black-and-white images to very few shades of gray, and the photo quality would degrade.

"Content on every page!" as the famous magazine designer Roger Black would say. As Doug and I talked, it became clear that the photographs themselves should be the site, rather than an entry door followed by an antechamber, then several gallery spaces. We wanted a metaphor that was understated, not architectural or literal.

Doug and I agreed on a loose interpretation of a professional photographer's contact sheet, enhanced by animated GIFs at the entrance and a different group of photos each time you visit the site.

This fairly technical chapter is much more effective if you see Doug's site on the Web before continuing – it uses animated GIFs and a Perl script running on the server to present random images (www.menuez.com).

Strategy

Digital Moments is a linear journey with a dramatic entrance, a simple intro page, 36 images, a behind-the-scenes parallel universe, and a closing page that gives visitors a chance to express their comments on the exhibition and its meaning.

I choose the number 36 as a theme, to take visitors through 36 images as though they were in Doug's private gallery, looking at a contact sheet for a single roll of film. There are 56 images total, but I want visitors to see a "roll" of 36 at a time. This site will use a script to randomly select 36 different images per visit. There's no reason for them to choose which photograph to see next.

Advertising the number 36 at the beginning tells visitors how long the journey is, setting expectations for the trip. There is no way to see all 56 total images. They can go through again if they want to see another selection of 36 taken from the total.

The impact of this site relies on randomness, on giving the feeling of a random walk. To set the tone up front, I take an idea from Ray Guillette's animated-GIF title page

for his groundbreaking site, "Sound Traffic Control."

To give the feeling of the contact sheet, I use an abstraction of the frame markers on film as a navigational element. As an added (undocumented) feature, visitors can click on the large images, taking them to the other side: a flipped, negative version of the image with the photographer's notes on the circumstances under which the shot was taken. This parallel universe enriches the site and creates an unusual behind-the-scenes view. I got this through-the-picture idea from Suza Scalora's enchanting "Mythopoeia" site (all sites mentioned are listed at the Book Site).

Entry, Exploration, Exit

This site has a *greeting page* that tells you about the gallery, warns you of the upcoming download, requests that you turn off underlining, and entices you to enter. The next page, with the animated GIFs, is the *title page*. I want to make everyone who sees it send the URL to her friends.

The next page is the *preamble*, where I put up a short statement from a curator's point of view. The exploration section is the journey through the 36 photos. There is no random access – no way to take a shortcut to the end page – you must go through the entire sequence to get to the end.

To finish, Doug would like an area where visitors can post their impressions for everyone to see. This is a way to build community and get reactions to the exhibit.

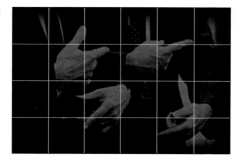

9.1 These three images and the black rectangle will become the layers of the animated GIFs.

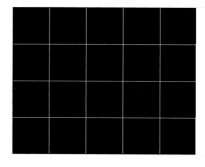

The Title Page

The first thing to do is make the site work statically, without the random-selector script. As usual, it's best to get into Photoshop to see what works and what doesn't. If I can make the first page and one of the gallery pages, I know I'll be in business. I like to do the hard stuff first, so I start with the title page.

Most of the tricks (discussed in other chapters) to reduce to 216 colors won't work here, where fidelity to the original is more important than being faithful to the color cube. Although I assume visitors will view this site with thousands of colors, I don't assume they have blazingly fast net connections or huge monitors.

I start with 70 of Doug's images on a Kodak PhotoCD. The high-resolution versions of each image are very good –

certainly good enough for my purposes. To use Doug's images on web pages, I must reduce the size and resolution of these large files. I choose and process a batch of 40 images, giving me enough to play with (see the "Processing Photographic Images" sidebar).

The Animated GIFs

To create the animated effect, I first make the title page in Photoshop using several layers. I need only three main images (two complete images and one made of four smaller shots) to cut up to make the grid elements. I set up the grid on yet another layer, giving each image enough area to show something, but not too much. I also tune the images to give them more contrast, which helps make the files smaller later. I must also make them lighter than normal, remembering that PCs will

182

show them darker than on my Macintosh screen. I add a fourth layer, containing a plain black rectangle, to break things up – the squares will seem to disappear occasionally on the black page background. Working with a large black background really helps show this page the way I intend it to look [9.1].

Doug likes the idea of blurring the edges, which makes me wish I could make animated JPEGs, because JPEG is the best way to store a photographic image, and blurry JPEGs really compress well. Unfortunately, animated JPEG images are not possible.

A quick experiment on a separate layer tells me I should use a 6 x 4 grid, in which each cell is 55 pixels square – the smallest square that still carries enough of the image to be worthwhile.

Before building animated GIFs, I need to reduce colors and determine the common palette they will share. I did some experiments, trying to influence the histogram at 32 colors, and I couldn't get the images to look perfect. To prevent banding and other artifacts, I had to go up to 40 colors to get enough tonal range so the images would look good on systems with thousands of colors. I could have indexed in 16 colors with dithering, but dithering would create distracting visual noise for these high-level visitors. Those with 8-bit systems will see dithering, no matter what.

I cut the images into squares using the grid as a guide and a 55 x 55 pixel fixed-size rectangle marquee. I do the same for the black rectangle. The trick is to place the type into the six images, so it appears to float in front while the

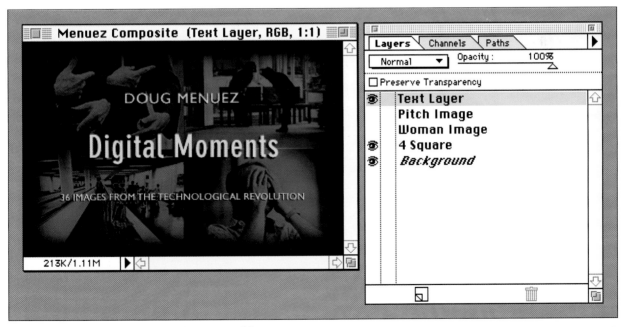

9.2 Make a type layer with as few colors as possible.

9.3 Slicing and dicing to make animated GIFs. Make them all the same size.

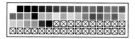

9.4 The three main images have a common (reduced) palette of 38 colors.

images change in back. The effect is quite three-dimensional and dynamic **[9.2]**.

I have chosen a typeface called DIN Neuzeit Grotesk Bold Condensed. It anchors the page and has a Bauhaus/retro look. I choose a pale green from the color cube to set it off. The subtitle is set in Gill Sans caps (I love the caps, but I rarely use the lowercase). I put the type on a front layer and make a separate drop shadow layer, which I move around until I get the effect I want.

When I have everything the way I want it, I build the animated GIFs. For each frame, I simply turn on the appropriate background layer and save the file as a GIF image. I want to save each 55 x 55-pixel square and let the GIF-building program make the GIFs for a high degree of consistency in processing the images. Because I already have the 40-color palette, I have everything I need to build the animated GIFs *(see "Animation," in Chapter 3 for hints on tools to use)*.

I flatten each image and cut it up, each time making the same sized cuts. I set the dimensions of the rectangle

tool to a fixed size to make cutting easier. Unless you have some particular effect in mind, it's best to build an animation by making all GIFs the exact same size **[9.3]**, and the exact same palette **[9.4]**.

Now I build all the animated GIFs before locking them together in a table. For each animated GIF, I load all the necessary images into the GIF-building program. I make sure to set the "Optimize" option, so I'll get the smallest files possible.

Once I have made these files, I give them different delay settings, randomizing the timing. I make sure to give them all different cycle times and infinite repetition, so the whole show keeps going but doesn't look like it's in a loop **[9.5]**.

Unfortunately, the total weight of all animated GIFs is just under 100K. After considering several options – including a redesign – I throw out one of the master images and use two photo layers, rather than three. That means I have to build every single animated GIF over again, a considerable amount of work. How could I have avoided this? By measuring the size of each GIF and multiplying by 24, I could have determined that each animated GIF must be under 3k. The files I have are around 4k each.

Fortunately, throwing out a layer is just a matter of rebuilding the animated GIFs; it doesn't take that long. Now the page is under 60K.

The 4 x 6 Table

Now that I have all the elements, the only way to test them is to build the

9.5 Different delays make the changing of the squares look random.

table and try the effect. I'll need a table with six columns and four rows, plus an extra column to space it over. The key is to get the cells to butt right up against each other (*see "The Invisible Table Trick" in Chapter 4*) [9.6].

This page has four rows in one large table. Each row has a left margin cell (a black single-pixel GIF), six cells containing animated GIFs, and a right margin cell. I link each animated GIF to the preamble page, so visitors enter the exhibit no matter where they click. I center this table in case people have large browser windows.

After a little debugging, it actually works. It's great to see this page come together on my screen for the first time [9.7]. A few tweaks of the timing parameters make it look nice and random.

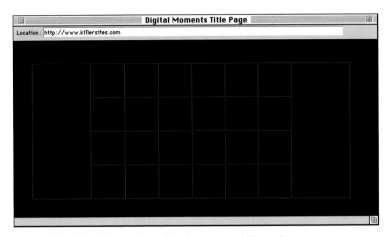

9.6 Position the table, make each cell 55 pixels wide, and use `CELLPAD-DING=0` and `CELLSPACING=0` for a thin border during development.

Broken GIFs

Unfortunately, with so many animated GIFs on a single page, there is a chance they won't all load. New changes to web protocols will help assure that all images on a page arrive together, but it will take a while for the new HTTP 1.1 standard to become universal. For now, a snappy server well connected to the Web really makes a difference. If this site sits on a shared server with a lot of traffic, there will be more than a few broken GIFs at lunch time. Reduce it to a 3 x 3 or 2 x 2 grid if your visitors get too many broken GIFs.

GifWizard

GifWizard is an online utility that takes your animated GIFs and optimizes them. It is not a program you can download; it's a free service. Simply specify where your images are (on the Web or on your hard disk), and GifWizard will reduce colors, scale, dither, and perform an analysis of your animated GIFs. It gives you a gallery of possible reduced-size images to choose from, which you can just take and put into your web site. It's a great resource, and an interesting model for software distribution. Try it!

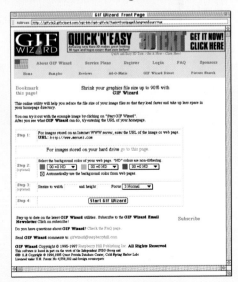

GifWizard is a free tool for optimizing your animated GIFs.

9.7 Get the animated GIFs running and make any adjustments to timing.

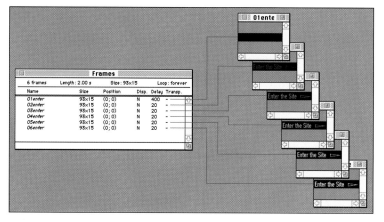

9.8 A gentle reminder fades in gradually and gets brightest right at the end.

Green Means Go

Throughout the site, I want green to be the navigation color. Anything green is a link that takes you to another page. After displaying this main animation, I have a small green arrow fade in to pull visitors into the site. This is done with a six-frame animated GIF.

I place the text and the arrow into a separate layer over a black background, then I save six identical copies. Leaving the first copy as is, I work back through the other copies, progressively applying the Gaussian Blur filter and decreasing saturation. The last frame must be completely black. I make the blur transitions to the title *nonlinearly* – in small steps near the title, but increasing the blur as I approach the black, so the fade-in accelerates when played **[9.8]**.

Using GIFBuilder on a Macintosh, I assemble the five frames in reverse order, setting the delay for the first frame at four seconds. This probably means (although it doesn't guarantee) that the title will appear after the main image loads. This is a single-pass animation; I set it to play once, stopping on the last image to let the surfer enter the site.

Finally, I add a simple navigation bar at the very bottom of this page. The navigation bar is made of seven text images set in Gill Sans caps. Following my rule, the clickable links are green, but the current page is always grayed out. By making all 14 images in advance, I have everything I need to make the navigation bars around the site (see the diagram at the beginning of the chapter). I make sure they are below the first 480 vertical pixels of the screen, so most people don't even notice it.

The Entry Page

Because the title page is big, it makes sense to put up a small greeting page at the front of the site, instructing visitors to turn off underlining and enlarge their browser windows, plus warn them that the site is graphics-intensive. The dinosaur image grabs their attention, sets the stage, and, I hope, compels them to enter the site. It's also a good place for a link to the site credits [9.9].

The Preamble Page

Doug wanted a preamble page to play the role of the words normally silk-screened onto the wall as you enter a gallery space. I make the page with a single image of type set in DIN Neuzeit Grotesk. After reducing colors (*see Chapter 5, "Rendering Type"*), the entire image weighs only 16K. I added the extra image at the bottom to tell visitors they are entering another world [9.10].

I want to remind visitors they are about to see 36 images, so I start the navigation graphics on this page. The arrow again fades in to reinforce the navigation scheme and beckon you on.

Finally, there is a little dot in the lower-left corner of the page. I hope you have to look closely to see it, because you're not supposed to notice it (in fact, you can't notice it here, but if you go to the site and look closely, you'll find it). It's actually the main image on the next page – a picture of

9.9 The greeting page lets people know they are about to enter a special space. It also warns that the next page contains a lot of graphics.

9.10 After reducing this large image to 8 colors, it is 16K. With the preload, the entire page comes in under 34K.

187

9.11 The site takes you through 36 images in a specific order. This shows one "train" of the gallery. The first image is always the Steve Jobs image.

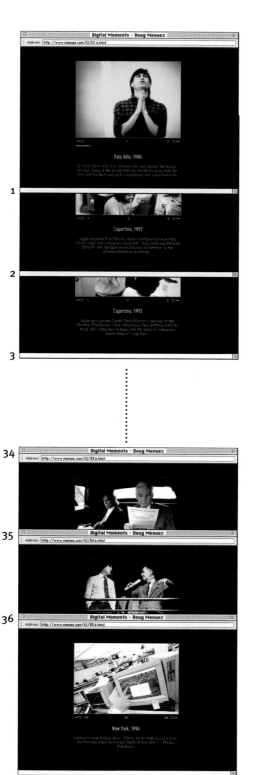

Steve Jobs – reduced to 1 pixel square. Unfortunately, `WIDTH=0` doesn't make it smaller than a single, visible pixel. The code for this image is:

```
<IMG HEIGHT="1" WIDTH="1"
SRC= "images/0.0jobs.b.jpg">
```

While visitors read the preamble, this image quietly loads onto their hard disks. When they click to go to the next page, the image flies onto their screens immediately. As they look at the first page, the images for both page 2 and the reverse of page 1 load in the lower left-hand corner. Whichever way they go, they always have the next images downloaded, so there is never a wait. With any luck, they won't notice. They'll just think I have the world's fastest server.

This is called a *preload*. It is one of the most user-friendly features you can put into a linear site like this. Preload included, this page weighs less than 34K, and you're reading the preamble while most of it loads. I don't interlace any of the images, since that would just increase their size.

The Interior Pages

Each of the 35 interior images follows the same format [9.11]. Each page has a high quality image that loads quickly, a title GIF, and an ASCII text caption in gray [9.12]. After reducing this large image to 8 colors, it is 16K.

To keep things organized as the project grows, I put all 72 JPEG images into a folder called "images," with logical names like "images/tokyo95.b.jpg". The negative version of this photo is "images/tokyo95.w.jpg". The slash means "get it out of the 'images' folder." I make another folder, called "titles," where I store all 112 title GIFS [9.13].

Image Processing

My first concern on each of these interior pages is to get the main images as small as possible while retaining the subtle details. I decide on a width of 298 and a height of 215 pixels. 215 pixels is as tall as I can comfortably make an image in a browser window that might be full of menu bars. The 298 is necessary to preserve the aspect ratio of the film. After resizing an image, I always apply the Unsharp Mask filter (a sharpening operation). Unsharp masking reinstates the fine details blurred during resizing. It's important to use this filter to correct, not manipulate – overdoing it will make the image look edgy. If I'm reducing an image by a large percentage, I reduce and sharpen in steps, preserving delicate details as I go.

Grayscale images require a full range of tonalities. In particular, I want the blacks to be completely black ("#000000"). Because some images have black at the edges, I decide to use a 50% gray, 1-pixel-wide border to denote the edge of each photograph. This will also help on the reverse side, where black becomes white. I save them as JPEGS using a medium quality setting. Now I make the title GIFS. I set each title in DIN Neuzeit Grotesk, using a light gray so as not to compete with the navigation color.

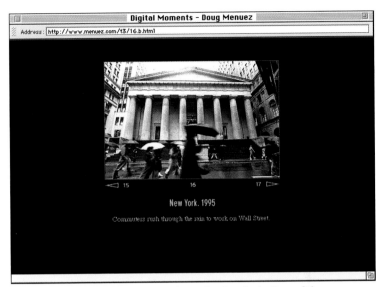

9.12 A typical interior page. Note the preload at the bottom of the screen.

Confirmation

In their excellent book, *Wayfinding in Architecture: People, Signs and Architecture* (McGraw Hill, 1992), authors Paul Arthur and Romedi Passini point out that people need three kinds of signs: 1) you are here, 2) how to get where you want to go, and 3) you are on the way. Most web pages have the first two by default. The third sign, confirmation, is very helpful when taking people on a journey through your site. If your site has five main areas, you might want to make sure visitors know where they are (area and page) at all times.

Site designers should use this kind of sign, a confirmation, more often. In the gallery site, the frame numbers under each picture indicate how far along you are. This information can be valuable to surfers, who unconsciously use a technique called *cognitive mapping* to get their bearings within your site. I highly recommend this book to anyone doing interactive design.

9.13 If your files have logical names, it's easy to keep everything straight.

```
<!-- Page Parameters -->
<HTML>
   <HEAD>
     <TITLE>
        Digital Moments Title Page
     </TITLE>
   </HEAD>
   <BODY BGCOLOR=#000000 TEXT=#CCCCCC ALINK=#FFFFFF
   VLINK=#CCCCCC>
     <CENTER>
        <IMG BORDER=0 WIDTH=524 HEIGHT=30 SRC="./resources/
        dot_black.gif">
        <BR>
        <!-- Begin Title Table -->
        <TABLE BORDER=0 CELLSPACING=0 CELLPADDING=0
        WIDTH=524>
          <!-- Start Row 1 Of Table -->
          <TR VALIGN=TOP>
            <!-- Left Margin -->
            <TD ROWSPAN=4><IMG BORDER=0 WIDTH=97 HEIGHT=1
            SRC="./resources/dot_black.gif"></TD>
            <!-- a 1 -->
            <TD><A HREF="preamble.shtml"><IMG BORDER=0
            WIDTH=55 HEIGHT=55 SRC="./animations/a1.gif">
            </A></TD>
            <!-- b 1 -->
            <TD><A HREF="preamble.shtml"><IMG BORDER=0
            WIDTH=55 HEIGHT=55 SRC="./animations/b1.gif">
            </A></TD>
            <!-- c 1 -->
            <TD><A HREF="preamble.shtml"><IMG BORDER=0
            WIDTH=55 HEIGHT=55 SRC="./animations/c1.gif">
            </A></TD>
            <!-- d 1 -->
            <TD><A HREF="preamble.shtml"><IMG BORDER=0
            WIDTH=55 HEIGHT=55 SRC="./animations/d1.gif">
            </A></TD>
            <!-- e 1 -->
            <TD><A HREF="preamble.shtml"><IMG BORDER=0
            WIDTH=55 HEIGHT=55 SRC="./animations/e1.gif">
            </A></TD>
            <!-- f 1 -->
            <TD><A HREF="preamble.shtml"><IMG BORDER=0
            WIDTH=55 HEIGHT=55 SRC="a./nimations/f1.gif">
            </A></TD>
            <!-- Right Margin -->
            <TD ROWSPAN=4><IMG BORDER=0 WIDTH=97 HEIGHT=1
            SRC="./resources/dot_black.gif"></TD>
          </TR>
          <!-- End Row 1 Of Table-->
        </TABLE>
     </CENTER>
   </BODY>
</HTML>
```

Contact-Sheet Navigation

The contact-sheet numbering scheme builds anticipation, displaces the usual Forward and Back buttons, and gives a familiar feel to the exhibit. The small triangle images are reminiscent of those found on contact sheets. I make the triangles into separate GIFS, so there are only two green triangle graphics to keep track of, and the frame-number graphics can be reused. I make the frame numbers into GIFS using a font called Interstate, which is reminiscent of the lettering used on film. The forward and back images, being links, are green, while the current frame number is gray, since it won't be clickable. While I have them in Photoshop, I change the color of all green GIFS to a dark red (the negative color of my navigation green) and flip them horizontally to get the reversed numbers to use on the behind-the-scenes page.

Centered Tables

I decide to use a centered table to hold the picture on the page. First, I use a single-pixel GIF to space down 30 pixels, giving me a consistent top margin. I create a table with a blank cell on the left, a cell for the image in the center, and a blank cell on the right. I then center the entire table. This assures me of a solid left margin, while giving the image more breathing room if people have wider screens [9.14].

This centered table with a firm left margin works wonderfully and is an excellent alternative to the four-column table for laying out text (*see* "Horizontal

Processing Photographic Images

Making images look good on the Web is a lengthy process; I've covered palettes, reduction, and other related issues elsewhere in this book. But photography and fine art images present a special challenge. Because fidelity is more important than download speed, I sometimes opt for better quality (larger file size). Here are a few hints to obtain the best results:

When scanning, capture the best tonal range you can. Guard against washout in highlights and shadows filling in. You'll never be able to salvage a bad source file, so it's worthwhile to pay attention and use your scanning software to get the most out of the original.

Scan sensitive images as large and at as high a resolution as possible. Color correct at a large size, then resample them down to the final physical size and resolution.

Generally use Unsharp Mask after resizing or resampling (changing resolution) to preserve detail and crispness.

As a general rule, highlights shouldn't burn out to full white unless they are highlights in shiny objects like chrome or point sources of light. Conversely, shadow tones shouldn't be completely black until you get to the darkest areas in a photograph (near blacks are very hard to see on screen).

Use Curve and Level adjustments in Photoshop to correct images to display proper midtone values prior to processing them for the Web. Keep cross-platform color issues in mind. When color correcting on the Macintosh, I recommend regularly switching your monitor settings to simulate the darker Windows screen representation.

When color fidelity is of primary importance, using the standard color cube and GIF format will change the colors unfavorably; use JPEG instead. JPEG distorts fine details, but the color stays substantially truer to the original scanned art.

9.15 A centered table makes a nice template for the interior pages. Notice the two preloads at the end.

```
<!-- Page Parameters -->
<HTML>
  <HEAD>
    <TITLE>
      Digital Moments - Doug Menuez
    </TITLE>
  </HEAD>
  <BODY BGCOLOR="#000000" TEXT="#CCCCCC" ALINK=#FFFFFF
VLINK=#CCCCCC>
    <!-- Top Margin Vertical Spacer -->
    <IMG BORDER=0 WIDTH=1 HEIGHT=30 SRC="../resources/
    dot_black.gif">
    <BR>
    <CENTER>
      <!-- Begin Image Table Table -->
      <TABLE BORDER=0 CELLSPACING=0 CELLPADDING=0
      WIDTH=524>
        <!-- Start Row 1 Of Table -->
        <TR VALIGN=TOP>
          <!-- Left Margin -->
          <TD ROWSPAN=7><IMG BORDER=0 WIDTH=112
          HEIGHT=1 SRC="../resources/dot_black.gif">
          </TD>
          <!-- The Picture For The Page -->
          <TD COLSPAN=5><A HREF="22.w.html"><IMG
          BORDER=0 WIDTH=300 HEIGHT=217 SRC="../images/
          tokyo95.b.img.jpg"></A></TD>
          <!-- Right Margin -->
          <TD ROWSPAN=7><IMG BORDER=0 WIDTH=112
          HEIGHT=1 SRC="../resources/dot_black.gif"></TD>
        </TR>
        <!-- End Row 1 Of Table-->
        <!-- Start Row 2 Of Table -->
        <TR VALIGN=TOP>
          <!-- Blank Vertical Spacer -->
          <TD COLSPAN=5 WIDTH=300><IMG BORDER=0 WIDTH=1
          HEIGHT=3 SRC="../resources/dot_black.gif"></TD>
        </TR>
        <!-- End Row 2 Of Table-->
        <!-- Start Row 3 Of Table -->
        <TR VALIGN=TOP>
          <!-- Previous Image Button -->
          <TD ALIGN=LEFT WIDTH=55><A HREF="21.b.html"><IMG
          BORDER=0 WIDTH=24 HEIGHT=13 SRC="../navigation/
          all.b.lt.gif"><IMG BORDER=0 WIDTH=24 HEIGHT=13
          SRC="../navigation/21.b.ltrt.gif"></A></TD>
          <!-- Blank Filler -->
          <TD><IMG BORDER=0 WIDTH=89 HEIGHT=1 SRC="../re
          sources/dot_black.gif"></TD>
          <!-- Image Frame Number -->
          <TD><IMG BORDER=0 WIDTH=26 HEIGHT=13 SRC="../
          navigation/22.b.ctr.gif"></TD>
          <!-- Blank Filler -->
          <TD><IMG BORDER=0 WIDTH=89 HEIGHT=1 SRC="../
          resources/dot_black.gif"></TD>
```

```
        <!-- Next Image Button -->
        <TD ALIGN=RIGHT WIDTH=55><A HREF="23.b.html"><IMG
        BORDER=0 WIDTH=24 HEIGHT=13 SRC="../navigation/
        23.b.ltrt.gif"><IMG BORDER=0 WIDTH=24 HEIGHT=13
        SRC="../navigation/all.b.rt.gif"></A></TD>
     </TR>
     <!-- End Row 3 Of Table-->
     <!-- Start Row 4 Of Table -->
     <TR VALIGN=TOP>
        <!-- Blank Vertical Spacer -->
        <TD COLSPAN=5 WIDTH=300><IMG BORDER=0 WIDTH=1
        HEIGHT=10 SRC="../resources/dot_black.gif"></TD>
     </TR>
     <!-- End Row 4 Of Table-->
     <!-- Start Row 5 Of Table -->
     <TR VALIGN=TOP>
        <!-- Image Title Cell -->
        <TD COLSPAN=5 WIDTH=298 ALIGN=MIDDLE><IMG
        BORDER=0 WIDTH=120 HEIGHT=30 SRC="../titles/
        tokyo95.b.txt.gif"></TD>
     </TR>
     <!-- End Row 5 Of Table-->
     <!-- Start Row 6 Of Table -->
     <TR VALIGN=TOP>
        <!-- Blank Vertical Spacer -->
        <TD COLSPAN=5 WIDTH=300><IMG BORDER=0 WIDTH=1
        HEIGHT=6 SRC="../resources/dot_black.gif"></TD>
     </TR>
     <!-- End Row 6 Of Table-->
     <!-- Start Row 7 Of Table -->
     <TR VALIGN=TOP>
        <!-- The Text for the Page -->
        <TD WIDTH=298 COLSPAN=5 ALIGN=MIDDLE>Japanese
        women bow in traditional greeting in the lobby of
        Apple Computer's Headquarters. </TD>
     </TR>
     <!-- End Row 7 Of Table-->
   </TABLE>
   <!-- End Table -->
 </CENTER>
 <!-- Bottom MarginVertical Spacer -->
 <IMG BORDER=0 WIDTH=1 HEIGHT=15 SRC="../resources/
 dot_black.gif">
 <BR>
 <!-- Preload for Next Image -->
 <IMG BORDER=0 WIDTH=1 HEIGHT=1 SRC="../images/
 zurich90.b.jpg">
 <BR>
 <!-- Preload for Negative Image -->
 <IMG BORDER=0 WIDTH=1 HEIGHT=1 SRC="../images/
 tokyo95.w.img.jpg">
 </BODY>
</HTML>
```

9.14 Adding a blank cell to a table and centering the whole thing ensures a left margin while opening up the left side if viewed with a larger screen.

White Space" in Chapter 4). I use the centered table trick on every page in the site **[9.15]**.

The last set of commands on the page preloads the next two images. I preload the next regular image first, because that is the more likely next page. Then I preload the negative version. By making the green arrows as separate images, I know they are already cached and load immediately. This ensures the best possible performance as visitors traverse the site.

The bad news: Surfers can have simultaneous connections that cause these two images to load concurrently. While I'd like to specify the actual order in which pages load from a server, there is no way to do that. Calling one first gives it a better chance, but there's no way to be sure one image will load before another. Sad, but true.

Building this site requires a lot of repetitive work. While it's not difficult, I must keep a chart of all the file names to avoid lots of debugging later. (I tape it to my monitor for easy reference.) The interior pages are quite easy to link. I use the first HTML file as a template, copying it for each new page and changing the numbers so they all hook together. After copying, I must change the following items in each file: the back link, the forward link, the names of the GIFs that show the previous, current, and next frame numbers, the name of the file that contains the photo, the through-the-picture link, the name of the file that holds the GIF for the title, the actual text caption for the photo, and the two preloads.

The first interior page links back to the preamble page, while the last page links to the feedback page. (The preamble page is called "preamble.shtml" – see the engineering section later in this chapter for why there's an "s" before the "html" in the suffix.) Other than that, the only thing I worry about are typing errors that cause pages to link up improperly. A quick run-through shows any mistakes immediately.

The Reverse Side

Once I have each positive image optimized for look and load, I simply invert and flip it in Photoshop. It takes very little extra time; the impact is well worth the effort [9.16].

The structure of the page and HTML are the same, but I must remember to link the photos backwards, so people move to the left to go forward (toward frame 36) and right to go back. I work with Doug to get the comments for each photo to be the same length as the caption, so when you go to the back side, you see the same amount of gray text for each photograph. I love the fact that it takes a second to realize there's something new to read back here.

The preload for this page first loads the next (left) image, assuming people will want to keep progressing down the line, then the main image for the opposing positive page, in case they arrived at that negative page from another negative page.

The Big Finish

The site experience is 36 images long. That's really too long for all but the most die-hard photography buffs. Probably 18 would be better. But we agreed that anything less than 36 would break the metaphor and would be unprofessional, because professional photographers use 36-image film. Because the site has done well, and we notice that people do actually go all the way through, we haven't shortened it. But we would if we saw that people were giving up before getting to the end.

Doug wanted visitors to see others' comments and to be able to leave comments if they wanted. I came up with a film-credits-style presentation that puts visitors' comments opposite their names [9.17].

My navigation bar goes at the top, with status information in gray.

9.16 The reverse pages add another dimension to the exhibit.

9.17 A form mock-up. I actually mock up the forms in Photoshop to play with layouts without being influenced by HTML.

The Feedback Form

Contrary to the fill-out form in Chapter 8, this feedback form is direct and simple. No need to make it span the page or include several fields. Just a comment and an email address are enough. I design it so visitors know they are still in the gallery, not yet back out in the world of default page design. They give their reactions first, then they can see what other visitors have said. On both pages, I give them a chance to go to the information pages or go back to the entrance.

I never make a form from scratch. I always copy one and work with it. There are plenty of good forms on the Web to copy. This file is called

"feedback.html", and the final file for presenting the selected comments will be called "comments.html" [9.18].

Engineering

The software engineering for this site presents challenges beyond the realm of the average graphic designer. While you may not be completely at home with the material that follows, the basic ideas should be clear. *I don't write the programs that go on my server. I work with my webmaster to achieve the effect I want. The better I understand what goes on behind the scenes, the more I can look for solutions that are technically feasible and robust.*

Note: In this second edition of the book, the basic engineering approach has changed. The first edition used a UNIX-based cron-event, while this edition discusses a more universal CGI-based approach. This method will work on more servers and is the method we actually use on the site.

Pseudo-Randomness

Once I have the site built with 36 interior images all hooked up, I test it out on several friends. They love it. I could stop here and save a lot of work, but the idea is to make it look like the exhibit is always changing, with a different 36 images each time you visit. To do this, I'll devise a way to show 36 images chosen from a total of 56, seemingly at random.

There are two ways to present random pages at a site like this: really random and pseudo-random. *Really random* involves a Perl script or a database that manufactures a temporary site containing 36 images chosen just-in-time. Each time visitors return, they see a completely random selection of 36 out of 56 images. The *pseudo-random* way is to prebuild a set of sites (enough that most people won't realize there's a limited number) and cycle the visitors through these prebuilt static sites.

The pseudo-random approach works well in situations where it's preferable to do extra HTML work in lieu of server or database programming. Think of it as building several trains and using a switch to put a new train on the track every time someone comes to the site. This "poor man's random" strategy is less technical and more tedious than dealing with databases **[9.19]**. In this case, I'll build three trains from a total of 56 images. If I want to, I can always make more.

Now that I have one train working, it's time to make three trains.

Building railroad cars. I want to make sure this idea works on my desktop before moving it to the server. After preparing another 20 images, I have 56 to work with. Doug has supplied 56 captions and photo notes. I make the positive and negative versions of all the photos, and I make the title GIFs for each page, including their reversed counterparts. Once I have all the ingredients, it's a matter of putting them all together.

All the images go into the "images" folder with logical names like "paloalto86.b.txt.gif". This folder now contains all 112 images (one for each

main image and one for its negative image). I make another folder, called "titles," where I store all 112 (positive and negative) title GIFs.

I make another directory on my hard disk, called "templates." There I make the HTML template for each picture and its negative counterpart. It's important to give each of these files a logical name, like "tokyo95.b.html" and "tokyo95.w.html," rather than a numerical one. I must put all 112 HTML files in place before taking the next step. It's important to associate

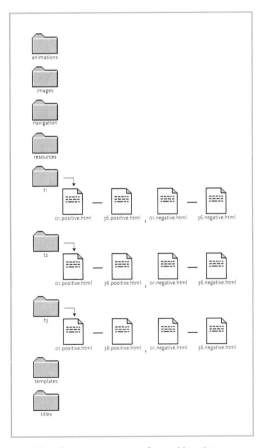

9.19 The directory structure for making three trains.

9.18 This particular form doesn't do anything fancy. It just sends Doug e-mail and lets him decide what to post on his comments page.

```
<!-- Begin Form -->
<FORM METHOD="post" ACTION="http://www.menuez.com/cgi-bin/
comment.cgi">
  <!-- Begin Form Table -->
  <TABLE BORDER=0 CELLSPACING=0 CELLPADDING=0 WIDTH=524>
    <!-- Start Row 1 Of Table -->
    <TR VALIGN=TOP>
      <!-- Left Margin -->
      <TD ROWSPAN=12><IMG BORDER=0 WIDTH=85 HEIGHT=1
      SRC="./resources/dot_black.gif"></TD>
      <!-- Top Margin -->
      <TD COLSPAN=2><IMG BORDER=0 WIDTH=354 HEIGHT=1
      SRC="./resources/dot_black.gif"></TD>
      <!-- Right Margin -->
      <TD ROWSPAN=12><IMG BORDER=0 WIDTH=85 HEIGHT=1
      SRC="./resources/dot_black.gif"></TD>
    </TR>
    <!-- End Row 1 Of Table-->
    <!-- Start Row 2 Of Table -->
    <TR>
      <TD ALIGN=LEFT WIDTH=60>Name: </TD>
      <TD WIDTH=294><INPUT TYPE="text" NAME="Name"
      SIZE="50"></TD>
    </TR>
    <!-- End Row 2 Of Table-->
    <!-- Start Row 3 Of Table -->
    <TR VALIGN=TOP>
      <!-- Blank Vertical Spacer -->
      <TD COLSPAN=2><IMG BORDER=0 WIDTH=354 HEIGHT=10
      SRC="./resources/dot_black.gif"></TD>
    </TR>
    <!-- End Row 3 Of Table-->
    <!-- Start Row 4 Of Table -->
    <TR>
      <TD ALIGN=LEFT WIDTH=60>Email: </TD>
      <TD WIDTH=294><INPUT TYPE="text" NAME="Email"
      SIZE="50"><BR></TD>
    </TR>
    <!-- End Row 4 Of Table-->
    <!-- Start Row 5 Of Table -->
    <TR VALIGN=TOP>
      <!-- Blank Vertical Spacer -->
      <TD COLSPAN=2><IMG BORDER=0 WIDTH=354 HEIGHT=20
      SRC="resources/dot_black.gif"></TD>
    </TR>
    <!-- End Row 5 Of Table-->
    <!-- Start Row 6 Of Table -->
    <TR VALIGN=TOP>
      <TD COLSPAN=2 WIDTH=354>I would like to be on a
mailing list announcing <BR>Doug Menuez's work: <INPUT
TYPE="radio" NAME="Mailing List?" VALUE="yes" CHECKED>Yes
<INPUT TYPE="radio" NAME="Mailing List?" VALUE="no">No
</TD>
```

```
    </TR>
    <!-- End Row 6 Of Table -->
    <!-- Start Row 7 Of Table -->
    <TR VALIGN=TOP>
      <!-- Blank Vertical Spacer -->
      <TD COLSPAN=2><IMG BORDER=0 WIDTH=354 HEIGHT=20
      SRC="./resources/dot_black.gif"></TD>
    </TR>
    <!-- End Row 7 Of Table-->
    <!-- Start Row 8 Of Table -->
    <TR>
      <TD COLSPAN=2 WIDTH=354>Your Comments: <BR></TD>
    </TR>
    <!-- End Row 8 Of Table -->
    <!-- Start Row 9 Of Table -->
    <TR VALIGN=TOP>
      <!-- Blank Vertical Spacer -->
      <TD COLSPAN=2><IMG BORDER=0 WIDTH=354 HEIGHT=5
      SRC="./resources/dot_black.gif"></TD>
    </TR>
    <!-- End Row 9 Of Table-->
    <!-- Start Row 10 Of Table -->
    <TR>
      <TD COLSPAN=2 WIDTH=354><TEXTAREA NAME="Comments"
      ROWS=15 COLS=53 WRAP=VIRTUAL></TEXTAREA></TD>
    </TR>
    <!-- End Row 10 Of Table -->
    <!-- Start Row 11 Of Table -->
    <TR VALIGN=TOP>
      <!-- Blank Vertical Spacer -->
      <TD COLSPAN=2><IMG BORDER=0 WIDTH=354 HEIGHT=15
      SRC="./resources/dot_black.gif"></TD>
    </TR>
    <!-- End Row 11 Of Table-->
    <!-- Start Row 12 Of Table -->
    <TR>
      <TD COLSPAN=2 WIDTH=354><INPUT TYPE="submit"
      VALUE="Send Comment"><INPUT TYPE="reset"
      VALUE="Never Mind"></TD>
    </TR>
    <!-- End Row 12 Of Table -->
  </TABLE>
  <!-- End Text Table -->
</FORM>
<!-- End Form -->
```

Directory Structure

I like to run a flat file system on the server. No matter how complicated the site, I generally use only one level of directories (directories and folders are equivalent). I put the "resources" directory and any other holding-tank directories at the top level of a site. For example, if there are five main areas of my site, I might have five main directories. I try not to have any directories deeper than this, unless they store a large group of images particular to the HTML for that directory only. **I never put HTML files more than one level down in the hierarchy because of the time wasted in debugging file references.** I keep almost all HTML files one level down from the top. Photographs are in the "images" directory, but they are called by HTML files one level down, in the different "train" directories, so each tag in the HTML file looks something like:

```
<IMG SRC="../images/
tokyo95.b.jpg">
```

The "../" means "up and over" in the directory structure. It works with the folders right on my machine as well as when I put it on the server later. I must refer to the title GIFs by typing "../titles/" rather than "titles/" before the file name. Because I'm working one directory down, I also have to add "../" to my "resources" folder references, or they won't work:

```
<IMG VSPACE=x
SRC="../resources/
dot_black.gif">
```

▷ 🗁	animations
📄	biography .html
📄	clients.html
📄	comments.html
📄	feedback.html
▷ 🗁	images
📄	index.html
▷ 🗁	navigation
📄	photolist.html
📄	preamble.html
▷ 🗁	resources
▷ 🗁	t1
▷ 🗁	t2
▷ 🗁	t3
▷ 🗁	templates
▷ 🗁	titles

the names of images and title GIFs with the right narrative text. There is much more linking to do, but it involves less thinking and more repetition.

I link each HTML page (railroad car) to its negative (but not evil) twin, but not by name. Because I don't know the names of the Back and Forward files, or which number each one will be, or which number the negative counterpart HTML file will be, I leave an "xx" in the code in these six places (you'll see why in a minute.) To make room for all the trains, I create three new directories (folders), called t1, t2, and t3. For each train, I will build railroad cars out of the template HTML files and fill up a new directory with a different combination of template files.

To make the first train, I open the "templates" folder and copy the 36 HTML files I want for that train (and their negative counterparts) into the first train's folder. Now here's the important part: as I copy each HTML file, I change the name from "tokyo95.b.html" to "01.b.html" or "22.b.html", or whatever number is next in the sequence. This leaves the logical names behind and sorts them in order of appearance in the folder, so I can see one entire train in the folder when it's sorted alphabetically. (Using the 01-09 prefix will assure that my files alphabetize properly in the folder.) I keep adding these files and changing their names until I get to "36.b.html", which is the last car in the train. Notice that I'm only copying HTML files here, not images, so the amount of data duplicated is quite small.

Now I have made all the cars for one complete train. The next thing to do is hook them up.

Hooking up the trains. Now that I have the HTML templates for that train in place, I hook them together by changing the links. This is repetitive, but it goes fairly quickly. I select 20 files (the first 10 pages and their negative counterparts) and open them all at once in my text editor. Searching for "xx", I can replace the numbers of each file without much thought. For file number six, for example, I put "06" into the "xx" part of the file, the name of the reverse file, "05" into the previous link and the back button's GIF filename, "06" into the text that shows which file this is, and "07" into the forward link and its GIF filename. I close the file and do the same to the negative version (remembering to switch the "05" and the "07" links so they point backwards). Finally, I switch the preload file names. This takes a little thinking. I do all the front pages in a group, then I go back and link the reverse pages. All together, each file has eight items to change [**9.20 A, B**].

I change links in groups of 20 files. It takes about 5 minutes to link 20 files, so each train takes about 20 minutes to assemble. After everything is in place, I hook up the first and last files. The Previous link of file "01.b.html" and the Next link of file "01.w.html" is "../preamble.shtml", while the Next link of file "36.b.html" and previous link of "36.w.html" is "../feedback.html". Note that I have typed "Digital Moments – Doug Menuez" into the titles of all the interior pages, so as to avoid

any extra work labeling specific page titles.

Now there's one last detail: the preload on the preamble page. If you recall, the preamble page is the same for all trains, so the image it preloads will also be the same. That means the first "car" of every train should be the page that contains the image of Steve Jobs. There are complicated (script-based) solutions to let me vary this image from train to train, but to preserve my navigation scheme and keep things simple, I decide that the best solution is to use the same image for the first page of each version. It's a little disappointing, but the preload is more important than avoiding repetition.

The fake randomness begins after the first train. After testing this train to

9.20 A (**B**, next page) Inserting the proper numbers hooks the trains together.

```
<TR VALIGN=TOP>
  <!-- Previous Image Button -->
  <TD ALIGN=LEFT WIDTH=55><A
  HREF="04.b.html"><IMG BORDER=0 WIDTH=24
  HEIGHT=13 SRC="../navigation/
  all.b.lt.gif"><IMG BORDER=0 WIDTH=24
  HEIGHT=13 SRC="../navigation/
  04.b.ltrt.gif"></A></TD>
  <!-- Blank Filler -->
  <TD><IMG BORDER=0 WIDTH=89 HEIGHT=1 SRC="../
  resources/dot_black.gif"></TD>
  <!-- Image Frame Number -->
  <TD><IMG BORDER=0 WIDTH=26 HEIGHT=13
  SRC="../navigation/05.b.ctr.gif"></TD>
  <!-- Blank Filler -->
  <TD><IMG BORDER=0 WIDTH=89 HEIGHT=1 SRC="../
  resources/dot_black.gif"></TD>
  <!-- Next Image Button -->
  <TD ALIGN=RIGHT WIDTH=55><A
  HREF="06.b.html"><IMG BORDER=0 WIDTH=24
  HEIGHT=13 SRC="../navigation/
  06.b.ltrt.gif"><IMG BORDER=0 WIDTH=24
  HEIGHT=13 SRC="../navigation/
  all.b.rt.gif"></A></TD>
</TR>
```

make sure it works, I go through the same process to hook up the other 2 trains. I can mix and match the order of the photographs as Doug wants, building each train from page 1 to page 36. I go through all 3 folders, making trains and hooking them up. It only takes a day (or maybe two).

Putting the trains on the track. To get the trains running, I mock up the behavior of the server script on my local machine. I change the "t1" reference in the file "preamble.shtml" to be "t2," and – sure enough – I'm in the second train [**9.21**].

Uploading to the server. Moving the site from my desktop to the server means moving everything over and

9.20 B (A, previous page)

seeing that it runs properly.

After re-creating my file structure exactly on the server, I go into my preamble page and "hard code" the link from the arrow to the first car on the first train. When I visit the site with my browser, I see the intended result: train 1 works fine. I rewrite the preamble page, changing the link to "t2," upload it again, and it does the right thing. I rewrite the preamble page and re-upload it a few more times, to make sure all trains are there.

To automate the switching of the tracks, I simply automate what I've been doing. I ask my webmaster to write a short server script called "switch.cgi." The script – it happens to be written in Perl – does two things: 1) it uses a system-provided random-number generator to set an internal variable called $num, and 2) it uses the value of this variable to print one of three statements into the HTML file, replacing the HTML statement that called it and serving the completed file to the visitor.

This is called a "server-side include." It's a way of substituting a CGI call for the text you intend to serve, only to have the CGI program install the correct text just as the page is served to the visitor. This particular script calls a subroutine named "srand" to choose a number and another subroutine called "int" to make sure it only yields one of three possible outcomes: 0, 1, and 2. These routines are part of Perl, which can be installed on almost any web server. The script then uses the value of the variable "$num" to substitute the final HTML and serve the file to the person who requested it.

```
<TR VALIGN=TOP>
  <!-- Previous Image Button -->
  <TD ALIGN=LEFT WIDTH=55><A
  HREF="21.b.html"><IMG BORDER=0 WIDTH=24
  HEIGHT=13 SRC="../navigation/
  all.b.lt.gif"><IMG BORDER=0 WIDTH=24
  HEIGHT=13 SRC="../navigation/
  21.b.ltrt.gif"></A></TD>
  <!-- Blank Filler -->
  <TD><IMG BORDER=0 WIDTH=89 HEIGHT=1 SRC="../
  resources/dot_black.gif"></TD>
  <!-- Image Frame Number -->
  <TD><IMG BORDER=0 WIDTH=26 HEIGHT=13
  SRC="../navigation/22.b.ctr.gif"></TD>
  <!-- Blank Filler -->
  <TD><IMG BORDER=0 WIDTH=89 HEIGHT=1 SRC="../
  resources/dot_black.gif"></TD>
  <!-- Next Image Button -->
  <TD ALIGN=RIGHT WIDTH=55><A
  HREF="23.b.html"><IMG BORDER=0 WIDTH=24
  HEIGHT=13 SRC="../navigation/
  23.b.ltrt.gif"><IMG BORDER=0 WIDTH=24
  HEIGHT=13 SRC="../navigation/
  all.b.rt.gif"></A></TD>
</TR>
```

If you go to the site and view the source, you'll see that the HTML is there, rather than the CGI call. The only place you can see the file as I actually wrote it is here in the illustration [9.22].

On many servers, it's customary to re-name your file to a ".shtml" file to indi-cate a CGI call in the HTML. Thus, the preamble page is actually named "preamble.shtml" and it's the only such page in this site.

Summary

Although the site has won several de-sign awards, this hand-coding method of presenting seemingly random imag-es really is a lot of extra work. In a per-fect world, this site would come out of a database. As databases become more affordable and easy to use, I would look into serving the site that way. The purpose of this chapter is to show that with determination and a few days of repetitive work, I can get a similar ef-fect without learning how to program a database. On the other hand, the site suffers from lack of flexibility.

I also used a lot of single-pixel GIFS to build the site, something I'd try not to do if I were building the site today. I could probably get the same basic design using non-breaking spaces.

In some cases, I look for solutions like the poor-man's random, where I can prebuild things and not have them running dynamically, because there is so much less to go wrong. This train-switching approach lets me focus on design, not programming. In this case, I simply make enough trains to make it

```
<!-- Enter the Site Button -->
  <TD><A HREF="http://www.menuez.com/t2/
  01.b.html">
  <IMG BORDER=0 WIDTH=93 HEIGHT=15
  SRC="animations/enter.gif"></TD>
```

9.21 In the preamble page, this HTML links the animated arrow image to the first car on the second train.

```
<!-- Enter the Site Button -->
<td>
  <!--#exec cgi="switch.cgi" -->
  <img border=0 width=93 height=15
  SRC="animations/enter.GIF">
</td>
```

9.22 What you see when you view the source *before* the script runs.

Aliases and Shortcuts

On the Macintosh, make an alias by selecting a file and choosing Make Alias from the File menu. In Windows 95, you can make a shortcut to a file by right-clicking it and selecting Shortcut. With Win-dows 3.1, you can't make an alias. You will either have to upgrade or put everything on the server to test your work.

feel random and add more if necessary later. The preloaded image trick works perfectly in a linear exhibit like this, provided people go down the one-way street the right way. Going against the grain of the preloads makes for slower surfing.

Though it is a complicated site, the HTML is fairly simple. Most of the work is in Photoshop. The hours are long, and the work itself is dull as toast. In the end, though, it pays off, because the site lets the photographs do the talking. Doug must be pleased. Among other awards, the site won honorable mention in *International Design Magazine's* annual interactive design competition.

Application

If you're making a gallery, another idea for the captions would be to use a pop-up tag as a design element. This can be a clever way to present information, like a caption, when you don't want it to show at first. In this case, I've put the title at the top of a pop-up menu and added the caption as several lines of options in the pop-up **[9.23]**. The form doesn't do anything. It just gives me the pop-up element **[9.24]**. I chose not to do it, because it forces the user to click the mouse more, but it might make a nice variation or give you an idea for making a gallery with a different theme but a similar structure.

9.23 Using a pop-up as a design element adds another tool to your toolkit.

```
<FORM>
<SELECT>
<OPTION SELECTED>
T O K Y O ,   1 9 9 5
<OPTION>Japanese women
bow in traditional
<OPTION > greeting in the
lobby of Apple
<OPTION > Computer's
Headquarters.
</SELECT >
</FORM >
```

9.24 Pop-ups are easy to add to any page.

The Perl Script

```
#!/usr/local/bin/perl
# Relocator Script for Menuez Digital Moments
- www.menuez.com
# Pick a random Number from 0 to 2 and go to
web page determined by number.

srand( (time/$$)*getppid );
$num= int(rand(3));

print "Content-type: text/html\n\n";

print "<A href=\"";

if ($num == 0) {
   print "http://www.menuez.com/t1/01.b.HTML";
}
   elsif ($num == 1) {
   print "http://www.menuez.com/t2/01.b.HTML";
}
   else {
   print "http://www.menuez.com/t3/01.b.HTML";
}

print "\">";
)
```

This Perl script chooses one of three "trains" randomly every time it's called and puts the correct command into the HTML file that called it, substituting for the CGI call in the HTML. Effectively, the script "prints" one of the following lines of text into the HTML file:

<a href= $\begin{cases} \texttt{"http://www.menuez.com/t1/01.b.HTML"} \\ or \\ \texttt{"http://www.menuez.com/t1/01.b.HTML"} \\ or \\ \texttt{"http://www.menuez.com/t1/01.b.HTML"} \end{cases}$

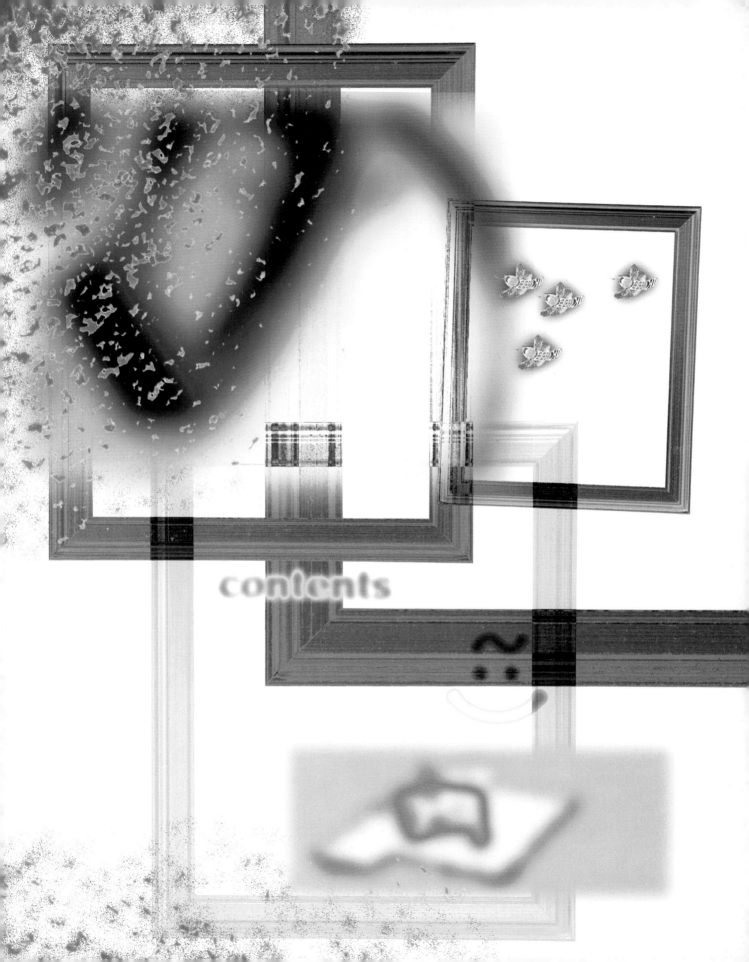

contents

CHAPTER 10

Creative Design Solutions

In this chapter, I present 15 solutions I think are worth noting. Twelve of these sites earned the High Five award (www.highfive.com) for excellence in site design. These examples show how to use the power of metaphor and theme to bring your web pages alive. Each has a particular tactic you can apply to your projects to achieve an effect or solve a problem.

Dennett's Dream
Matthew Lewis

www.cgrg.ohio-state.edu/~mlewis/
Gallery/gallery.html

Matthew Lewis finished his wonderful exhibition, *Dennett's Dream*, just as the Netscape 1.1 extensions arrived in 1995 to give him a black background for presenting his work. It shows a number of paintings he did for a multimedia project at Ohio State University. The site won a High Five and much recognition from other award givers. Matt gives us two versions, a high-bandwidth and a low-bandwidth site. The high-bandwidth site is really engaging. He uses a set of ephemeral navigation arrows to provide a familiar interface.

This gallery shows an alternative version of the linear gallery structure of Chapter 9. Matt gives us two ways to walk through the space: either by advancing and turning or by stepping sideways. No matter how you go through the space, each page gives you hints of where to go next. You never look at a full painting all by itself. You can see small parts of each painting to the left and right. These visual cues keep us moving toward the end, which is a U-turn that sends you back to the entrance. If you take the hint at the beginning and sidestep down the left side, you'll follow the paintings around the U, coming to the big finish at the end. It's an excellent example of a linear exhibition space with a beginning, middle, and end.

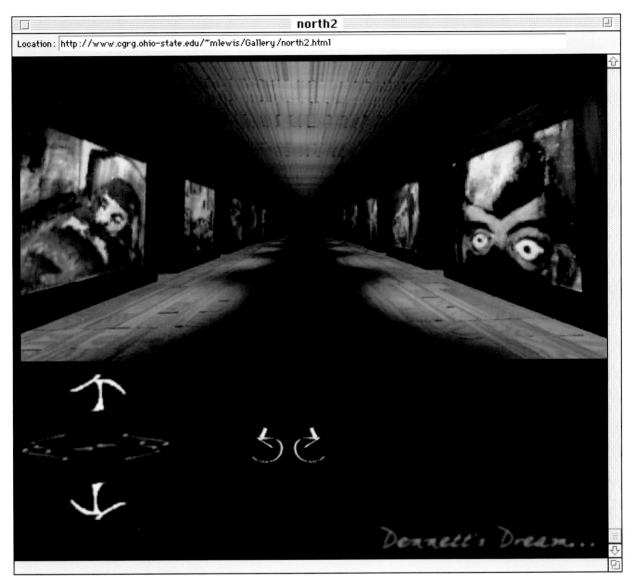

Dennett's Dream: you can walk down the middle or you can sidestep down
the left side, make the turn, and come back up the right.

The Idea Factory
TBWA/Chiat/Day

www.chiatday.com

Good ideas aren't born, they're made. By describing their advertising agency TBWA/Chiat/Day as "The Idea Factory," John Avery and Dave Butler make good use of a good idea – metaphor. Good metaphors tell a story, explain a concept, and provide a practical format for mapping information. What better way to describe the nebulous world of advertising than the concept of turning raw materials into a product?

Avery and Butler kept their site simple, letting the metaphor do its work. Their company information is contained within three areas, and well chosen graphics illustrate the manufacturing process visually. A sheep provides Raw Materials, which becomes a ball of yarn in Manufacturing, which becomes a sweater in the final Product. Within each section, TBWA/Chiat/Day has ambitiously attempted to describe the various raw materials and processes that go into making their creative ad campaigns by including articles on, for example, the color red and food.

Note the construction of the animated GIF on the home page. If you look at the code, you'll see it's actually four images, only one of which (factorysmoke.gif) is animated. The other three images are static GIFs mortised together in simple table, giving the look of one large animated image.

Good metaphors explain a concept. Great metaphors do it simply.

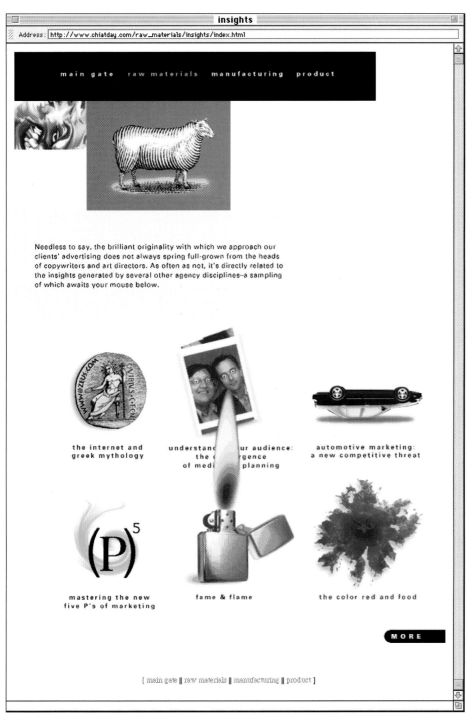

The minimal design keeps download time to a minimum.

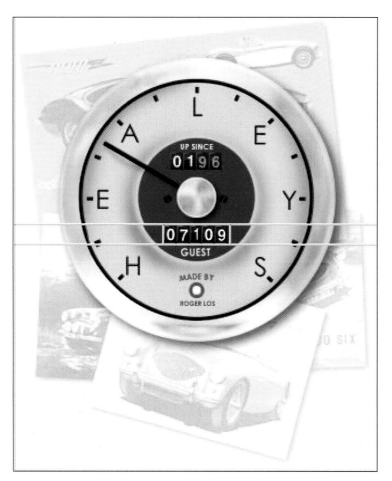

Roger's clever trick exposed: using a table to mortice four static images around one dynamic one. Visit the site to see it with table borders turned off.

Big Healeys
Roger Los

los.com/healey/big. html

Don't try this at home! Roger Los, an independent designer (and English sports car enthusiast) in Seattle, has created a very sophisticated frame-based site, using nested frames and JavaScript to keep the frames behaving well. Roger is a site designer with a rare blend of visual and technical acumen. The showpiece of the site is the speedometer dial that tells you what number visitor you are. Many sites have rotating counters; this is the only one I've seen that uses one appropriately.

It's a simple enough trick: take a photograph of a speedometer, cut it up, and replace the odometer with an active access counter. Doing it well is something else. Each digit is a separate GIF. A special program correlates the number to be displayed with the proper GIFS, spits out the HTML, and the whole page serves up dynamically. Go try it and see for yourself.

Locating Graphic Elements

To see how a page is built on the Mac, click on individual graphic elements with your cursor and move the mouse around slightly. You'll be able to "pick up" an image and move it around, pulling its outline out of place on the page so you can see how it fits with other elements. You can also use the View > Document Info command in Netscape Navigator to dissect a page.

Urban Diary
Joseph Squier

gertrude.art.uiuc.edu/ludgate/the/place.html

Joseph Squier is an Assistant Professor at the University of Illinois at Urbana-Champaign who teaches photography and electronic media. Joseph's site, called The Place, has received critical praise from around the world. I learned to turn off underlining from this site just a few days after I first started surfing. Joseph is responsible for opening the eyes of hundreds of thousands of visitors who find his site refreshing and visually stunning.

This page from his piece, the Urban Diary series, is one of several image maps using photographs of graph paper to display an entire page. This page, while somewhat memory intensive, is perhaps the first page on the Web to break the grip of HTML. The numbers at the bottom tell you which page you are on, almost everything links to something interesting, and every time you come back you discover something new. Visit the rest of The Place to see what may have been the world's first third-generation site.

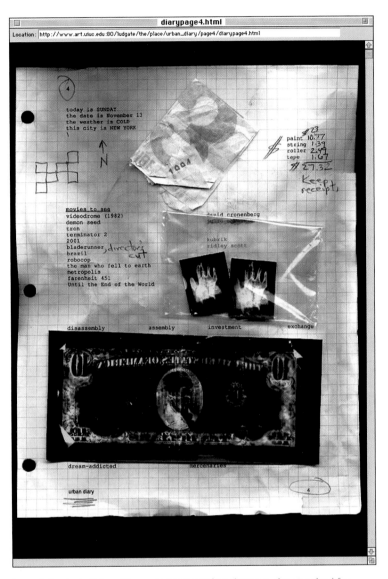

Joseph Squier's Urban Diary uses a metaphor that sets the standard for third-generation designers.

Dial It
Peter Horvath

www.6168.org/tv/tv_2.html

Peter Horvath is part of a two-person design team (along with Sharon Matarazzo) called 6168. Peter's design for a TV dial is an excellent way to couch a pop-culture exhibition in a pop-culture metaphor. The TV dial plays center stage, evoking memories of *Gilligan's Island* and *Dragnet.* To flip channels, select a hotlink. The links turn dark as you hit them, so you keep coming back to the dial for the pages you haven't seen yet.

This is simply a tour-de-force of table work; with the tables turned on, you can see how it all works. Rather than put the code here, I encourage you to see the 6168 site and view the source *in situ.*

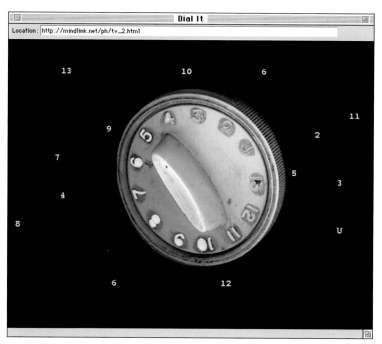

Can you see the table structure of this page?

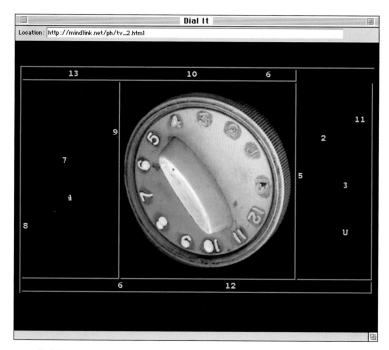

A TV dial is a great interface for dissecting popular culture.

214

Zoloft Intro Page
Josh Feldman

www. spectacle.com/zoloft/initiation/
letter.html

This clever page was designed by Josh Feldman of Prophet Communications for his interactive adventure, Zoloft. The amazing wood panel background image was made from a scan and made into a seamless JPEG in Photoshop. This page makes excellent use of the LOWSRC argument. An image can have two sources, the low source and the so-called high source. The low source loads first. It is meant to be a proxy for those with slower connections, so the user gets an idea of what is to come. If the user waits, the higher quality image loads on top of the low source image. In this case, Josh has made two separate images: the first

a torn-open envelope and the second an open letter. Note that he has copied a piece of the envelope to preserve continuity after the transition to the high source image. This is a brilliant use of the LOWSRC option. You occasionally see it used well, but rarely this well.

This page has an extra little gift. There is a Shockwave movie preload that loads the exterior shot of the church for the next screen while you're reading the letter. It's scaled into a small image in the upperleft corner. Although on the next page there are many images to load, this one is already in the cache.

  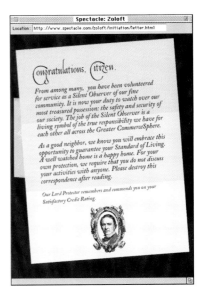

The background, the low source, and the high source.

This animation captures an otherwise hard to visualize concept.

Fila
Foote, Cone & Belding
Modem Media
R/GA Interactive

www.fila.com

Peter DePasquale and Steve McGinniss of Foote, Cone & Belding worked with Michael Hedgepeth of Modem Media and Natalie de la Gorce and Scott Prindle of R/GA Interactive to create this site for Fila athletic shoes.

Note how the animated GIFs in the Design Lab – I especially like the flexing pods – manage to make an otherwise uninteresting aspect of their product seem fascinating. Animated GIFs are too often used as whizzy window dressing, whereas Fila shows us they can illustrate hard-to-visualize concepts. A less practical but definitely cool animated GIF shows Grant Hill morphing from nice to imposing in the "Camp Tough Guy" entry tunnel.

As you travel further into the site, keep an eye on the navigation bar. The designers use different text effects to set each section off rather than relying on useless icons or confusing images. Type treatments emphasize some sections and downplay others. *See Chapter 5, "Rendering Type," for more ideas on using type to enhance your site.*

216

Fine Magazine
Gene Na, Peter Kang
Kioken Design

www.finemagazine.com

When you present your entire site in a pop-up window with no browser buttons, navigation becomes critical. Plus, Gene Na, Peter Kang, and the creative team at Kioken Design in New York had another problem: they didn't want a standard table of contents for Fine Magazine. They managed to find a creative solution for both by organizing the content "elements" with a creative, natural metaphor: the periodic table. Art becomes Ar, Affairs becomes Af, Music becomes Mu, and so on. This simple, condensed presentation of the site's departments also makes an unobtrusive toolbar for the top of each page. Meanwhile, the department you're in appears at the right, as well as the name of the article you're looking at.

Navigation within each article varies. The David Seltzer photography exhibition does it best – new periodic table elements Ba(ck) and Ne(xt) guide you through the exhibit. These nav elements work beautifully with the metaphor, but unfortunately, this is the only article in which they appear. In some sections, "back" and "next" is missing altogether – you have to go back to that section's main page just to see the next photograph. The articles, however, handle the navigation nicely. Not only can you click between pages, but the design shows what page you're on and how many pages there are. The navigation complements the periodic table look while reinforcing the magazine's brand.

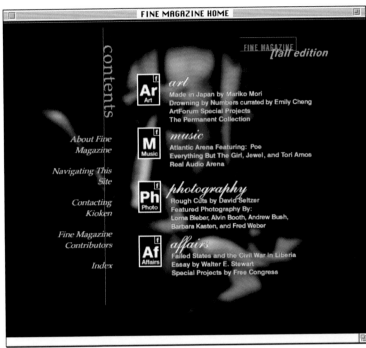

The home page explains the metaphor, making it easy to use as a toolbar on other pages.

These navigation elements extend the site's periodic table metaphor.

The Fray
Derek M. Powazek

www.fray.com

Formerly of Hotwired and Electric Minds, Derek M. Powazek created The Fray in his spare time. Powazek got his first High Five back in 1995. Since then The Fray has become well known for its innovative HTML tricks and

Pull the frames apart to reveal the narrative.

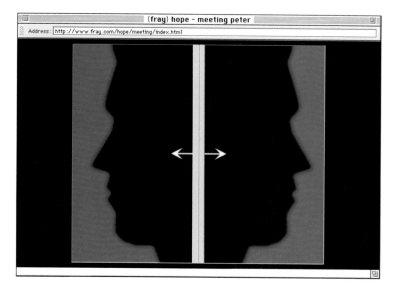

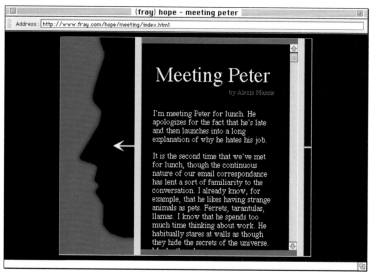

design, as well as its good writing. Designed by Powazek and Alexis Massie, the "Meeting Peter" article in the Hope section uses a truly innovative frame set. The page uses nine frames to achieve its effect: three across, three down, and three in the middle – the two faces plus the hidden frame containing the text beneath them. Any frame set is adjustable if the borders are turned on, and this design depends on it. Move the middle border apart to reveal the narrative. Visitors who don't know that they can pull the frames apart can just click on the arrows, which link to a new frame set with the doors open.

Frames work to advance and enhance the narrative on other articles. Check out Powazek's and Adam Rakunas' design for "Booze" in the Criminal section – you have to click on the last few words of each section to get to the next part, and then the story appears in a different frame. This layout forces you to interact with the text instead of passively scrolling though it. The same graphics repeat throughout the article to make new pages and frames load quickly. In "Reality Check," designed by Powazek and Jennifer Lind, a more complex frameset allows the text about riding a San Francisco bus to appear in seemingly new frames running across the page. This creates a sense of time and scenery moving past – or at least landscape moving past bus windows.

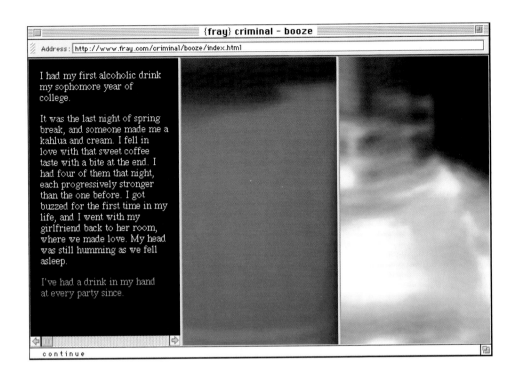

Visitors click often to advance the narrative – the frames add interactivity.

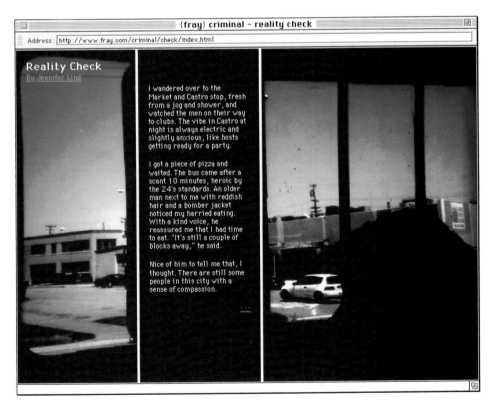

Pioneer Electronics USA
Eagle River Interactive

www.pioneerelectronics.com

Pioneer Electronics USA's navigation makes exploring this mammoth site as easy as changing your radio station. Eagle River Interactive's creative director Charles Field, senior art director K. Lee Hammond, art director Clay Jensen, illustrator Michael Morrison and 3-D artist Danny Sublett worked with senior producer Bruce Maurier, producer Andy Hawks, and project manager Blaire Hansen on this High Five winning site.

The navigation is innovative but remembers to include the basics. The top left frame provides basic info like the name of the section and subsection, showing you at a glance how deep you are in the site. Hop from section to section with the top right frame's rollovers – shiny, technical looking dots well in keeping with the site's mad scientist look. The bottom right frame usually provides text lists of products. Colored arrows next to items in the list, reminiscent of the Mac interface, give visual cues that more information awaits within certain sections.

Using small elements like these arrows floating near text lets you go to any particular page in that area, or off to any other area. It's not true random access – it's too complicated to link every page from every other page – but it gives visitors two levels of choices, which is just right for most sites. You either walk around your local neighborhood, or you go to another neighborhood and start at the top. In this way, you can slice through the site either by product or by category (CD players, equalizers, and so on).

Once you're in each neighborhood, you'll notice the navigation gets more creative. Animated graphics suggest paths you can take, some real, some facetious. In one sequence, elevator buttons appear in the right frame, which when clicked take you to the next level – a succinct use of metaphor. Other sequences take advantage of the right frame to explain how to navigate more complicated image maps in the main frame. Note the unusually complex frame set – this site uses five frames to present information, while most sites are content with just two.

Note how Eagle River's attention to detail goes beyond the navigation – take the colored table cells in the Home Theater section. Just add a BGCOLOR tag plus a hex value to the TD tag, and you've got instant color with almost no bandwidth. These small details combine to create a seamless, creative user interface that will keep you poking around this engrossing site for hours – without ever getting lost.

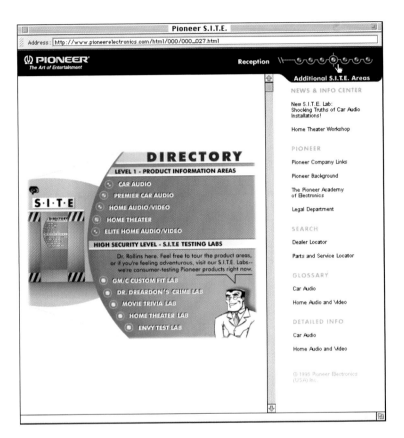

Rollovers in the top right frame allow you to navigate between sections (above), while navigation within each section gets creative (below).

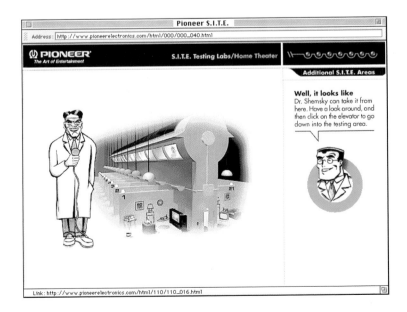

Elliott/Dickens

www.elliottdickens.com

Silicon Valley-based ad agency Elliott/Dickens takes advantage of oft-forgotten space by presenting their site not down, but sideways. Their creative team bucks the non-scrolling trend by placing essential nav elements far, far to the right – as the JavaScripted ticker-tape proclaims, "Scroll over, scroll over, scroll over. This site is full of surprises!"

This design makes practical use of the horizontal space with long layouts of menu items, like their portfolio. The horizontals contrast effectively with the photography. Shot from an angle above the subjects, the photos pop – not just vertically, but practically out of your monitor. By breaking the layout into three large images – keyword, photo, menu – the site reduces download by taking advantage of GIF compression of same horizontal colors.

Check out the rollovers in their interactive portfolio. As you roll over an option, a new window pops up, and the contents of this window change as you roll over different options. The rollover creates an event not only removed from the menu, but in another window altogether – pretty slick. Another cool effect is in their office tour – a quick slide show takes you through a series of pictures quickly and eliminates a tedious click-and-download procedure. Clearly, good things happen to those who let design and technical talent work together creatively.

222

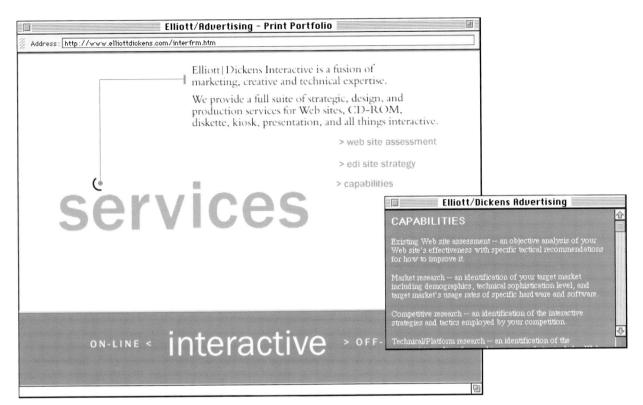

Roll over each option, and the text in the pop-up window corresponds.

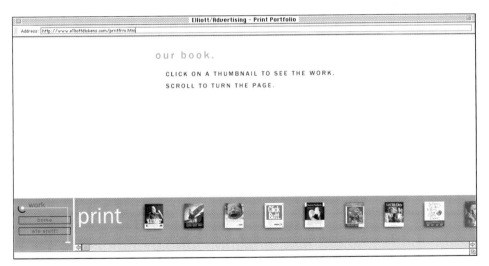

Elliott Dickens takes advantage of the extra space to display their portfolio.

Disappearing Inc's Font Arsenal
Red #40

www.disappear.com

Disappearing Inc. is a type foundry run by five guys who take hit-and-run typography seriously. The digital design group Red #40 (with members not coincidentally including Disappearing Inc. font designers Jeff Prybolsky and Jason Lucas) designed and implemented the site.

The Disappearing Discourse section uses a database of names and thoughts and cranks out text GIFs on the fly. How many online font sites do that? The big backgrounds throughout the site don't hurt much here, because they're contained by the frame. And

the select use of animation is another good idea – lots of sites tell you where you are by indicating your section on a nav bar, but in "Re: Disappearing Inc.," a glowing red light tells you you've hit the bull's-eye. Make your way through the legal jargon and hit their CPU by pretending to order some fonts. Their online order feedback system is great! Now, aren't you compelled to buy? Be the first on your block to own Disappearing fonts. Raskolnikov, Galatek, Fragile, and Storybook are my favorites.

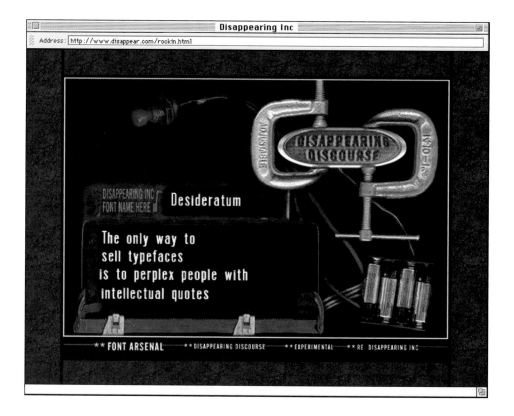

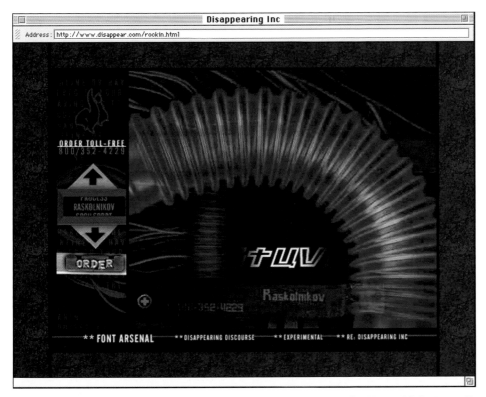

The ordering system alone makes you want to buy the fonts. Below: A flashing red light "warns" you of your location.

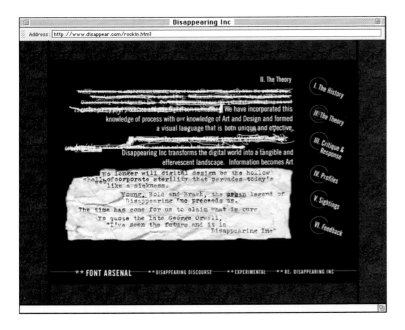

Samsung
Phoenix Pop Productions

www.phoenix-pop.com/samsung

Design gurus Simon Smith and Bruce Falck of Phoenix Pop initially won the Samsung project by proposing that the huge company could be encapsulated by a haiku-like entry into the site. Since the beauty of the haiku resides in its smallness of subject, the site's haiku could only be about a tiny, representative part of the company. This is an example of using metonym instead of metaphor – using part of your subject to stand in for the less graspable whole.

As Phoenix Pop developed the haiku idea, they changed it into a graphical metonymic representation, rather than a verbal one. The core page contains three differently sized graphics of the same image – of either a tree, a ripple in a pool of water, or a kid playing soccer, depending on what the server randomly serves up – that suggest different aspects of Samsung. For example, the expanding ripple evokes Samsung's vision of growing value. Each graphic changes into an explanation of the site's areas as you roll over it.

Choose a category, past, present, or future, and you'll see more rollovers in action. Here rollovers add functionality, as each becomes a sort of table of contents for each item. Note the JavaScript handiwork in the site guide – a pop-up window gives you a menu of more choices, and it follows you around the site so its menu corresponds to where you are on the main screen. An added bonus – if you accidentally lose the window behind another screen, just click on "site map," and it will return to the front. Too many sites provide a pop-up window that disappears as soon as visitors click on the main screen.

This JavaScript pop-up window "follows" you around the site – the options it displays correspond to where you are in the site.

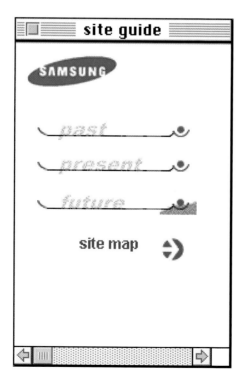

While the Samsung site has been redesigned from its launched version, you can see the original at the URL listed above.

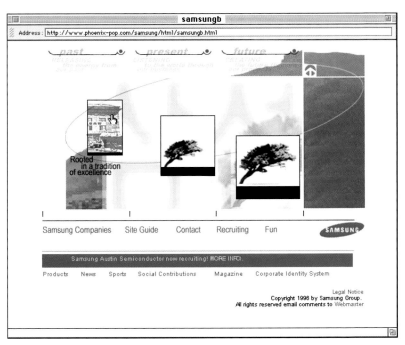

The simplicity and beauty of the tree captures one aspect of Samsung, while the rollovers lead you to the site's three main categories.

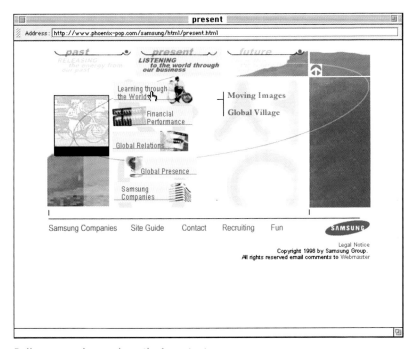

Rollovers preview each section's contents.

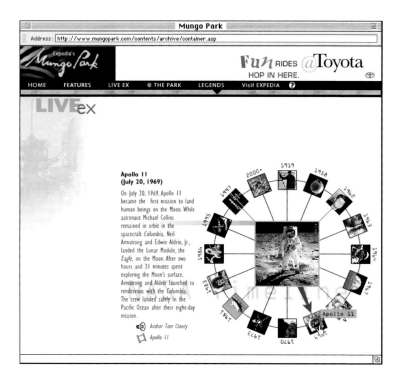

Apollo 11
(July 20, 1969)

On July 20, 1969, Apollo 11 became the first mission to land human beings on the Moon. While astronaut Michael Collins remained in orbit in the spacecraft *Columbia*, Neil Armstrong and Edwin Aldrin, Jr., landed the Lunar Module, the *Eagle*, on the Moon. After two hours and 31 minutes spent exploring the Moon's surface, Armstrong and Aldrin launched to rendezvous with the *Columbia*. The crew landed safely in the Pacific Ocean after their eight-day mission.

Author Tom Clancy

Apollo 11

Mouse quickly from year to year to see the smooth Flash transitions.

Mungo Park
Microsoft's Live Expedia

www.mungopark.com

Mungo Park demonstrates a number of important design principles, but I want to focus here on its excellent use of Flash (also known as Flash 2, Shockwave Flash, and previously called FutureSplash). Editor-in-chief Richard Bangs, art director Jonathan Cowles, and designers Doug Montague, John Griffin, Roger Los, and Heidi Flora created this innovative site. Before looking around the site on your own, make sure to download the incredibly small Shockwave Flash player from Macromedia.

This site has some of the best applications of Flash on the Web. Notice how quickly the animation loads and runs – Flash's vector-based animations keep the file sizes tiny and resolution-independent. You can resize or zoom in without a loss in quality. Look in the Legends archive for the "STS-81: Live from Space" article's gorgeous timeline – rollovers explain what event happened that year. As you mouse from year to year, you'll notice a certain smoothness in the transitions between rollover graphics, as opposed to the more jerky JavaScript. It's like the difference between the second hand on a Rolex versus an imitation – on the Rolex, it sweeps.

It's fun to play with Flash animations. In "Mungo's River Road," an animated map traces the journey of an explorer. This not only shows you where each dispatch on the site comes from, but the vehicles change, showing you how the explorer traveled from place to place. Flash offers both visitors and designers a lot of advantages for just a small download, but the authoring tool's awkward interface is of no advantage to anyone. *(See Chapter 12, "Transitional Strategies," for more information on Flash.)*

228

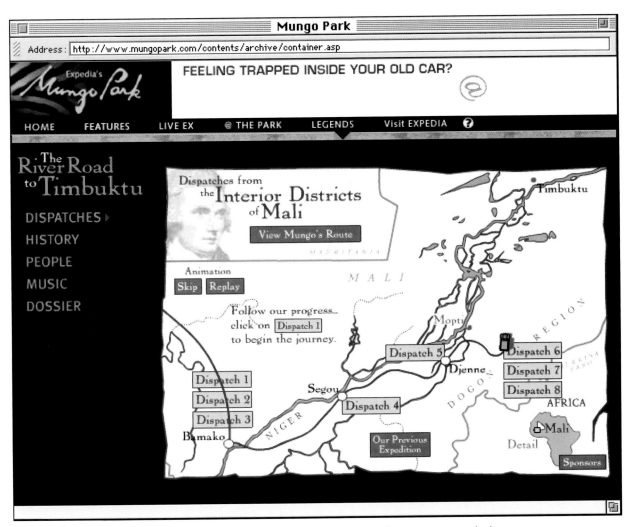

This Flash animation shows where each dispatch was written, as well as how the team got to each place.

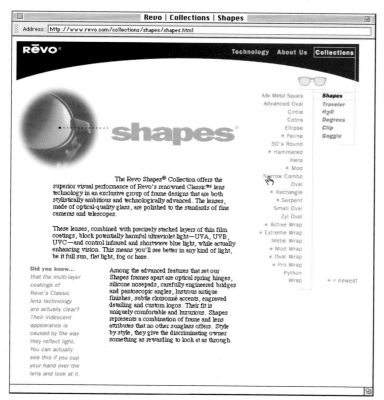

Customers know their favorite shapes, not the names – Revo's rollovers provide a preview of each style's look.

Revo
Studio Archetype

www.revo.com

Web-design leaders Studio Archetype, with the skills of manager Karen Roehl-Sivak, design director Jack Herr, senior designer Brooks Beisch, designer Karin Bryant, and producer Nick McBurney, produced this well designed site for Revo. Note the slick JavaScript rollovers that trigger a tiny image of each style to accompany each name – these thumbnails are small, yet effective enough to let the visitor browse the shapes.

Not only can you see the shapes, but you can also check out your options. The style pages use a matrix to list whether you can get prescription lenses to color choices for each frame and lens. The designers chose to retain control over their table by presenting the information in well rendered text GIFS (see Chapter 5, "Rendering Type"). Several small images make up these matrices so that repeated elements cache and load quickly with each new choice.

Notice how Studio Archetype neatly sidesteps the temptation to make a bulleted list in the technology section by setting off their lists with white space. Words, not bullets, bear the burden of assigning each item status. This is one of the few sites on the Web that does this well. Although Archetype gets extra points for omitting bullets, they lose points for all the blank-line typography. Indented paragraphs would make the site more readable.

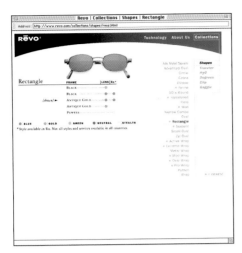

Text rendered as individual GIFs gives designers control of the matrix and downloads quickly.

Deadly Sin Number Six

Aliasing, Dithering, and Halos

Aliasing means you can see jaggies. Think of jaggies as bugs: they creep into your images and eat away at the quality of your site. Although they make images smaller, they also make images look like they've been nibbled by leaf-cutting ants. Strive to eliminate jaggy lines or pixelated areas of images that should be smooth.

Dithering is a form of jaggies, since the pixels are usually noticeable. Dithered images generally look bad, unless they are in photographs, which should probably be JPEGs, not GIFs.

Halos are the biggest symptom of pixel rot. Halos often occur when you assume people have a certain background for surfing (like gray) and anti-alias your images to this background. Visitors with white backgrounds in their surfing preferences see gray halos around all the images.

Part III

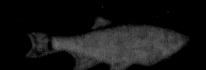

CHAPTER 11

A CSS Primer

What you'll learn in this chapter:

What is css?

css Pitfalls

Degradation-conscious Design

Browser-specific css

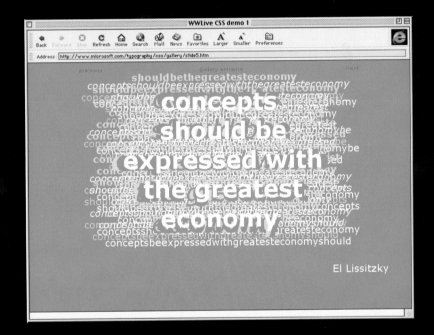

The 10 Commandments of CSS

1. Use CSS to separate content from style. CSS is the wave of the future for web-site design.

2. Learn and support the W3C specifications for style sheets and related protocols.

3. Take responsibility for keeping up with the current status of style-sheet support in browsers.

4. Encourage browser vendors to ship CSS implementations that follow W3C specifications to the letter.

5. Experiment with this technology now to prepare for the day when a majority of browsers will render CSS pages properly.

6. Document and report to the browser developers all departures from the W3C's CSS specifications. Don't let today's broken implementations become tomorrow's standards.

7. Adopt style sheets as soon as practical for your sites and for your clients' sites. Be prepared to revisit your work as CSS support improves.

8. Educate clients and prepare them to switch to CSS when the time is right.

9. Use a script to detect which browser people are using. As necessary, serve style sheets to reasonably complete CSS implementations, like IE 4.0, and withhold them from dangerously substandard ones.

10. Begin with a good comprehensive set of style sheets and modify them to meet your needs instead of starting from scratch. Choose style sheets as you would choose a browser: carefully.

EVERYTHING YOU KNOW about designing with HTML could be very wrong. Your pages will start disintegrating. Your visitors will start complaining. Newbie designers will produce faster, better-looking sites than yours in less time. What could be happening? A superior technology is making most of the HTML coding techniques discussed in this book obsolete: Cascading Style Sheets.

Many books show how Cascading Style Sheets (CSS) should work. To a certain extent, this chapter represents an exercise in futility – it demonstrates the appalling degree to which the browsers fail to deliver on the promise of style sheets in August 1997. This new technology is so important for web designers that the people who work at Verso and I invite you to look over our shoulders as we try to work with the CSS implementations the browser vendors have given us.

What's a Cascading Style Sheet?

Today, graphic designers use style sheets with PageMaker, Quark, and even Microsoft Word. Joe, who is in charge of laying out this book, keeps a style-sheet definition for all subheads in each chapter. With a few changes to the style sheet, he can change every subhead in the book. To keep this flexibility, he must take the time to designate paragraphs, major headings, second-level headings, and so on. Cascading Style Sheets work in similar fashion, but more powerfully and subtly.

All browsers use style sheets, even Netscape 1.0 and Lynx. Before CSS, style sheets were hard-wired into browsers, where they couldn't be changed by authors or by users (except to change default colors, fonts, and so on). The internal style sheet in most browsers is the one that makes <H1> headings really big, with "blank lines" before and after them, just as with <P>s and many other HTML elements. Most tags by themselves imply no particular formatting.

In CSS, each possible HTML tag and each specific item the author wants to style set a style definition. You can write a style sheet as a text file, then refer to that style sheet from any HTML document. All you'll have to do to use a Dave Siegel style sheet – or any of the pre-made style sheets that will become available on the Web – is include its name and location at the top of your file. The document itself needn't change, except for the link to the style sheet.

In addition to giving designers control over the elements on a web page, complete CSS implementations allow personal style sheets. Just as users now can select their preferred fonts and colors, personal style sheets will let users specify a preferred look for all HTML elements. There's a fairly elaborate tug-of-war mechanism for resolving conflicts between designers' and users' styles, with the author's style sheet getting slightly higher priority. If the designer really wants a certain definition, she gets it. Unfortunately, the CSS-1 spec says that even if the user really needs to use her own style sheet, rather than the designer's, she's out of

---

CSS Resources

www.w3.org/Style/ The World Wide Web Consortium's web site is the best starting point, full of up-to-date links to specific tools, articles, tutorials, discussion groups, etc.

www.htmlhelp.com/ Highly recommended, this site features an excellent CSS reference page, an online CSS "Lint," or debugger/coach, as well as help for writing the syntactically valid, non-visually-oriented kind of HTML that CSS was designed to complement.

www.mcp.com/hayden/internet/style/table.html Before pulling your hair out over some CSS feature that doesn't seem to be working, refer to this table to see whether your browser implements it.

news:comp.infosystems.www.authoring.stylesheets A newsgroup devoted to web style sheets, which at this point means CSS. It may eventually mean something called DSSSL, too, but that's another story.

Cascading Style Sheets, by Håkon Wium Lie and Bert Bos (Addison-Wesley, 1997) is a thorough explanation of the standard and its place in the larger scheme of the Web – written by the two lead architects of CSS.

Håkon Lie, the father of Cascading Style Sheets

---

luck. Authors get final control. While you might expect me to be in favor of this approach, I'm not. I think designers should specify exactly how their work should render, and if the user needs to override that, it's her business.

There are two approaches to using CSS. There's the pragmatic approach, where css is merely a supplement to the familiar set of HTML tricks and workarounds, and there's the "orthodox" approach, where css serves as a radical replacement for these tricks. There is, of course, a middle path between the pragmatic and the orthodox, but finding it safely can be difficult without a solid knowledge of both extremes. If you're reading this book, you are familiar already with the status quo of HTML tricks, so the exercises in this chapter take the "orthodox" approach to explore both its promise and the realities of its implementation.

Central to the orthodox css approach is the importance of starting with valid structural markup. Structural markup is a way of tagging the elements in a document according to the structural hierarchy of the document and the logical significance of its parts, rather than their intended appearance. Most structural tags are containers – they have beginning and ending elements. The format is `<TAGNAME>Contents</TAGNAME>`, and contents can be as short as a character or as long as an entire document. Valid markup observes a complex set of rules governing what elements are allowed to be within others. Cascading Style Sheets build upon these formal relationships to let designers change the appearance of documents without changing their tags.

This means, of course, that the "duct tape" tricks and workarounds of the preceding chapters have only a tenuous place in a Web ruled by css. To take full advantage of the power of style sheets, site designers will have to start with correctly marked-up content and stop relying on HTML as a visual tool.

Why Style Sheets?

The reason we're doing all this is to gain three important advantages over the hacks espoused elsewhere in this book:

1. Maintainability. You might think that books don't need to be maintained, but they do. Because we've set up the style sheets for this book in advance, producing a second edition is quite easy. We take a chapter, copy it, and use it as a template for a new chapter. Web sites are constantly changing. Even a medium-sized site is easier to maintain if you separate your marked-up content from your typography.

2. Searchability. By marking up our content in a standard way, we let the

---

The Evolution of Style Sheets

CSS-1. This original specification includes a number of typographic controls, many of which I explore in this chapter. The specification was released in December, 1996.

CSS-P. This branch of css introduces relative and absolute coordinate-based positioning of elements, as well as z-axis layer ordering (hooray!). CSS-P is particularly interesting in conjunction with scripting languages. The combination of nonvisual markup, css, and scripting languages is marketed as "Dynamic HTML."

CSS-2. The latest specification combines CSS-1 with CSS-P and adds a few other extensions, including Aural css (for rendering HTML into speech), as well as support for alternate style sheets in media like print and overhead projection systems.

search engines "peer into" our sites with more accuracy. As I'll discuss in the final chapter, this is only a small step toward better searchability, but it is a good start.

3. Flexibility. All around the world, people are surfing with different modems, displays, languages, and browsers. Some day, we'll be able to modify our style sheets to accommodate different viewing conditions. For that, we must mark up our content independently. In other words, for designers to maintain complete control over look and feel, they must get the look and feel out of their content and into style sheets. Similarly, if we are to present layered information so the user can see as much granularity or resolution as she wants, we must have a way of specifying the layers. Structured markup is the way to go.

css is most compelling for large-scale sites or longer-term web projects, like intranets. By working with a single page, I hope to illustrate what can happen to dozens – or thousands – of linked pages simultaneously.

Because working with current css browsers is mind-numbing work, I will chronicle a four-day journey of style-sheet exploration (if you're working along with me, give yourself time to absorb everything; I deliberately skip certain details to keep the pace up). Warning: this is not a tutorial! This is a sad story, so read along and see where it leads.

Day One: Laying the Foundation

If you're going in here, put on your hard hat. I'll try to do things properly, but they won't work. I'll be using Internet Explorer 3.0 and Netscape 4.0, the only two shipping css browsers available at this writing. Don't be dismayed – this should all be working by the fourth edition of this book.

Markup

I mark up an initial test document, one with enough material to let you see how elements interact with each other [11.1]. Note the lack of any tables for layout, color specification, <FONT> tags, or other visual formatting except one instance of <i> (you'll see why in a minute).

Looking at the file through the browser's default style sheet doesn't show me anything very interesting [11.2].

Style

Creating the style sheet. I'm going to give this page a typographical bath with css, almost without touching it. The first step is to create an empty css document – I'll call it "test.css" – and link to it from the HTML document.

To link to the external css file, add the following line to the document <head> section:

```
<link rel="style sheet"
type="text/css" href=
"./style/test.css">
```

```
<!doctype html public "-//W3C//DTD HTML 4.0 Draft//EN">
<html>
  <head>
    <title>
      Playing with CSS
    </title>
  </head>
  <body>
    <h1>
      The most important heading
    </h1>
    <p>
    This is a test of the Emergency Webcasting System.
    <i>
      This is only a test.
    </i>
    This site, in voluntary cooperation with the W3C and other authorities,
    is conducting a test of the Emergency Webcasting System. This system has
    been developed to help keep the World informed in the event of an
    invasion from space.
    </p>
    <p>
    Were this an actual emergency, critical fight/flight/suicide instructions
    would be pushed simultaneously through all available data channels and
    other orifices, free of spam and gratuitous animations, yet attractively
    formatted in organic proportions, with proper leading and indentation, as
    well as an aural style sheet modelled after the inflections of the late
    Orson Welles. This concludes our test of the Emergency Webcasting System.
    </p>
    <h2>
      A less-important heading
    </h2>
    <p>
    The next characteristic of the book, after the title page, is the page
    opening. Earlier one learnt: a page opening is a symmetrical thing, the
    margins likewise, the numbering, everything arranged around the axis of
    the book, according to specific proportions. All these things are very
    relative. Now we often place a wide left margin on the left-hand page and
    only paginate on odd-numbered pages.
    </p>
    <img src="./cube.gif" alt="The Color Cube">
    <ol>
      <li>
      Pre-dithering to the cube is
      <strong>
        Bad
      </strong>
      (with special-case exceptions).
      <li>
      On-the-fly dithering is
      <strong>
        Good
      </strong>
      (or at least often the least of evils).
```

```
    <li>
    Diffuse dithering, either pre- or on-the-fly, is
    <strong>
      Ugly
    </strong>
    (pretty much always).
  </ol>
  <hr>
  <a href="foo">
    Next</a>
  |
  <a href="foo2">
    Previous</a>
  |
  <a href="foo3">
    Home</a>
  </body>
</html>
```

11.1 The source code for my example (see 11.2, below).

CSS is something like a parallel universe to HTML, possibly involving its own directory structures and many interlinked files. I put CSS files in a separate "style" directory to keep things tidy.

Selectors. Now I'll work on the CSS. Look at the HTML source [11.1]. All the displayed content is contained by the `<body>` element. To make global changes (like margins or background color), I apply them to `<body>`. In CSS parlance, `<body>` is my *selector*. Think of selectors as handles or hooks within HTML for CSS formatting instructions.

Setting margins. I want to set up a nine-unit visual design grid for this project that looks good no matter what the window size, so I specify horizontal white space in units of 11% (100/ 9=11.1). Left margins and alignment points will be multiples of 11%, while right margins will be adjusted, because

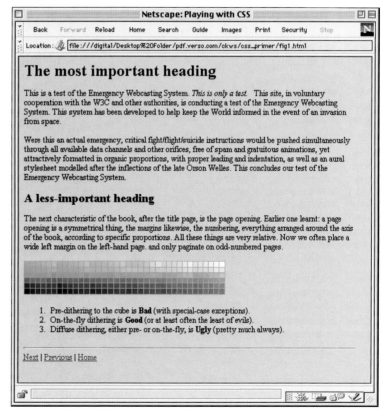

11.2 The browser's default style sheet renders the document with classic first-generation panache.

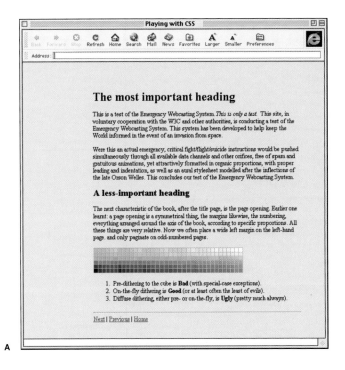

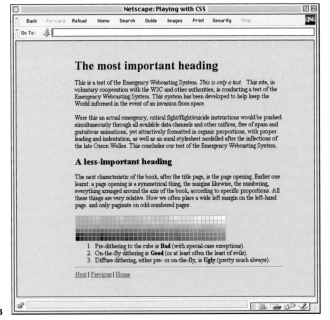

11.3 A quick check in the two CSS browsers currently available on the Macintosh, Internet Explorer 3.0 (A), and Netscape Navigator 4.0 (B), shows all going according to plan, give or take a few pixels.

the optical margin of ragged-right text falls short of the real margin somewhat. I'll also throw in some white space at the top and bottom of the page [**11.3 A, B**]. (I can't do this in percentages of the window height as I'd like, because the CSS-I formatting model doesn't know about window height.)

In CSS, the syntax looks like this:

```
body {
    margin: 2em;
    margin-left: 22%;
    margin-right: 8%;
}
```

Specificity and inheritance. I specified just "margin," and then left and right margins. There is some redundancy and conflict here, but CSS is designed to handle it gracefully. In CSS, later-specified values override earlier-specified ones – they have greater *specificity*. "Margin" is shorthand for all four margins, while margin-left and margin-right have more specificity. In this case, the result is top and bottom margins of 2 em, and right and left margins of 8% and 22%, respectively. This evaluation process – early to late, general to specific – is one meaning of "cascading."

Style attributes cross boundaries according to an outside-in inheritance model. Any local values override more global ones, so if you don't specify a value for, say, font color in a paragraph, the browser looks at the style values for the next largest container – in the case of this example, that's BODY.

Background colors and graphics. Next I'll specify a subtle background graphic, as well as some color and font information:

```
body {
    margin: 2em;
    margin-left: 22%;
    margin-right: 8%;
    background: #FFFFFA url(./
    textura.gif);
    /* this color will shift to
    white for 8-bit displays;
    image path is relative to
    style sheet */
    color: black;
    font: 0.8em/1.4em Verdana,
    Gillsans, sans-serif;
}
```

The background color is in the familiar hex notation – a cream color – while the foreground (text) color is called by name: "black." You can specify most common colors by name in css. Whatever language you use, always specify background and foreground colors together to assure good contrast – you don't know if the user specified white as her default text color, which would be hard to read on a cream background. My background image, "textura.gif," lives in the style directory along with the style sheet.

One nice feature of css background images is that you can specify whether they tile horizontally, vertically, or not at all – it is no longer necessary to make oversize backgrounds to avoid unwanted tiling.

Comments. Slashes and asterisks delimit comments in css. As in

HTML, comments are very useful for debugging style sheets – you can temporarily de-activate individual lines or whole sections.

Font specs. On the "font" line, the first two numbers specify font size and line-height (leading) respectively. The slash traditionally means "on," so 12/14 means "twelve on fourteen," a typographer's way of specifying 12-point type with 14 points of leading.

The list of fonts works the same way the FACE attribute of the FONT tag does, but you can also specify broad font families like serif, sans-serif, monospaced, and "fantasy," just in case the user has none of the faces you name. You don't need to specify font size, line-height, and face together like this, but typographers usually do.

I've set the font size to be 80% of what the user normally looks at .8em).

Dial "em" for Killer

What is an em? An "em" unit is equivalent to the point size of the font in use. If the user's default font size for <body> were 18 point, 2 em would be 36 point. Fractional values are allowed, so 0.67em would be 12 point. css has many unit systems, including pixels and points, but em units are among the most powerful, because they are always relative to the browser's font size.

I do not recommend using point units in css because they are interpreted differently across platforms, with potentially unreadable results at smaller sizes. Pixels are more consistent, but pixels are different sizes on different systems. Besides, a bug in Internet Explorer 3.0 makes pages styled in css pixel units unprintable. Em and percentage units are generally best.

243

Why? Sans-serif faces generally look better at smaller sizes than serif faces, and leaving it at 100% would likely make it look too big and horsey. This is especially true with the killer cross-platform TrueType font Verdana, available free from Microsoft.

User preferences, defaults, and overrides. Just as users can now select their preferred fonts and colors, personal style sheets will let users specify a preferred look for all HTML elements.

What happens when both designer and surfer specify their preferred style sheets? They cascade, or resolve to a unified appearance. In case of conflict, the designer's style sheet wins – usually. Users with special needs or unusual browsing setups can declare any or all of their preferences as "!important," and these will override designer preferences. Designers can, in turn, declare their specifications !important to override surfers' preferences. This will generally be a foolish thing to do. I wish users had the final say, but they don't, so I make it a policy not to declare anything as !important.

CSS designers wishing to avoid unpredictable interactions with user style sheets should start with comprehensive

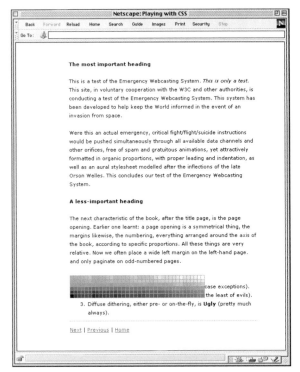

11.4 Because of a bug, Netscape 4.0 can't find my background image. It looks for the image along a path relative to the HTML document instead of to the CSS file (as called for in the W3C specification).

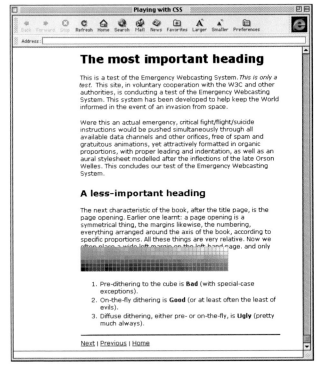

11.5 Internet Explorer 3.0 doesn't support background images in linked style sheets.

style sheets for generic HTML as a base and edit them, rather than specifying only a few modifications to the presumed "browser default" style sheet. This approach will also be far easier than building up style sheets incrementally to accommodate new content as it arrives. Look for such style sheets to become available on the Web as css browsers become capable of handling them. Check the w3c site for news on core style sheets.

Viewing the results. Note how both browsers have crashed the image into the text, each in a different way **[11.4, 11.5]**. Apparently, the line-height I applied to the contents of BODY affects the IMG element without regard to its dimensions.

While both browsers display the correct typeface, only Netscape 4.0 applies the appropriate font size and leading. This is because Internet Explorer 3.0 doesn't support the "em" unit properly. This also explains why the top margin, shown correctly in figure **11.3A,** is too large.

Finally, notice how the headers and links have inherited the properties set on BODY differently. Netscape 4.0 applies a single font size to the entire document, headers and all, but it has not applied the black color to the links at the bottom of the page. Conversely, Internet Explorer 3.0 has applied black to the links but has retained a variety of sizes for the headers. What's going on here? Who knows! The people in the war rooms at Microsoft and Netscape shipped the browsers this way, and tens of millions of people have downloaded them.

Now is probably a good time to take a break and come back for another adventure on the style-sheet roller coaster.

Day Two: One Forward, Two Back

If you recall, Netscape and IE rendered the same style sheet with their own sets of problems. Revising the style sheet works around a few problems, adds several new features, and introduces several new problems. Study this style sheet **[11.6]** to understand the differences.

Instead of a single "font" specification, I have now specified font family and font size on BODY separately, saving line-height for other, more specific selectors. This fixes the problem with the image running into the text, but the results are still different.

Netscape 4.0 has now found the subtle background image, because I included the name of the style directory in the path statement. This is not a very robust fix, however, as any additional HTML documents pointing to this style sheet must be in the same location as the first.

The next declaration in the style sheet applies leading to paragraphs <P>, ordered lists <OL>, and link anchors <A> – everything in the document except the headers and the image.

Next, I remove the blank lines ("margins") preceding the paragraphs <P> and apply an indent equal to the leading. Note that Internet Explorer 3.0 applies the indent but retains the blank lines. There is simply no way to control vertical white space on most HTML elements in IE 3.0.

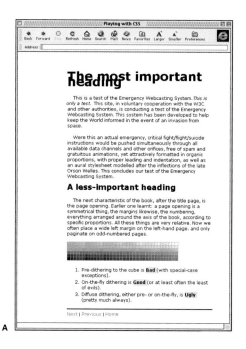

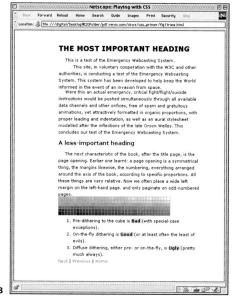

11.7 Is it my imagination, or are things getting worse? IE (A) and Navigator (B) each has its own problems.

11.6 This more comprehensive style sheet addresses several more selectors.

```
body {
    margin: 2em;
    margin-left: 22%;
    margin-right: 8%;
    background: #FFFFFA url(./style/
textura.gif);
    color: black;
    font-family: Verdana, Gillsans, sans-serif;
    font-size: 0.8em;
    }

p, ol, a {
    line-height: 1.4em;
    }

p {
    margin: 0;
    text-indent: 1.4em;
    }

h1 {
    font-size: 1.4em;
    text-transform: uppercase;
    letter-spacing: 0.1em;
    }

h2 {
    font-size: 1.2em
    }

i {
    font-style: plain;
    text-decoration: blink;
    }

strong {
    font-style: normal;
    background: yellow;
    }

a {
    text-decoration: none;
    }

a:link {
    color: red;
    }

a:visited  {
    color: #336666;
    }

a:active {
    color: #FFFDF3;
    }

hr {
    display: none;
    }
```

246

Netscape 4.0, meanwhile, has set the inter-paragraph spacing to zero, but it has discarded the leading. This means there is less space between paragraphs than between lines within paragraphs. This is a bug.

For the H1 selector, I have specified a reasonable size for the header, and I've even set it in caps, gently letter-spaced – without touching the HTML! How does it look? [11.7] Internet Explorer 3.0 – well, this browser needs to be put out of CSS misery; I will only ask that Microsoft forget about backward-compatibility with IE 3.0. Netscape 4.0 has done the right thing with the sizing and case transformation, but it doesn't implement the letter-spacing part of the CSS specification, so the characters aren't tracked out the way I'd hoped. (Internet Explorer 4.0 betas implement letter-spacing, so we should keep these kinds of declarations in, but we shouldn't count on them.)

I have turned the italics specified in HTML into plain, blinking roman text (figure **11.7B** captures it mid-blink). This is not a good design choice, but it demonstrates that CSS can make presentational tags like <i> redundant and meaningless. To avoid confusion, avoid presentational markup with CSS.

Similarly, I have set the <strong> tag (strong emphasis – usually rendered bold) to display with a yellow background and in a normal font weight. This effect cannot be achieved without CSS. (Note, however, that Netscape 4.0 fails to set the font weight correctly.) A very handy CSS feature I've employed lets authors turn link underlining off *(see Appendix 1: "Dave's Guide to Better Surfing")*. Color-blind

surfers can set up their personal style sheets to override my specification as necessary.

Last but not least, I have nuked the horizontal rule <hr>, simply by setting its display property to "none." Imagine doing that to thousands of web pages with a single declaration! That's control!

Day Three: Browser-Specific Style Sheets

You've probably noticed that the promise of style sheets is not exactly shining through. Each CSS implementation has its own quirks [11.8]. Each browser company puts up wizzy demos (called propaganda by designers and facts by the press) to make you think its implementation of style sheets is actually useful [11.9 A, B].

Here's the question: Should designers write and try to maintain individual style sheets to get around particular browser deficiencies? If we do, we'll be ahead, stabilizing our marked-up pages and gaining the advantages that come

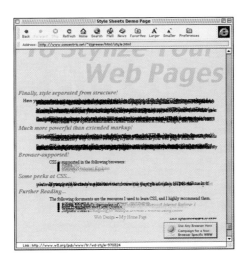

11.8 Browser-war biohazards. This page, earnestly cheerleading the wonders of CSS, uses correct "browser-independent" HTML and CSS, but it would clearly be better with no CSS at all in Internet Explorer 3.0 (Mac OS). While they helped get CSS taken seriously in the first place, early implementations are now a serious obstacle to the full deployment of CSS on the Web.

247

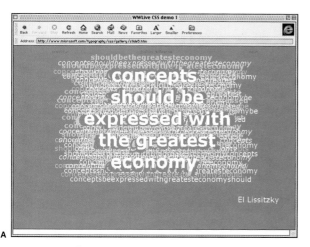
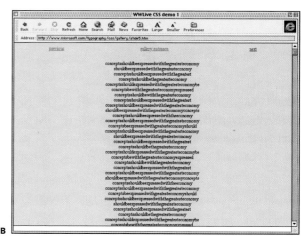

11.9 Browser boosterism or style-sheet terrorism? This selection from the Microsoft-sponsored "css Gallery" is fairly impressive (A), until you realize that it's redundant gibberish without css support (B). While Microsoft demonstrated a willingness to support style sheets, their early demos encouraged designers to make pages that rendered as meaningless gibberish in Netscape 3.0, the then-current version.

```
<SCRIPT> <!--
  if ((navigator.appName == "Netscape") &&
  (parseInt(navigator.appVersion) == 4))
  {
  document.writeln("<link rel=\
  "stylesheet\"
  type=\"text/css\" href=\
  "./style/testns.css\">")
  };
// -->
</SCRIPT>
```

11.10 This simple script detects one browser and serves up a particular style sheet. See the Book Site for a more elaborate, annotated example of a script to serve css to other implementations.

even if that means working around bugs. I do it for the sake of making progress, hoping Netscape will release a patch or a fix that will let us do style sheets properly. Hang on. This is going to get messy.

Remember, take this as an exercise! By the time you read this, the browsers may behave differently – I hope they do.

One Browser at a Time

If I'm to keep working on this page, the only practical solution is to create css files for one browser at a time and serve them by means of browser-detect scripts. I write one set of content/structure files (HTML) and develop a set of browser-specific style sheets just for Netscape 4.0. Visitors with all other browsers will see the ugly (but familiar) default layout.

with style sheets. But we'll also encourage the browser companies to retain their legacy bugs, because as soon as they ship a browser that fixes earlier problems, lots of pages will fall apart.

My answer is that we should work with style sheets but perhaps not deploy them widely, meanwhile insisting that the browser companies get it right. This section is about cutting the worst implementations out of the loop and moving forward with the better ones,

To serve a style sheet exclusively to Netscape 4.0, I replace the style-sheet link in the HTML document's HEAD section with a script [**11.10**]. Note that I've renamed the style sheet to "testns.css".

Now that the script lets me concentrate on a single browser's implementation, I can work around some of the bugs. To address Netscape 4.0's inter-element margin bug, I restore the missing line-height to the top margin:

```
p {
    margin: 0;
    margin-top: 0.4em;
    text-indent: 1.4em;
}
```

(I won't show the result just yet, but this does the job.) Next I attempt to remove most of the white space beneath H2, so it appears associated with the paragraph below, rather than floating ambiguously in the breach between paragraphs. Setting H2's margin to 0 has no effect. In fact, not even setting a negative bottom margin will remove the space. This is another bug. A final, desperate hack, mixing CSS1 and CSS-P features, gets the white space right but chops my text off at the waist [**11.11**]:

```
h2 {
    font-size: 1.2em;
    margin: 0;
    margin-top: -0.8em;
    position: relative;
    top: 1em;
}
```

The final two lines in this definition invoke CSS-P to position the H2 header by brute force.

There's just one thing more I can do before I run out of selectors for this document: I can try to bring the alignment of the ordered list <OL> into harmony with the paragraph indents. Setting the left margin of OL to zero has no effect. This is – you guessed it – yet another hole in Netscape's implementation. Setting the margin to -1.4em does the job, at least until the bug is fixed and my work-around breaks [**11.12**]. (I hope Netscape will not hesitate to break my work-around.)

Day Four: Finer Granularity

For good typography's sake, I'd like to lose the indents on the first paragraphs following the headers and add a little white space around the image. I also want to move the navigation links at the bottom of the page down a bit, so they stand by themselves as navigational elements. And those vertical barriers between the links have to go, too. Finally, I'll investigate the possibilities for rescuing that dangling H2, lost in mid-space between paragraphs.

I'm out of selectors to modify. To address any of these things, I will enrich the HTML with more selectors – more control points for adding style.

CLASS and ID

I can't add any more tags to HTML. To differentiate any group of elements from others of the same kind, however, I can attach CLASS attributes to their tags and call them by that class name in CSS. To differentiate a single item from others of the same kind, I attach an ID attribute to its tag and call it by name.

249

well as an aural stylesheet modelled after t
Welles. This concludes our test of the Emer

A less-important heading

The next characteristic of the book, afte
opening. Earlier one learnt: a page opening
margins likewise, the numbering, everythin
the book, according to specific proportions.

11.11 Rats! Resorting to the use of CSS-P exposes another bug in Netscape.

11.12 I've specified every selector in the document and done my best to work around Netscape's bugs. This is about as good as I can do without touching the HTML.

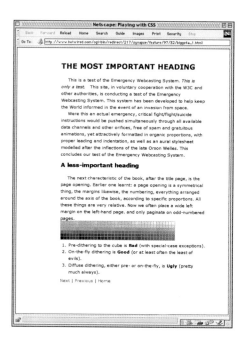

To differentiate the paragraphs following headers from the rest, I mark them up as `<p class="initial">`. To remove indents from all elements of this class, I add this to the style sheet:

```
.initial {
    text-indent: 0;
    }
```

Note the dot preceding the class name: that's the syntax for calling classes instead of elements in CSS. Classes can extend not just to multiple instances of a single HTML element but to multiple HTML elements. For instance, I could set up a "test" class and apply it to headers, paragraphs, list items, or any others, then easily change the display attributes in all instances with a single line in CSS.

To position the color-cube image, I could address IMG in the style sheet, but that would apply to all images in any documents that ever refer to this style sheet – a potential problem in the future. To address a particular image, I give it a unique identifier in HTML:

```
<img src="./cube.gif" alt=
"The Color Cube" id="cube">
```

In the style sheet, I address it like this:

```
#cube {
    margin-top: 1em;
    margin-bottom: 1em;
    }
```

In CSS, the pound sign preceding the ID name addresses a unique HTML element. (See the results of these two operations in [**11.14**].)

250

Special Cases: DIV and SPAN

The DIV (division) element has been around in HTML for a while now. Most people use it for alignment, in conjunction with the ALIGN attribute. In fact, <DIV ALIGN="center"> is functionally identical to Netscape's CENTER tag, even in pre-CSS browsers. In CSS browsers, DIV's usage expands from being merely a hook for an ALIGN or NAME attribute to being a hook for the full range of CSS styling through CLASS or ID attributes. DIV has a grouping function – it's a generic block container for any sequence of elements. DIVs are typically preceded and followed by a line break when rendered. I can create any number of DIV groupings, each with its own style definition.

To address the three navigational links at the bottom of the page, I wrap them in a DIV with the class "nav" [11.13].

By changing the 2 to a 2.4 or a 2.6 I can dial in the exact spacing I want. That's third-generation typography without the single-pixel GIFs! To add vertical white space, I give the "nav" division a top margin:

```
.nav {
  margin-top: 2em;
  }
```

Now to hide those vertical bars. Just as horizontal rules are a primitive substitute for vertical white space, vertical bars are a poor substitute for horizontal white space. Because some people will see this page without my style sheet, I leave them in and simply hide them for CSS viewers.

```
<div class="nav">
  <a href="foo">
    Next
  </a>
  |
  <a href="foo2">
    Previous
  </a>
  |
  <a href="foo3">
    Home
  </a>
</div>
```

11.13 Use of the DIV element.

```
1. Pre-dithering to the cube is
2. On-the-fly dithering is Goo
3. Diffuse dithering, either pre
   always).

Next | Previous | Home
```

11.14 Use DIV to create a margin around a group of elements.

The SPAN Element

HTML 4's new SPAN element is a generic container, just like DIV, except it does not imply that the enclosed material is a block. Rather, it is internal to a block – an inline element. Unlike DIV, which will at the very least produce a line break in pre-CSS browsers, SPAN will be gracefully ignored unless associated with CSS rules in a CSS browser through CLASS or ID attributes. A complete CSS implementation would let you make DIVs render inline, and SPANs render as blocks.

251

11.15 Using css-p's "visibility" attribute, I hide everything in the division except the links. The invisible vertical bars still take up space, separating the links. Isn't that better?

```
   2. On-the-fly dithering is G
   3. Diffuse dithering, either
      always).


   Next   Previous   Home
```

To get rid of them, I could wrap each in a SPAN of a certain class and hide that class with css. If I set their css "display" attribute to "none", they would disappear, but then the space they occupy would collapse. Instead, I hide the entire division, using css-p's "visibility" syntax. Hiding something renders it invisible, so it still takes up space, while setting its display attribute to "none" effectively removes it from the page.

```
.nav {
   margin-top: 2em;
   position: relative;
   visibility: hidden;
}
```

Next, I take advantage of css's contextual selector mechanism to select only the actual links (a) within the division (div) whose class is "nav", and I turn the links back on.

```
div.nav a {
   position: relative;
   visibility: visible;
}
```

This leaves the navigation links nicely positioned and spaced with no visible vertical boundaries, yet they're still there for folks with non-css browsers. This is called degradation-conscious design [**11.15**].

A Brief Foray into CSS-P

So far I've been using css-1 to make fairly fine adjustments to the typography of this page. css-p offers a somewhat more radical degree of control over the positioning of elements. To show the power of css-p, I'll move the navigation links at the bottom of the page one by one into the left margin near the top of the page – all without using tables or otherwise interfering with the order of elements in HTML. I start by assigning unique IDs to each of the links in HTML:

```
   <a href="foo"
   id="next">Next</a>
|
   <a href="foo2"
   id="prev">Previous</a>
|
   <a href="foo3"
   id="home">Home</a>
```

Then I write the css-p syntax to position these three links relative to the upper-left corner of the document "canvas" [**11.16, 11.17**].

It's cleaner than tables, and it works! There's just one problem – the links have now lost their functionality. You can't click 'em anymore. I have no idea why this has happened, and I can't fix it. I send email to my friends at Netscape asking them to take css more seriously. So much for css-p in Netscape 4.0. I undo my style-sheet work and proceed.

Cheating the Markup

Remember the floating H2 tag? Part of Netscape 4.0's brain damage is that all tagged header elements force a blank line of space after them, even if the style sheet says otherwise. One way to work around it is to remove the H2 tag and replace it with something less descriptive, something like DIV. This is definitely cheating, but I've been doing that for a while now. In the HTML, I replace:

```
<h2>
    A less-important heading
</h2>
```

with

```
<div class="h2">
    A less-important heading
</div>
```

In the style sheet, I simply add a dot before the pre-existing H2 declaration, sneakily changing the selector to a class designator instead of an element:

```
.h2 {
    font-size: 1.2em;
    margin: 0;
}
```

At last, the browser lets CSS have its way [11.18]. But I also see that I was unconsciously relying on the browser default style sheet to take care of a few things. When you roll your own pseudo tags with DIV or SPAN, you must build your descriptions from scratch.

I fill out the H2 class declaration with the missing instructions and have a look [11.19]:

```
#next {
    position: absolute;
    top: 2em;
    left: 5%;
}

#prev {
    position: absolute;
    top: 4em;
    left: 5%;
}

#home {
    position: absolute;
    top: 6em;
    left: 5%;
}
```

11.16 The "position" line calls CSS-P into effect. The two modes are absolute and relative positioning.

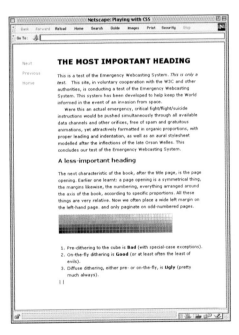

11.17 Using CSS-P to move my links. Note also the results of the CLASS and ID work on the paragraph indents and the space around the image.

```
.h2 {
    font-size: 1.2em;
    font-weight: bold;
    margin: 0;
    margin-top: 1.4em;
}
```

modelled after the inflections of the late Ors
concludes our test of the Emergency Webca
A less-important heading
The next characteristic of the book, after th
opening. Earlier one learnt: a page opening

11.18 Replacing common HTML elements with generic D I V or S P A N markup gives you a clean slate typographically. A little too clean, alas, for non-css browsers.

modelled after the inflections of the late Ors
concludes our test of the Emergency Webca
A less-important heading
The next characteristic of the book, after the
opening. Earlier one learnt: a page opening

11.19 Victory – at a price.

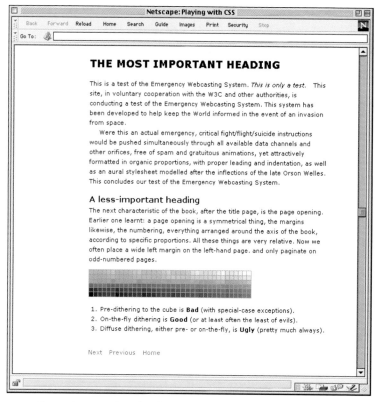

11.20 There, that wasn't so hard!

By replacing H2 with D I V to force these results in Netscape 4, I've compromised the intelligibility of the document in non-css browsers. This is a step down the slippery slope toward style-sheet terrorism. Furthermore, users with personal style sheets can anticipate and style standard H2 elements, yet nobody can anticipate class="h2" in a personal style sheet. This means this document won't cascade so well anymore – it can't survive in another style context. As a workaround, I add <BIG> and <B> tags to the HTML, so most non-css browsers see a headline that's a little bigger and set in bold type [**11.20**] (compare with [**11.2 B**]). If you think this is ridiculous, you're right.

```
<div class="h2">
  <big>
  <b>
    A less-important heading
  </b>
  </big>
</div>
```

Summary

Anyone who has read this far sees the promise – and the pitfalls – of style sheets. I've covered only a small part of the css-1 specification's features and found terrible bugs in every direction. By the time you read this, however, the situation will surely have improved somewhat. Microsoft Internet Explorer 4.0, for instance, appears poised to become a worthy "reference" css implementation, and we can only hope that Netscape will strive to do better.

I admit that this primer did not develop an exciting, thematically compelling page. That was not my aim, but you can see from this exercise that we can't rely on css for such things until browser support improves dramatically.

Where are you on the adoption curve? Are style sheets your buzzword of the week? Are you "keeping tabs" on style-sheet developments? Are you watching your access logs to see when 80% of your visitors come with decent css browsers? Are you willing to try style sheets on some pages, knowing that many people will see "default" style? Or are you willing to go whole-hog, detecting which browsers people use, innovating with workarounds to get what you want, adding new classes and DIV elements to your markup, and changing your scripts and style sheets with every new browser release?

I'd say it depends a lot on your audience and your volume of work. If you can serve a site with 10,000 ugly, but not broken, pages, style sheets will pay off quickly. If you're serving a magazine, you might want to hold off or attempt a cautious, compromised approach.

My recommendation is to start slowly. Develop good habits and be willing to rework your style sheets as you learn. Target certain pages or areas within your site for conversion and experimentation with css. Work from the outer pages in toward your core page in logical steps.

Will we be able to use style sheets to create well designed third-generation sites? The answer is in the final chapter. Before that, I'll cover a number of other exciting developments.

The Lowdown on CSS Support

Microsoft Internet Explorer 3.0. This first major css browser was released long before the specification was finished. It implements only about 40% of css, with many major bugs that can easily turn the best of style sheets into document-destroyers. It's often best to serve plain HTML to IE 3.0, rather than let it mangle your css.

Netscape Communicator 4.0. Far better than Internet Explorer 3.0, but unfortunately still a long way from getting it right in the css department. Supports most css features, but many omissions and bugs are critical.

Internet Explorer 4.0. Still in development at this writing, this browser looks like it will be better than 90% true to the w3c specification once released – at least the Windows version.

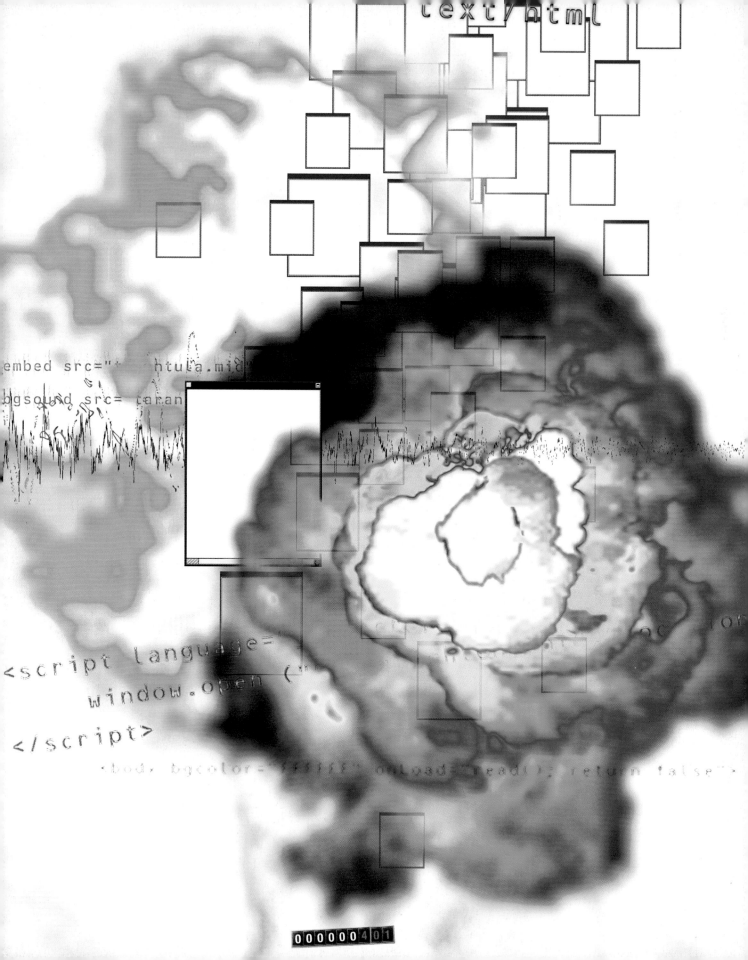

text/html

embed src=" htula.mid

bgsound src= taran

`<script language=`

`window.open ("`

`</script>`

`<body bgcolor="#ffffff" onLoad=fread(); return false">`

Transitional Strategies

What you'll learn in this chapter:

Using vector graphics formats

How to solve the font problem

Sound and virtual reality on the Web

The role of WYSIWYG tools

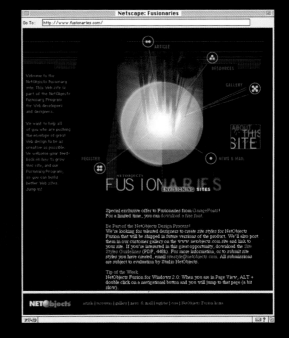

2.1 Navigator and Internet Explorer claim the vast majority of the browser market, but there will always be room on the Web for good design.

DESIGNERS ARE FACING new challenges: how to design sites during the awkward transition from version 3.0 and 4.0 browsers **[12.1]** to the version 5.0 and (more important) 6.0 browsers to come. The limitations of 3.0 browsers require designers to resort to workarounds and tricks I call duct tape, many of which I've introduced in this edition of *Creating Killer Web Sites.*

As the previous chapter demonstrates, the 4.0 browsers aren't quite ready to let designers take advantage of Cascading Style Sheets. Early adopters will separate markup from style, suffer the slings and arrows of the 4.0 style sheets, and let their sites "degrade" on today's browsers. Late adopters will keep applying duct tape until style sheets work properly, adding ticking time bombs to their content. When CSS is ready, we will be able to separate our content from our design, and we will work with tools that let us focus on design, not workarounds.

So much to look forward to! For now, let's look at some exciting developments that will help make third-generation site design easier in the interim.

Design

No amount of technology can make you a good designer. Design is a muscle – you must build it up and then maintain it. Good designers have been able to create compelling web sites since browsers gained the ability to handle images. Study the use of line and form, color and atmosphere,

12.2 Not only are there some good design magazines on the Web, there are also some good design magazines on paper!

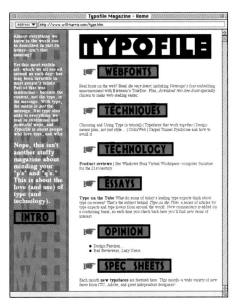

typography and illustration, animation and narrative, and, most important, how best to attract and satisfy the customers you want at your web sites.

Spend time surfing. Visit the High Five (www.highfive.com) every week, and go to other design resources on the Web. Get inspired by what others are doing. Create a "play space" on your web site and just experiment. Challenge yourself. If you don't have a design degree, enroll in a local course on typography, layout, illustration,

book design, and so on. Most good-size cities have a bookstore that specializes in architecture and design books – go drench yourself in delicious design books! There are several wonderful magazines just for designers, and many of them now have columns on web design. Sure, the techie web journals have a design column now and then, but I'd rather spend time looking at a design magazine like *How*, learning from good designers **[12.2]**.

Fusion

Maybe you don't have time to learn how to build third-generation web sites using the various techniques I've explained in this book. Maybe you don't have the budget to hire a design shop to create your killer web site. Yet you still want to get up and running as soon as possible with a visually appealing web site, one that will draw surfers in and keep them there while you do your best to turn them into customers. Or, perhaps you need to beef up your intranet and make it a more compelling experience for its target audience.

Net Objects' Fusion, located at www.netobjects.com, enables site creation following many of the design principles described in the first edition of this book. In fact, in the sincerest form of flattery, the people who designed Fusion used my file-name nomenclature. Fusion also includes powerful site-management tools that ease the process of adding new material and updating a site [12.3].

12.3 Fusion implements my web design principles in a WYSIWYG editing environment and provides powerful site management tools, too.

Once you learn how to use Fusion (and the learning curve can be steep), you can use it to develop pages and sites quickly [12.4]. We used it at Verso Editions to develop the web site for my recent book, *Secrets of Successful Web Sites* (www.secretsites.com).

The best thing about Fusion is that it uses its own internal, proprietary technology to code web page and site elements as you move them around on the page and within the site, and then it outputs HTML. Fusion can create different versions of a site to accommodate different browsers – push a button for Netscape 3.x, push another button for Internet Explorer 3.x, select all the browsers you'd like your site to be compatible with, and so on. While it's not quite as magical as it sounds, it is the right approach. Other WYSIWYG tools store a site as HTML, and that means you're stuck with it when new browsers come out. As long as you work within Fusion and its future updates, you should be able to build sites that take advantage of the market-dominant browser technologies, including style sheets: Fusion will output HTML that works with the latest browsers.

Some professional designers use Fusion to make good looking sites in a hurry. Others use it to "storyboard" or plan the navigation for a large site, to create proposals and presentations for clients. Many amateurs use it to build sites for their small businesses. The quality of the HTML Fusion generates is acceptable, especially for sites with a limited audience.

To work its magic, Fusion as we know it today exports bloated pages of unwieldy tables and single-pixel GIFs.

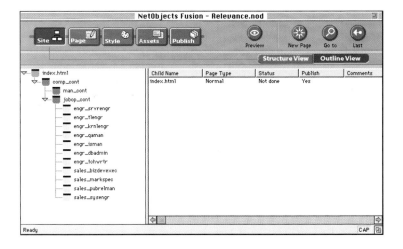

It takes longer to download a Fusion-based site than it takes to download a hand-crafted one, but then it takes a lot longer to build the hand-crafted site. Because Fusion's HTML is really only a by-product, it's impractical to edit the code produced by Fusion, so you must play within the rules set by the program. Fusion probably won't be the best choice if you need to stretch things to the limit of browser feature sets or add extra functionality, though you can add scripts and even your own hand-edited bits of HTML. But keep in mind that this can change as NetObjects releases new versions that write cleaner code.

Fusion's site management capability is a big improvement over maintaining code-based sites. Some day, no one will have to maintain a site by doing multiple character-based search-and-replace actions across dozens or hundreds of files.

For now, there's no substitute for hand-coding HTML for maximum control over web page design. Professionals will keep an eye on Fusion's development, while people who don't have much time and would like to build simple sites will find it quite useful [12.5].

JavaScript

First things first: JavaScript, the scripting language, is not related to Java, the programming language. They have nothing in common except the first four letters of their names. JavaScript, Netscape's language for controlling elements on a web page, has quickly

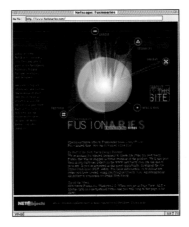

12.4 Fusion implements my web-design principles in a WYSIWYG editing environment and provides powerful site-management tools, too.

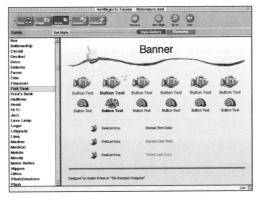

12.5 Fusion has its own styles to choose from.

12.6 Designers have embraced Java-Script's ability to execute subtle mouse rollover effects.

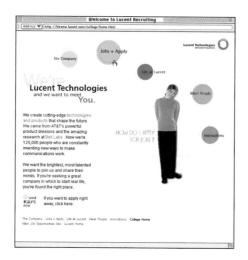

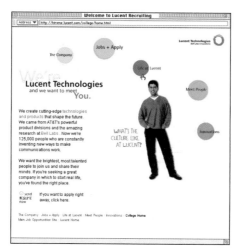

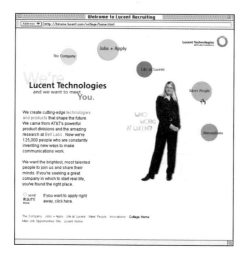

found a place in the web designer's tool kit.

The most popular use of JavaScript is to create gratuitous rollovers that cause images to change when the cursor moves across a hot spot on a web page. Although rollovers can often be a good form of feedback to the web surfer, most sites use them to change the color of some GIF text, which is more a technical than a visual feat. Other uses include "ticker tape" scrolling text, pop-up windows, and validation of forms. Far down on the list of popular uses of JavaScript is the creation of nongratuitous, useful rollovers that add information when rolled over – very few sites use rollovers to good advantage [12.6].

Microsoft's version is called JScript. So far, Microsoft has man-aged to implement most of the Java-Script capabilities, albeit one browser version behind. Internet Explorer 3.0 had Netscape Navigator's 2.0 Java-Script capabilities, and at the time I write this, it looks as though IE 4.0 will have Netscape 3.0's capabilities. Microsoft has promised to catch up in version 5.0, but Netscape promises to imple-ment its own special extensions that do extra tricks with each release of its browser. Even though both companies have committed to making their ver-sions comply with a new European Computer Manufacturers Association standard, you can be sure that Net-scape's browser will support nifty new features that other browsers don't.

Java

Java is a cross-platform language that will make programming in a networked world much easier than it was before. Java applets are small programs that download quickly and execute on a web surfer's system (the client) [**12.7 A**].

I mention Java because it has an imaging model. It may be primitive, but it's vector-based, which means you can actually program an entire web site in Java and it will download quite quickly. One product that lets designers create Java sites is Coda, by Randomnoise [**12.7 B**].

Coda is an entirely different kind of tool for web designers. Because visitors must download a set of special Java classes to see a Coda-based site, there is some initial cost to visitors. But in an environment like an Intranet, it can be quite handy. Rather than suffering with the limitations of HTML and poor browser implementations, Java runs quite well on all platforms (except the Mac, where it is still quite slow) and has a stable imaging model. Using Coda, you can build action into your sites easily. If you have an online annual report, for example, you can link your data right from the database and have all your charts display from live, real-time data. It makes graphics a snap, because the graphics are all driven by numeric descriptions, not raster images (*see Chapter 3, "Preparing Images"*). It's like having a dynamic version of Illustrator that works off of a spreadsheet. Change a few numbers, and your page or your graphics change accordingly. Coda can be very powerful for specific applications. I'm sure we'll

12.7 A Java enables powerful client-server applications on the Web but requires industrial-strength programming skills

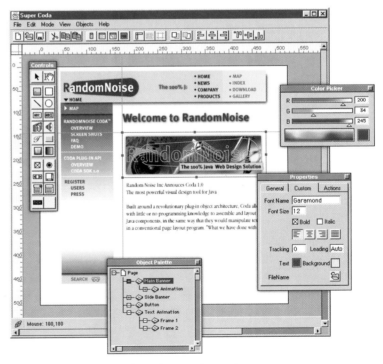

12.7 B Coda lets you build a web page almost the same way you build a page in Illustrator.

see this program add features and become easier to use as others enter this same market. Coda works today. It may be just the thing you need to get around problems you're having, or it may be something to keep an eye on as more and more Java products attract designers' attention.

PDF

The first edition of *Creating Killer Web Sites* contained two chapters about designing web pages with Adobe's Portable Document Format (PDF), a page-description file format based on PostScript that gives designers precise control over the look and feel of pages. You'll find those chapters on the Book Site.

PDF remains a good tool for web designers in certain circumstances – especially where the designer can safely assume that web surfers will be using browsers configured to view PDF files, as in a company intranet or an extranet project site.

On the Web, surfers who want to view PDF documents still have to download and install Adobe's free Acrobat Reader, then configure their Web browsers to use it. As with any plug-in, this poses a barrier to entry. Requiring people to get and install a viewer is sort of like asking them to run out and pick up their own chopsticks before they can eat any of the Japanese delicacies on your menu.

However, PDF is not an obscure plug-in. I'm often pleasantly surprised to hear that many people already have it. PDF represents a transitional strategy for designers who demand more precise control over their pages than they can otherwise get with today's browsers. Unfortunately, the way things are going, it looks like PDF offerings will remain more of a specialty side dish than the main course at most web sites.

Unlike HTML, PostScript is a page-description language that offers total graphical control of fixed-size pages. Designers have as much control over PDF as they do over paper, but PDF offers many of HTML's interactive features as well. Because it's largely a vector format, PDF is resolution-independent, or scalable. You can zoom into a PDF page in any increment, up to 800%, or view it at smaller than actual size, with excellent design fidelity. PDF is a fixed output format. Like hard copy, you can annotate, rearrange, add, or delete pages (but it's not practical to edit their contents substantially).

PostScript on the Web

In the first edition of this book, I described how PostScript would form the basis for Java's imaging model. I was wrong. PostScript has lost momentum as a data type on the Web, even though bits and pieces of its capabilities are being assembled to suit different needs. The big disappointment is that web designers are still making GIF text when they should be sending outlines. It seems Adobe hasn't been able to part the waters of the Web and introduce PostScript as a native format. It looks like we'll have to take the *à la carte* approach, which means that people who divine HTML and browser standards for a living can look forward to several more years of prosperity.

The best thing about PDFS is that they embed fonts and print beautifully. Browsers still do a poor job of printing web pages. If you have documents that are meant to be printed, you should strongly consider requiring people to use PDF to view and print them.

Learn more about making and serving PDF documents and get detailed, step-by-step instructions for how to create a PDF-based web site at the Book Site. Make sure you have the PDF plug-in installed first.

Shockwave

What's happened to Shockwave? No longer hailed as the be-all/end-all multimedia authoring tool for the Web, Shockwave once promised to make every web page come alive with sounds and animation. Like PDF, Shockwave animations have become more or less specialty items, relegated to a page or two on a site, or at best a "Shockwave gallery" of games. I've seen only a few uses of Shockwave for information design or presentations on the Web. Perhaps it is the fact that Shockwave animations are not that easy to make, even though many people can use Director, its main authoring platform. I can see Shockwave being used for intranets and corporate training sites, and it has been used with some success in various reference works on the Web. But web designers who don't know Director haven't been able to get over the hurdle and expense of learning how to master this fairly effective medium. Like PDF, this all-in-one, Swiss Army knife solution has not

caught on, but several of its basic capabilities have fared better individually.

Flash

Flash, formerly called FutureSplash, is a vector-graphics format that has acquired momentum in web design since its acquisition by Macromedia in 1997. Flash produces lean, resolution-independent, vector-based art work. It's especially good for detailed line art and is easily produced by a program like FreeHand. Of course, you have to get and install the Flash player (which comes with the Shockwave plug-in) to see Flash illustrations [12.8]. Flash 2, now available, includes support for rollovers, embedded graphics, vector fonts, sounds, and other nifty tricks.

Resolution-independent means you can resize or zoom in on Flash graphics with no loss of quality: Flash graphics resize on the fly as the web browser window resizes, a key capability, since designers cannot know in advance how big a web surfer's browser window will be or how it might change during viewing [12.9]. Flash graphics are anti-aliased on the client – the computer renders them smoothly, without any jaggies.

Because the rendering happens on the surfer's computer, Flash files are tiny compared to GIFS. They're scalable and print nicely. They don't work with photographs, but for line art and display type, they are just what the HTML terrorist ordered. You can use Flash to create extremely lightweight animations. Flash images can also incorporate sound (WAV for Windows and AIFF for the Mac) files. Although the

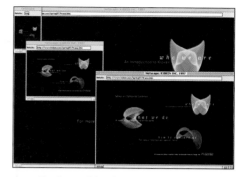

12.9 Flash graphics dynamically re-size when a user changes the size of the browser window.

files become considerably larger with the addition of sound, their sound compression scheme is said to be excellent.

Flash's downside is that it's proprietary, so the authoring environment is controlled by one company. Although it's still fairly primitive, the authoring environment will surely get better. While Macromedia remains in control of the format, it's unlikely to become standard equipment on both major browsers. Still, as more people pick up the plug-in and Microsoft lends support, I'd say Flash is the best bet for bringing vector graphics into mainstream use on the Web.

PNG

On January 1, 1995, UNISYS and CompuServe announced they would soon charge a royalty on GIF compression software. That day, a group of concerned technologists got together and defined a new public-domain format, called PNG (unambiguously

12.8 Flash animation brings life to a web page at the cost of a small plug-in.

pronounced "ping"). Some day soon, PNG will replace GIF with a superior, patent-free compression method, better color capabilities, and – finally! – an alpha channel.

PNG is an example of how a bunch of people can collaborate to create a truly versatile and appropriate standard without any profit motive. For starters, PNG supports bi-directional interlacing, color depths up to 48 bits, grayscale depths up to 16 bits, a full 8-bit alpha channel, gamma correction for cross-platform "brightness" control, and file-corruption checking, all while remaining open and extensible into the future. PNG compression is based on a public-domain version of LZW that usually results in 10%-30% smaller files for the same quality image [**12.10**].

One of the most important features of PNG images is the alpha channel. An *alpha channel* is simply an extra "color" added to each pixel. This phantom color can be used for transparency, masking, and holding other information. PNG gives us up to 256 levels of transparency, similar to the way Photoshop behaves when you move layers around – it will automatically anti-alias your images.

PNG lets you add an arbitrary amount of text-based metadata to an image file, including URLs or any database-friendly information you want to add. This completely replaces the ALT attribute and gives search engines the clues they need to know what is on your pages.

PNG is not GIF on steroids. PNG is GIF done right.

Support for PNG images has been building slowly. Although all the major players say they support PNG, the implementations so far haven't been worth using. Microsoft has adopted PNG and is likely to give it the boost over GIF it needs. But both Microsoft and Netscape 4.0 browsers do not do justice to the format. Neither lets you take advantage of the transparency levels on a web page, and for Netscape, you must download a plug-in. I predict that in late 1998, PNG will take over.

PNG Reading

I highly recommend reading *The Web Designer's Guide to Graphics: PNG, GIF & JPEG*, by Timothy Webster, Paul Atzberger, and Andrew Zolli (Hayden Books, 1997).

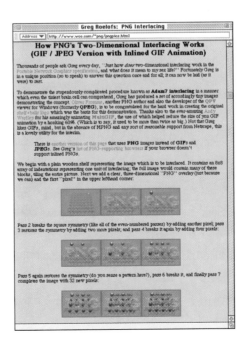

12.10 The PNG home page, where you can learn everything you always wanted to know about PNG.

The PNG Advocates

Siegel & Gale, a New York-based design firm, created a free PNG viewer called PNG Live, www.siegelgale.com. Some 250,000 people have downloaded the PNG Live 2.0 plug-in, which works with Netscape Communicator for Windows 95 and Mac.

With any luck, GIF will be eradicated like the Small Pox virus by the end of 1999.

Adobe Photoshop 4.0 supports PNG in the same way that 3.0 initially supported GIF: badly. Adobe wanted to show support for PNG even before a good implementation was available. Let's give them credit for trying, but let's not use Photoshop to make PNGs until they produce a good export filter that can do the job well.

Web hot-shots will be disappointed to know that the same holds true of Equilibrium's DeBabelizer, the versatile can-opener of all images. At this writing, neither DeBabelizer nor DeBabelizer Pro will save a PNG image you'd want to present on the Web – the files come out way too large. But the first major update of DeBabelizer Pro should have full support for 8-bit PNGs with a full alpha channel. (Watch the book site for pointers to new developments.)

As PNG extends to animation with a new set of extensions in the new standard known as "Multiple-image Network Graphics," or MNG (pronounced "ming"), I expect that when we can animate PNGs we can start kissing GIF goodbye.

Wavelets

Most people don't realize that JPEG is about as useful a format as GIF – it's old and it's substandard. It works, but there are much better ways to compress photographs, and the most promising technology is called wavelets [12.11].

12.11 Wavelet technology is the next step beyond JPEG.

CHAPTER 12: TRANSITIONAL STRATEGIES

Wavelets start where JPEG leaves off. I think the most important thing to know is that JPEG was really not a good idea in the first place, and wavelets are not a big rocket-science advance. They just make sense. Here's how they work.

JPEGS know that color in photographs usually follows a gradient. That is, the color values ramp smoothly from one to the next with fairly predictable transitions. JPEG replaces the actual pixels with a sine-wave representation of the major color changes – one for the color information and one for the brightness information. In essence, JPEGS lay a wavy color blanket over a black-and-white blanket, or sine-wave description, of the image. Higher quality JPEGS have a higher frequency sine wave for the entire image. Lower quality (called Q-factor) JPEGS use a lower frequency that throws out lots of information, resulting in fewer modulations and a much smaller file.

Wavelets combine the best of both high-and-low quality JPEGS. If an image has a large, smooth area, like clouds, wavelets use a low-frequency sine wave. For sharp details, like buildings and shadow edges, wavelets use a higher frequency sine wave to represent the transitions. In fact, wavelets use straight lines to represent hard "square wave" transitions, so the compression scheme is basically tuned to the area of the image being compressed.

Infinop (www.infinop.com) makes a good wavelet plug-in you can download today. Their plug-in, called Lightning Strike, is free, and their compressor is quite affordable. If I were mounting a photo gallery today, I would compress

the images using this technology and require my visitors to get the plug-in, because the difference is well worth the trouble. Some day we'll see wavelet-based images native in the Dominant Browser, and everyone will be able to enjoy wavelet technology. Combined with FlashPix (see below), wavelet technology should become the standard for photographic compression as we enter the next millenium.

FlashPix

FlashPix is a graphical file format developed by Live Picture (www.livepicture.com), Hewlett-Packard, Kodak, and Microsoft [12.12]. It's a great example of a standard developed for online image transmission. FlashPix essentially takes the concept of progressive JPEG one level further – it does bi-directional interlacing to several levels.

FlashPix takes an image of any size and stores it in a multi-resolution "pyramid," with the highest resolution image at the bottom, then one that is 1/4 the size, then another that is 1/4 the size of that, and so on, until finally the image is represented by a single 64 x 64 pixel tile. Each layer of the pyramid is stored as tiles and represents a version of the image you can access directly. Using a special server component that uses the IIP (Internet Image Protocol), a web designer can designate that a certain version of the image be served with an HTML file. Because there is more data in the image, the person receiving the image can click on it as it arrives to zoom in, triggering a server request to send more detailed information for that particular cell (or

269

group of cells). This way, you get more relevant information sooner, and you can stop when you've seen all you need to see. Once you've downloaded an entire FlashPix image, you can zoom into it to reveal more information, up to the final resolution of the image. FlashPix

images can also be rotated or manipulated quickly without destroying the original image data.

The FlashPix format is not proprietary – anyone can create tools or viewers for it – and it will work with both JPEG and PNG.

12.12 FlashPix promises to be a good online image format.

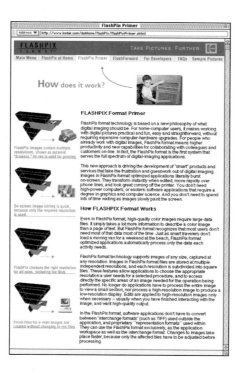

Fonts

If we're lucky, we'll be able to stop sending GIF text by the end of the century. Right now, you can specify `<FONT FACE="verdana">` and if the viewer has that typeface, she will see your text in Verdana.

Fortunately, both Verdana and Georgia are available from Microsoft for free. These excellent fonts, designed by Matthew Carter and implemented by Tom Rickner and others, are a great first step away from using Times Roman for everything on the Web. Some day we will have a large number of fonts to choose from for presenting headlines, logos, attention-getting graphics, tabular data, captions, text, perhaps even handwriting.

Netscape is shipping the TrueDoc technology, developed by Bitstream, with its 4.0 browser. TrueDoc takes existing fonts, uses the operating system's capability to render them at a large size, and creates an outline version of the font that is free of any royalty or U.S. copyright obligations. It sends that outline version of the font with your web site. Because Netscape's implementation isn't very good, and because font designers are completely against it, good designers have embraced TrueDoc as eagerly as they embraced the `<BLINK>` tag.

12.13 SGI's Cosmo plug-in is currently the hottest VRML viewer in town. SGI is dedicated to making VRML more capable and ubiquitous.

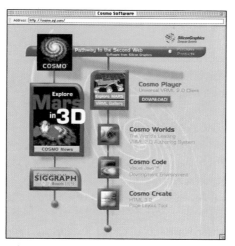

Microsoft and Adobe, meanwhile, proposed the OpenType solution, which is a system-level font format that will completely replace today's warring TrueType and Type-1 fonts. OpenType is cool. The technology hasn't been commercially released yet, and it will take some time before everyone converts, but I hope that within five years all fonts will be in this new format. The distinction between platforms and font formats will go away. There will simply be one standard, and it will be rich enough to accommodate both print and online designers' needs.

OpenType has too many good features to list here. Web designers will be able to embed them in sites, and people visiting will see placeholder text until the proper fonts download. Because these are outline fonts, and because the system will break them up into subsets so only the characters needed arrive with the page, they will come down the wire quickly. Just think – you'll be able to present an entire web site in fonts you control! Because it is a system-level feature, OpenType will work with any browser.

The biggest concern of type designers is security. Because there are still a few people left who design fonts for a living, and because a growing number of companies sell quality type, it's important that users can't just download fonts from web sites and use them for everything else. Here's the rub: you download fonts to your hard disc so you can see a particular web site. Now you have the outline data. Someone, somewhere, will able to write a small utility program that gets to these fonts and repackages them as fonts your

system "owns," giving you the use of any font you can download off the Web. As in any situation, more security is more of a hassle, so it remains to be seen what the exact tradeoffs will be in using OpenType fonts in web pages safely.

Ideally, OpenType will spawn a new era of type design, one aimed at fonts for web sites. Designers will buy these specialty fonts, perhaps with the rights to put them on a small number of sites, with upgrade licenses for larger sites. Or they will buy one font and use it for all their sites. But every designer will buy a fair number of fonts, revitalizing the type market. No one knows whether this will happen, but if students ask me about getting into type design, I advise them to go to business school – or at least graphic design school – instead.

OpenType is a big undertaking. It will take some time to implement correctly. I expect to see OpenType fonts emerge in 1998 and take off in 1999, as the type vendors and designers convert their libraries. I imagine Open-Type will kill TrueDoc if it is implemented well.

Virtual Reality

The term virtual reality is about as well defined as multimedia. While these exciting developments in technology don't always translate into compelling surfing experiences, there are a few things to watch for. If nothing else, it helps to know what they are when you go to a white-wine gathering of digerati, or even just a gathering of digerini sharing beers and talking about what happened to the server that day.

VRML, the always-promising Virtual Reality Modeling Language, is almost as old as the Web itself **[12.13]**. Its proponents keep saying that web sites will become walk throughs, and places will turn into spaces. Perhaps when every-

one has a cable modem, that will be true. Until then, I suspect VRML will be reserved for special 3-D applications, like giving fly-through or walk-through demos of a building in an off-line presentation. It will be quite a while before we go to a web site, click on a button, and enter a 3-D world where other avatars walk, creep, fly, and slither around us as we explore a jungle, a city, or an alien planet.

QuickTime VR (QTVR) is a technology from Apple that extends Quick-Time to do more than just present linear film clips **[12.14]**. Basically, QTVR is a way to stitch a movie or a series of pictures together to form a seamless "loop of film" that viewers can see as though they were in one of two points of view. You can either have a first-person view, as though you are swiveling a camera around in a 360-degree arc, or you can have a second-person view, as though you were walking all the way around an object. You can also add hot zones, so the visitor can click through and go somewhere else, presumably to another QTVR clip.

OliVR is a new image format that goes beyond QTVR to deliver a streaming, server-based experience. It's analogous to FlashPix in that it features progressive rendering from its special server. OliVR images can be of very high quality, so you can pan around an image then zoom in to get more detail, and the server will send that information on request. OliVR is more of a streaming model, and it has excellent compression. (Live Picture Corp. recently acquired OLiVR Corp.)

I first saw Ipix, which used to be called Photobubble, on the Carnegie

12.14 QuickTime VR is a software solution from Apple that stitches a movie into a 360-degree view of something or somewhere.

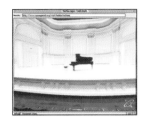

12.15 Ipix gives you a floor-to-ceiling, 360° view of Carnegie Hall.

Hall web site [**12.15**]. Ipix is a plug-in that allows you to see full spherical representations from one point of view. It takes two back-to-back photographs shot with a fish-eye lens and stitches them together seamlessly with some special technology. Then it lets the viewer look up, down, and all around from a single vantage point. I vividly remember exploring Carnegie Hall from the conductor's point of view – it was worth getting the plug-in.

Sound

For me, surfing the Web is mostly a quiet experience, with pockets of noise and atrocious design, and a few oases of well-designed sites and occasionally soothing sounds. Just as there are two basic kinds of images (vector and raster), there are two basic kinds of sound files: wave files and instruction files.

A wave file sends a compressed version of a sound wave, like a human voice or a tree falling in the woods. Microsoft Internet Explorer 4.0 and Netscape Navigator 4.0 both support the AIFF, AU, and WAV audio formats, but neither includes the most popular audio plug-in, Progressive Networks' RealAudio player. The first set of formats are encapsulated into single files, whereas the RealAudio solution is a

streaming data type – you get it as it comes to you over the Internet. RealAudio is used for voice-overs, music, distance-learning, and could even be used for two-way conversations. Since so many people have the plug-in, many sites now pay license fees to use the RealAudio server software.

Because many people have decent speakers hooked up to their computers, you can actually play an orchestra of instruments over the Web. MIDI files transmit musical-instrument instructions, which are then synthesized in software on your CPU and sent to your speakers. MIDI is the vector format of sound. A decent MIDI player is built into QuickTime. Another comes from Thomas Dolby's company, Headspace (www.headspace.com), which offers a cool MIDI plug-in called Beatnik [**12.16**]. It works with Netscape Navigator 2.0 or higher on Windows 95/NT and Macintosh PowerPC systems and with limited support on Internet Explorer. It plays files in several music and audio file formats, including RMF, MIDI, MOD, AIFF, WAV, and AU files. MIDI files are small, even playing several instruments simultaneously, and they sound great. Once you've sent a set of MIDI instructions to the visitor, you can change their tempo, volume, range, and other factors all on the fly

273

for practically no extra download charge.

While it is fairly easy to add sound to your site, adding sound as a design element is a different story. Web designers can learn from Hollywood's sound wizards and from sites that do it well. It's not fair to your visitor to shove sound at them just because you figured out how.

While there may not be a Michael Jackson or a Sofia Coppola voice synthesizer, there are generic voice synthesizers on the market. These readers can actually read a page to you, letting you decide whether to take various hot links they express as they read. They may not sound as nice as Michelle Pfeiffer does, but they have

Sharon Stargazer beat. This is great for blind people surfing the Web. Today, the best way to accommodate these people is to provide an up-to-date, text-only version of the site, so people with alternative browsers can get through your text.

It's a bit beyond the scope of this book, but I want to mention a voice-input system that lets you surf the Web by speaking into a microphone rather than clicking your mouse. This is a great solution for people with nerve damage to their hands. One solution in particular is Surftalk, from Digital Dreams (www.surftalk.com). Surftalk lets you navigate with a set of pre-defined commands, bookmark and visit bookmarked sites, and activate live text links just by speaking the text [12.17].

Database-Driven Sites

When you go to a web site and you see a bunch of funny-looking characters in the URL of each page, you know you're surfing a site that resides in a database. For today's large web sites, this is really the only way to go. This is the subject of several other books, and I actually find it quite interesting. I want to mention it here because as sites grow they tend to get out of hand, and databases are an important option to remember.

In a database-driven site, designers create templates for HTML pages ahead of time, and databases pour content into these templates according to the choices each visitor makes on every page. These sites usually come with content-management systems that help writers and editors check their content

12.16 Headspace lets you play MIDI files on your own computer. Visit their sound gallery and rock to the beat!

into the system, make the proper as-
signments of what should go up when,
track users through the site, and adjust
the ad-banner mix accordingly. As you
can imagine, it all gets pretty compli-
cated. Sites like HotWired, c|net, and
ESPN Sportszone really have no choice
but to use databases to serve their sites.

Another use of databases, of course,
is to present complex information that
you can't present easily any other way.
Comparing airline tickets, searching
parts catalogs, fetching a bank statement or a stock price – databases do
these things better than static sites can.
Suffice to say that user-interfaces on
most database-driven web sites are fair
to poor.

For more on this subject, see *Secrets of
Successful Web Sites*. I wish a designer,
rather than an engineer, would write a
good book on designing for database-
driven web sites – I'd love to read it.

12.17 Surftalk lets your voice do the walking!

Summary

The Web is always going through a
transition. Books like this are always
"under construction." But there is a
fundamental change afoot, and I hope
I have the chance to chronicle it. The
shift is toward separating content from
design. In the next chapter, I hope to
shed some light on what it will take to
get to that promised land. Meanwhile,
we will hack and scratch and use
whatever plug-ins are necessary to
create our third-generation sites.

Perhaps the reason we're seeing
various *à la carte* solutions win over
the big, do-it-all formats is that each approach must run the gauntlet of competition to emerge as the one best adapted
to the Web. A company has a good idea,
they build a plug-in, and if it truly serves
a need, people flock to the site and
download the player. Then the company
hopes to make money on the authoring
tools or by having Microsoft buy them.

The Color Cube

ON THE FOLLOWING PAGES I present my own look at the color cube mentioned throughout this book (and described in detail in Chapter 3) for your reference. Most graphic representations of the cube show all 216 colors, either laid out in a big table or arranged as slices through the cube. The problem with these approaches is that they don't show the various color combinations possible when looking at the cube in different ways. Both versions shown are different from other representations in that they have more than 216 entries. They have as many as necessary to show their perspectives. Many colors are repeated, but that's the idea.

I hope you will find these two presentations both stimulating and useful when choosing colors for your images. You should also pick up the color-cube graphic from the Book Site, where you can get instructions on how to load it into your color picker for easy reference.

Transitions Between Fully Saturated Colors

The first version [A2.1] is a transition table, showing possible transitions between prominent colors. This shows the intermediate steps between each of the colors at the eight corners of the color cube. Transitions between primaries, like the pure red of FF0000 and pure blue 0000FF increment one color and decrement the other by hex 33 for each step. Transitions between secondaries are the same as for primaries. The most complex transitions are those between a primary and a secondary made from the other two primaries. Blue to yellow involves blue decreasing as red and green increase.

The Cube Unfolded

The second [A2.2] is the cube peeled, so you can see the outside layers and the inner core. These groupings can be helpful when choosing colors that go together or making transitions from one area of color to another.

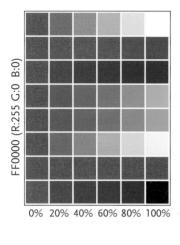

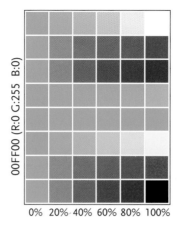

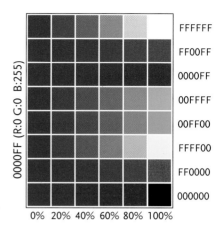

FFFFFF
FF00FF
0000FF
00FFFF
00FF00
FFFF00
FF0000
000000

0% 20% 40% 60% 80% 100%

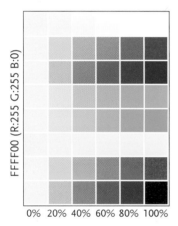

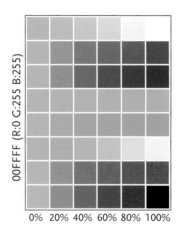

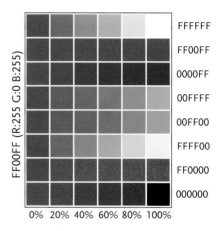

FFFFFF
FF00FF
0000FF
00FFFF
00FF00
FFFF00
FF0000
000000

0% 20% 40% 60% 80% 100%

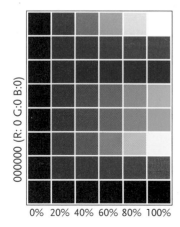

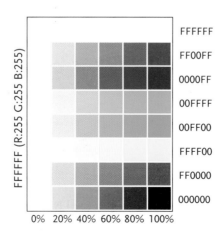

FFFFFF
FF00FF
0000FF
00FFFF
00FF00
FFFF00
FF0000
000000

0% 20% 40% 60% 80% 100%

A2.1 This shows the intermediate steps between each of the colors at the eight corners of the color cube.

The outside faces of the color cube are dominated by pure, saturated colors. In the depths of the cube, colors are noticeably murkier. The eight colors in the center of the cube are middle grays and muted tints with little variation.

Converting Hex Triplets to Decimal RGB Values

The hex (hexadecimal) values for each color are shown on the swatch. Use the following table to translate hex to RGB. Example: FF00CC, a hot pink, translates to 255 red, 0 green, 204 blue in the decimal Photoshop palette. 9966CC, a faded plum color, would be 153 red, 102 green, 204 blue.

HEX	DECIMAL
00	0
33	51
66	102
99	153
CC	204
FF	255

A2.2 These groupings can be helpful when choosing colors that go together or making transitions from one area of color to another.

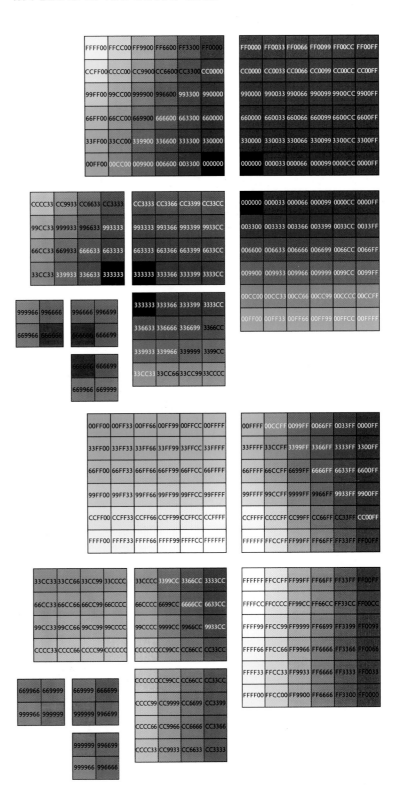

Image Optimization for the Web

WEB DESIGNERS who are ready to move beyond the basic techniques discussed in Chapter Three will be interested in this automated, industrial-strength procedure we've developed here at Studio Verso. If you process a lot of images for the Web, this script will save you time and reduce the file sizes of the images as much as possible automatically. At the time I wrote this, it was available for Macintosh users, but by now there may be a Windows version available. This solution was initially coded as a DeBabelizer script; Photoshop-based solutions may already be available.

The idea of the procedure is to reduce the colors in your image and then run one of two versions of this script, which will map near-color-cube colored pixels to the cube exactly. This avoids dithering in cases where a pixel that is close to a color-cube color can be shifted to be exactly a color-cube color without doing any damage to the image.

The WebScrub Script

First go to the book site and find the WebScrub section (don't be surprised if we've renamed it, but seek and ye shall find). Follow the instructions for downloading and installing either the native DeBabelizer script or the Apple-Script application. Note: you must own a copy of DeBabelizer for this to work (check the Book Site for other programs and platforms). You'll want both the 10-grit and the 5-grit versions.

This script works well on images destined to be GIFS or PNGS, but you might find that on certain photographic images it produces a smaller GIF than the alternative JPEG.

1. Reduce (index) your full-color image to the least acceptable number of colors, without forcing to a generic (web or system) palette and avoiding dithering, using DeBabelizer, Photoshop, or another program. You may use any

These images represent a gif before and after processing with the "10-Grit WebScrub" script.

Before: (RIGHT) 34,285 bytes. Note the measles in the type images at 8-bit. This is typical Photoshop damage

After: (BELOW) 31,124 bytes - 3K smaller. Do the math: how many downloads at 28.8 before you save a life?

specialized tools at your disposal, like HVS ColorGIF, BoxTop PhotoGIF, influencing the histogram, etc. *(see Chapter 3, "Preparing Images," for more on reduction)*. Save a copy as a GIF for reference.

2. Open the indexed image in DeBabelizer. Here are some examples, indexed initially with Photoshop and the HVS ColorGIF plug-in.

3. Run the DeBabelizer script "10-grit WebScrub," and save the resulting image as a GIF.

4. Inspect in web browser(s) at 8-bit and higher color depths, noting any dithering or banding. Compare with the "prescrubbed" reference version you saved in step 2. The scrubbed version should be visually acceptable and quite a bit smaller.

5. Note the file size compared to the reference version you saved in step 2. Depending on the image, the scrubbed version should be between 5% and 20% smaller than the reference version. If the image looks good and is smaller than the reference version, you're done.

6. If banding or color shifts are evident and objectionable, run the DeBabelizer script "5-grit WebScrub" on the original GIF.

7. Repeat steps 4-6. If this procedure does not produce excellent results (smallish, good visual quality when viewed at all depths), then the image should probably be prepared as a JPEG – start over with the highest-resolution version you have, and use JPEG tools to compress.

How the WebScrub Scripts Work

The scrubbing operation (216 steps) tells DeBabelizer to look for color values within either 5 or 10 units of any of the 216 cube values. So, for example, if you have the color 54, 109, 201, the 5-grit script will leave it alone, but the 10-grit script will map it to 51, 102, 204. Colors not remapped will dither only as necessary in 8-bit surfing environments. Scrubbing increases the runs of similar colors, boosting the effectiveness of lossless compression schemes like LZW. If the 10-grit script is too strong, use 5-grit.

The scripts can be useful when you have a JPEG that looks bad when viewed through a browser on a 256-color system. Run one of the scripts on the full-color (unreduced) image, perform a mild Gaussian blur to take the edge off any banding, and see if that improves the appearance.

For Extra Credit

This script-based approach is new here at Verso. Our first choice is that all surfers in the world get systems that can see more than 256 colors. Our second choice is that web designers can specify the exact 256 colors for any web page they build. Back in reality, it is possible that programs like Photoshop will build these scripts in as an indispensable tool for web designers.

There is more to do. The scrubbing scripts, for example, treat all three colors the same rather than trying to understand more about the image or human perception. Real perfectionists who want to produce intermediate and extended grits are encouraged to seek counseling, write a plug-in with a slider and live preview, or both.

With more experimentation, we will be able to further optimize visual quality and compressibility. New techniques like these and new tools like Ditherbox give designers at least a few more weapons in their assault on ugly web graphics.

Index

Symbols

32-bit images, alpha channel, 35

A

absolute cell width (tables), 79-82
absolute margins, 71-72
adaptive color palettes, 50-51
adding captions to images, 109-110
Adobe Multiple Master Fonts, 101-102
Adobe PageMaker
    typography, 77
    Web site, 46
aliasing, 231
aligning images on Web pages, 77-78
alpha channel
    32-bit images, 35
    PNG images, 266-268
anchor images
    reducing, 156-158
    small business Web sites
        building, 154-155
animated GIFs
    finite looping, 48-49
    infinite looping, 48-49
    optimizing, 48-49
anti-aliasing
    addition of colors, 40-43
    background correction in images,
        43-44
    effect on selected shapes, 40-43
    images, 40-43
    less compressibility, 40-43
    type, 96-101

B

background correction, 43-44
background image registration,
    132-135
backgrounds
    colors, selecting, 288-289
    tiled, 119-120
    Web sites, 146
banners, Web sites makeovers,
    120-124
BBEdit program, 82-84
Big Healey's Web site, 212
bitmaps, 34-35
blending, colors, 39-40
borders, eliminating from tables,
    78-79

bounded initial caps, 108-109
browsers (Web)
    and support of PNG images, 267-268
    and third generation Web sites, 15
    cascading style sheets, 236-238
    conflicting displays, style sheets,
        245-247
    development by Netscape, 5-6
    fonts, 289
    image offset problems, 77-78
    Internet Explorer development, 6-7
    Macintosh platform, screen resolution,
        111-113
    supprt of cascading style sheets,
        280-281
    Windows platform, screen resolution,
        111-113
building
    audiences, net equity, 21
    themes in third generation Web sites,
        24-26

C

captions, adding, 109-110
carriage returns, eliminating in tables,
    82-84
cascading style sheets
    advantages, 250-251
    background colors, 243
    browser support, 280-281
    comments, 243
    creating, 237-238
    defined, 236-238
    font specifications, 243-244
    implementing, 237-238
    inheritance, 242
    margin setting, 241
    markup, 239
    selectors, 241-242
    specificity, 242
    style sheet creation, 239-248
    system defaults, 244-245
    "Ten Commandments", 236
    use in browsers, 236-238
    user preferences, 244-245
    Web future, 278-281
    z-order layering, 279
cell width (tables)
    absolute, 79-82
    relative, 79-82
cellpadding, 82
cellspacing, 82

X - Y - Z

About the Author

DAVID SIEGEL is the chairman of Studio Verso, a third-generation site design and web strategy consultancy in San Francisco. Verso, widely known for its quality web sites and forward thinking, has made sites for Hewlett-Packard, Lucent, Klutz Press, Sony, Relevance, Giga, and others. Visit Verso at www.verso.com.

David is also chairman of Vertebrae, a database and e-commerce consulting company in San Francisco.

His personal site (www.dsiegel.com) has been linked thousands of times and won 2nd place in the 1995 Cool Site of the Year competition. His Web Wonk site is widely regarded as one of the best sources of HTML tips on the Web.

David received an undergraduate math degree from the University of Colorado at Boulder, where he studied algorithms under professor Hal Gabow. He received a master's degree in Digital Typography from Donald Knuth and Charles Bigelow at Stanford in 1985. His masters project was to produce a typeface drawn by calligrapher and type designer Hermann Zapf using a type-description program called Metafont. In 1986, he worked for Pixar before working for himself. He started a company painting Macintosh computers, designed some of the country's best-selling typefaces (Tekton, Graphite, and Eaglefeather).

David is president of Verso Editions, a content-publishing company in San Francisco, where he consults, writes, and lectures full time. He is the publisher of the High Five web magazine of design, which each week points surfers to the best design on the Web. Since June of 1995, the High Five has been the most coveted design award on the Web.

David has taught graphic design at Pratt Institute and The New School in New York. He is an advisory member of w3c committees on HTML and STYLE. He has written numerous magazine articles on type, technology, and the Web. He has lectured at Yale, Stanford, Columbia, the School of Visual Arts, and at conferences worldwide.

David has published a book on environmental, population, and women's issues and continues to express his views and concerns through his web site. He is an ardent vegetarian, an avid skier, and writes screenplays in his spare time. He lives in San Francisco and dreams of sitting in a sidewalk cafe on the French Riviera writing THE BIG BOOK OF LIFE.

Contrary to popular belief, his cat, Gizmo, was not responsible for the unseemly demise of *The Spot*, the first-place winner in the 1995 Cool Site of the Year Competition. Gizmo, a third-generation cat, has been known to make phone calls from Verso Headquarters soliciting contributions from officers of cat food conglomerates in his effort to lobby for the legalization of catnip for personal, nonmilitary use.

David Siegel can be reached at:
david@killersites.com

This is the best book on project management I have ever seen. It is indeed a producer's secret weapon. I would buy it myself if I were alive today.

– Thomas Jefferson, architect, US Constitution

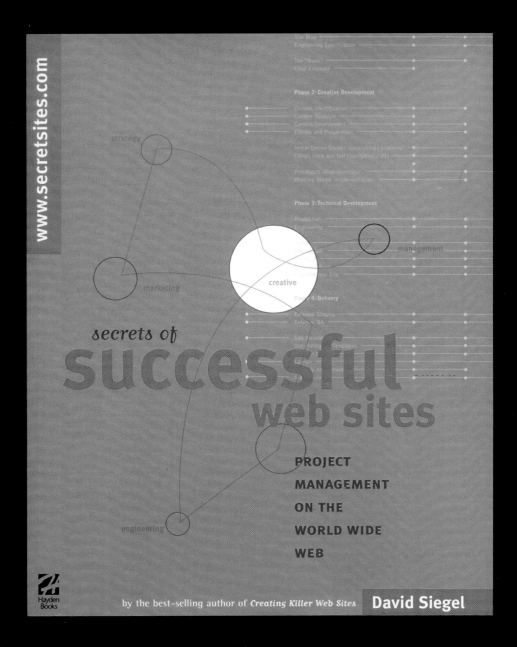

MACMILLAN COMPUTER PUBLISHING USA

A VIACOM COMPANY

Technical Support:

If you need assistance with a particular situation in the book, please feel free to check out the Knowledge Base on our Web site at **http://www.superlibrary.com/general/support**. We have answers to our most Frequently Asked Questions listed there. If you do not find your specific question answered, please contact Macmillan Technical Support at **(317) 581-3833**. We can also be reached by email at **support@mcp.com**.

CHAPTER 13

Looking Forward

What you'll learn in this chapter:

Positioning

Promise of Style Sheets

Dynamic Object Model

5.0 and 6.0 browsers

XML

Metadata

Scripting

Profiles

UNPREDICTABILITY HAPPENS. Microsoft has won the browser wars. Structuralists and designers are starting to say friendly words to each other. Here in the last minutes of the millennium, it's time for us to get on with the business of connecting every human being on earth, building the E-Tower of Babel as one of the Seven Wonders of the Electronic World (I'll talk about the other six in the sequel to this book – hint: America Online and Marc Andreesson are not on the list). The first language of the E-Tower was HTML. More will follow. Children who grow up in this world will speak several markup languages natively.

We are building the Seven Wonders of the Electronic World on standards. Though standards change slowly, few can tell which will dominate just six months from now. Everyone wants to know what is ahead, especially designers. People up front should holler back and say what they can see. As you can tell by comparing the first edition of this book with this one, almost half of my predictions have come true. Take that for what it's worth – in school, you get an F for getting it right 40% of the time; in baseball, they put you in the Hall of Fame.

I'll take this opportunity to lay out the Grand Scheme now envisioned jointly by the Framers of the Web and the designers who have contributed to its visual enrichment. When it works, it's going to change our lives. It's going to happen in two phases.

Phase One: HTML & Style

Style sheets will let us design third-generation sites as the browsers improve and several ingredients come together. In my view, this is how it will shape up. Much of what I'm about to explain builds on the material of the previous two chapters.

Content will continue to be an explosion of offerings on the Web. English, the *lingua franca* of the Electronic World, will continue to dominate, though online translation services will actually serve English-based web sites in other languages – unbeknownst to the author! The quality of the content could certainly improve, but I doubt it will. Content on the Web should and will remain a free-for-all.

New web-native data types are quickly emerging. These new formats for images, speech, music, animation, and other creative forms of expression will be matched by ever more sophisticated authoring tools. Unfortunately, the tools will continue to lag behind the data types. When tools become

The 6.0 Browsers

I believe the 5.0 browsers will continue the tradition of patching holes in previous releases, but I think the engineering teams working on 6.0 browsers will have the time to build a better product. They will rewrite the browsers to enable them to parse HTML and thus solve today's CSS implementation problems. By then, Netscape will be unable to introduce new tags unilaterally and Microsoft's IE 6.0 will be quite a formidable style-sheet engine.

more flexible, they will better serve all content creators. We may have to wait until all our tools are in Java, so that everything is modular and we can just plug in the latest Java-Bean module to export the latest data type on the Web.

HTML contains the rudimentary tags needed to publish a hyperlinked physics paper, and that was the original intention. It is not a particularly good markup language, but it is light weight and has served its purpose. It is extendable by adding class attributes, but if we let everyone define his own class attributes going forward, the future will likely resemble the movie *Brazil.*

We must do two things with HTML. First, we must stop changing it. If you mark up your content once, you shouldn't have to do it again. The latest version, HTML 4.0, has a few new structural tags and has earmarked all presentational tags for eventual disposal in preparation for the arrival of CSS to handle presentation. This division of responsibility between HTML and CSS enables the creation of better, more stable tools that will encourage web designers to follow the rules and move on to the real creative work. As Tim Berners-Lee, the inventor of the Web, states:

Information to be published on the Web must also be formatted according to the rules of the web standards. These standardized formats assure that all web users who want to read the material will be able to view it.

Now that HTML is maturing and finding its proper place, we can build

on its foundation with more powerful markup languages to handle the kinds of complex, real-world applications we want to do on the Web. Dan Connolly, a standards architect at the W3C, says:

By the time Mosaic took off worldwide in 1993, people were using HTML as a hammer and were seeing nails everywhere. Unfortunately, HTML is not a (universal) hammer; even HTML 4.0, released in July 1997, only furnishes an elegant but small tag set, and no single tag set will suffice for all of the kinds of information on the Web.

Style is something you apply to a marked-up document, subject to the capabilities and wishes of the user. Style sheets will give designers the control they seek, but today's browsers are far from delivering on that promise.

Style sheets enable positioning of elements and, in combination with new data types, will let designers create true, interactive multimedia effects on web pages. Better implementations of CSS's layer model will let designers position page elements behind or in front of other elements. They can be positionable in space, either relative (anchored) to other elements or in absolute measurements. Elements that are relative flow with text, while absolute measurements are always specified from the upper-left corner of the *canvas* – the white space of a web page.

CSS gives us *z-order layering*. Soon, I hope, we will laugh as we remember the old days in which there was one background image and one page of

foreground content. With an unlimited number of layers, we can accomplish so much more, making today's modem speeds bearable. If we can put a JPEG in back and a PNG image in front, we can put fancy type on top of images in less time with greater efficiency. We can use PNG's transparency to tint and reuse already downloaded graphics in new and interesting ways. We can collage and overlap things, only to find them rotated and repositioned on a different page. We can use clipping paths and masks to see through in the foreground and filter things in the background. The advantages are endless.

css is thus central to the continued evolution of design on the Web. HTML extensions, like Netscape's <LAYER> tag, are simply red herrings to get analysts excited about new browser features. I predict that the mainstream of content providers will wait until the 6.0 browsers dominate before switching completely to css to do these things. By then we'll be learning about DSSSL (Document Semantic Style Specification Language), an emerging programming language that will let us do even more amazing things with marked-up content.

Profiles. One thing we're missing in this equation is a *universal surfing profile* each visitor can put together to describe herself to the sites she visits. A surfing profile might combine a visitor's *technography* (whether she is using a hand-held cellular browser, a TV, a high-end graphics workstation, etc.), *geography* (where she lives, her native language, her country's cus-

toms, etc.), *psychography* (the kinds of places she likes to visit, things she likes to do, and a list of preferences for sites she visits often), *demography* (whether she wants to indicate her age, sex, income, and other factors – this should be up to her), and *physiography* (whether she is hearing impaired, color blind, etc). All of this should be at the control of the consumer, but the profile should be as important as the information you put on your driver's license – it should not be buried somewhere so that most people don't even fill it out. The more designers know about their visitors, the better they can create style sheets to serve up the content in a way that suits both provider and consumer.

The object model. Web pages need not be static. Their elements should be able to appear, disappear, move, rotate, and do other things we haven't even thought of yet. To do that, page elements need *handles* you can call them by, and they need to respond when they hear their names called. This is a way of saying elements need an *object model* complete with inheritance. *Inheritance* says that if an image is part of a larger group of objects, and the group is moved, then the image must move. Or if the group disappears, the image must disappear. The w3c is hard at work on the DOM, the Document Object Model. It is behind all the "Dynamic HTML" propaganda you hear from the browser companies. The key here is to agree on a standard so that a Java applet, a script, a browser, or other program can accurately identify elements and their associations. DOM

will help add true interactivity to our web sites.

Scripting and event control. Once page elements have handles, you can use handlers to make them do things. A *handler* is a script that causes an element to take a given action. Scripts should be able to manipulate any element on a page, and this is why a common object model is so important.

Scripting combined with css will allow many of the multimedia effects designers are used to: transitions, animation, pop-ups, hiding and showing graphics, etc. Using a push model and an open connection (HTTP 1.1), designers will be able to create television-like interfaces where you can simply watch everything happen on a single page. Time- and event-based scripting will allow visitors to enter gamelike environments, online events, simulations, community or club spaces, as well as interact with web sites in ways we can't today.

Phase 2: Beyond HTML

As I mentioned, we will leave HTML alone and supplement it with more powerful, specialized markup languages. HTML mostly addresses document structural features – whether something is a heading or a paragraph, etc. – as opposed to semantic issues. While knowing that something is a paragraph has its uses, it might also be helpful to know something about its contents. We need metadata that describes meaning. This is known as *semantic markup.*

Here's an example. Suppose I write a movie review. To tell you that *The Godfather, Part II* is a film title, I'd put it in italics. In HTML, I might put it between `<I>` and `</I>` tags, using presentational information (the italics) to make up for HTML's inability to describe it semantically.

If we had a tag for `<MOVIE TITLE>`, then we could display it properly, depending on the environment. People searching for a movie on their handheld cellular PDA would see "The Godfather, Part II," because on a tiny screen, you can't display italics. In this case, the browser itself adds the quote marks – *they would not be part of the document.* The `<MOVIE TITLE>` tag

What Happened to Load Order?

While some people are hard at work on everything mentioned above, no one is interested in addressing load order. As long as modems carry data at speeds measured in kilobits/second, designers will want to specify the load order of images on their pages. Generally, designers want the top screenful of content to load first – and perhaps even a single image or a set of images first – so that visitors can have something to work with rather than having to wait until the entire page loads. Today, the images at the bottom of a page compete with those at the top for bandwidth, and that makes the whole Web look slow.

I've figured out why people's eyes glaze over when I ask them about load order – it's not their department. Load order would have to be negotiated between the browser and the server. It would have to become part of the transfer protocol, and the browser companies don't have that much to do with it. I'm afraid load order won't be a switch designers can throw for some time.

What about Fourth-Generation Sites?

I'm looking forward to writing a book on fourth-generation sites. The Web remains technology driven. I am waiting and watching for a shift in the wind, where designers and content producers collaborate to build sites that are truly well designed, not just whiz-bang techno-marvels. I think I personally have a lot more to learn about design on the Web.

When I am able to articulate my vision for fourth-generation sites, the technologists will be disappointed. We have the tools at hand today. There will be a seamless change, not a radical one. But it will take another book to describe. The Fourth Generation will come, and it will be based on third-generation design principles. Design, not technology, will make the difference.

provides *semantic meta-information*. The User Agent (browser) interprets the content using the meta-information in whatever way is appropriate for the target display.

The killer app in this department is XML – the Extensible Markup Language. XML was defined in 1996 as a solution to the semantic-markup problem. It is a small subset of a much larger, more complicated language called SGML (Standard Generalized Markup Language). XML is suited to the Web and is quickly being adopted by both Netscape and Microsoft.

What is XML? XML provides a way to create a custom markup language to suit a particular kind of document. For a given set of information, you define a *document type definition*, or DTD, that helps you tag the contents meaning-fully. If you want to build a restaurant menu (or, let's say, a database containing 10,000 restaurant menus), you could construct a document type called Menu [13.1].

Anyone who's worked with data-bases can see that a DTD defines a *schema* – a database term for a mean-ingful taxonomy of the anticipated content. To serve a database-driven web site, you must design a schema for its documents. We can all have data-bases serving our sites, or we can just prepare our data properly and have the search engines do the heavy lifting. Think of XML as an extensible schema for the Web that lets us define certain document types, so we don't have to re-invent the wheel every time we want to figure out how to tell everyone about our particular kind of document.

Designing a DTD is similar to de-signing a form for future content own-ers to fill out. Using XML, different groups can decide on standard tagging schemes for their documents. Play-wrights can define the elements of a play then define various style sheets for printing or displaying written plays. Cooks can define a DTD for recipes. There will be standard DTDs for movie reviews, sports scores, chemistry papers, travel brochures, catalogs,

residential real estate listings, phone books, architecture plans, tax forms, contracts, wills, coupons, bank statements, Shakespearean sonnets, assembly instructions, patient charts, screenplays, waltzes, stock tables, and any other kind of document.

New tools are already springing up to help us create and manage XML documents. Microsoft based its Channel Definition Format on XML – and look for more radical support in Internet Explorer 5.0 and beyond. Netscape thinks it's a big deal, too.

You can combine different DTDs within a web site, even within a single page. XML is going to fix the search engines. The key is to tag content with semantic metadata on our web sites, so that it emerges from behind the closed

13.1 XML lets you define a document type definition that contains the special tags you need to describe your content meaningfully. Here is a hypothetical application of a markup language defined by a restaurant menu DTD. The DTD (not shown) specifies the nesting structure and any required elements. The result is a set of tags for marking up a menu. While this shows only one item, imagine that the DTD includes tags for main dishes, desserts, wines, etc. Marked up this way, the web content now becomes available to search engines or other applications that might want to index or compare vegan restaurant menus.

```
<!DOCTYPE menu "http://www.killersites.com/
DTDs/menu.dtd">
<menu>
   <?xml default menu
   restaurant = "Sofie's Place"
   phone = "1.415.550.4537"
   email = "sofie@sophiesplace.res"
   homepage = "http://www.sofiesplace.res/"
   ?>
   <appetizer>
     <title>
     Napa treasure
     </title>
     <desc>
        Roasted red peppers with braised
        leeks
        <dietary>
           vegan
        </dietary>
     </desc>
     <price cur="USD">
        4.50
     </price>
   </appetizer>
</menu>
```

doors of databases to turn the Web into one big searchable database – one of the Seven Wonders of the Electronic World.

Summary

CSS promises to deliver third-generation typography and layout to web designers. XML promises to be the Alexandria of our electronic future. It will let us build great libraries simply by building our own sites. It will let the average person put together very sophisticated and powerful applications simply by tagging everything properly so it fits into the larger schema of the Web. In a perfectly tagged world, the big search engines do all the work for us by searching the Web and storing not only the data, but also the metadata. Style sheets, user profiles, and the object model will provide the layout capabilities to make it look good.

With good CSS implementations on the horizon, I am in the process of turning in my black hat. Yes, I will continue to commit HTML terrorism to accomplish my design objectives on today's browsers. I may even have to combine HTML terrorism with style sheets for a while, until the browsers improve. But over time, the black hat will find itself gathering dust, and I'll be off creating new DTDs and style sheets and looking for *well-styled* third-generation sites to showcase at the High Five design-award site.

In closing, I'd like to present an email message I received from Charles Goldfarb [13.2]. Goldfarb invented SGML, which was standardized in 1986. His interest in web designer's needs tells me that the designers and markup mavens are both working hard to meet in the middle, for the benefit of designers, surfers, and the Web in general. In the grand scheme of things, it's not a big deal. But to me, the ability to include everyone in this global enterprise we call the Web is a step toward our own self-enlightenment. I am happy to be part of it.

From: Charles F. Goldfarb
To: david@killersites.com
Subject: Your article in Web Review
Date: Thu, 17 Apr 1997 10:58:43 GMT
Organization: Information Management Consulting

Hi,

Tim Bray, Co-editor of XML, told me about your article in Web Review and I really enjoyed it.

Despite being the father of SGML and (therefore) the grand-father of HTML and XML, I'm not an extremist of the kind you mentioned. Structure and style go hand-in-hand; the more detailed and interesting the structure, the more places for a creative designer to hang style variations. (Ask any fashion designer - there's a reason they like models with well-defined bodies.)

Also, what you called "structure" is abstract information. The result of laying it out is a rendition, which necessarily has a style. SGML can be used to represent information in either state - abstract or rendered - though the extremists don't think so. And both states have structure. In fact, one person's rendition is often another person's abstraction - consider indexing a paginated book. The HyTime standard, which uses SGML to represent hypertext and multimedia, is necessarily heavily into renditions.

I was delighted to see you promote the user-profile idea. Not only is it necessary for making intelligent style-sheet decisions, it also addresses the accessibility problem for the disabled. If color isn't available, it doesn't matter whether the reason is a monochrome display or the user's color-blindness.

Finally, I think you are right on about who should determine the style of a rendition. There is an analogy in classical music: the score describes an abstraction - notes with rela-tive duration values. The performer interprets the score and renders it in real time. The composer might choose to influ-ence the style of the rendition by including tempo direc-tives, but the end-user (i.e., the performer) has the final say.

Welcome to the SGML/XML fold (liberal branch),

Charles F. Goldfarb
Information Management Consulting
Charles@SGMLsource.com

13.2 Welcome to the fold – a letter to me from Charles Goldfarb, the inventor of SGML, the grandfather of all markup languages. (The *Web Review* article is linked from the Book Site.)

Paralysis

Possibly one of the most difficult things to do on the Web is to make a single page as good as it can possibly be. You can always do something to make it better. If you have a site, you know there are places you haven't touched in a long time, and two months is a very long time on the Web.

We all start with horizontal rules and blank-line typography. It's part of the learning curve. As we gain control of our pages, we raise the bar on ourselves, striving for better pages as we add tools to our toolkit. It doesn't get easier, the results just get better.

Possibly the best piece of advice I can give any designer is to roll up your sleeves and dig in. Start pushing pixels and tables around to see what works and what doesn't. I never get a page right on the first, or second, or third try. I'm always re-thinking my pages, realizing in the middle of the night how I could have done something more simply or cleanly.

A web site is an adventure. It's like surfing. You pick a goal, you start the journey, you end up somewhere else, but it turns out to be more inter-esting than where you thought you were going. While I advocate control over your pages, I hope this book has expanded your creativity by freeing you from the narrow, linear thought process imposed by HTML programming.

HTML is not for dummies. It can't be learned in a week. Making great pages is exacting work, and you can always do better. Third-generation site de-signers work their way up the hard way, sweating the details and using whatever tools are at hand to make balanced, beautiful, communicative pag-es. I hope that after you make a third-generation site, people you have never met will come visit, enjoy, send you mail, and connect in ways you never expected. Then you will know why it's all worth the effort.

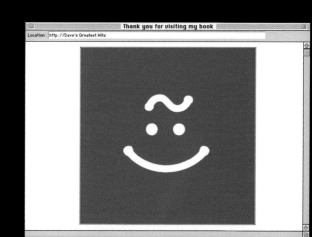

Dave's Guide to Better Surfing

Because I insisted, my publisher let me squeeze in a few notes on surfing. Though it is beyond the scope of this book, I would like to make a few recommendations to increase your surfing pleasure.

Link Colors: Brain Damage on the Infobahn

The Framers of the Web decided to denote links with underlining and special colors. They decided to make unvisited links blue and visited links purple. They avoided using red, probably because they thought red universally meant "STOP!" Also, they might have figured that some people can't see red, and many people (at the time) had black-and-white monitors, so underlining links was a good idea.

At user-interface school, they teach us that the color red has a prominent place in the evolution of our visual system. In the jungle, the color red serves as a strong warning of danger. Red is a "flag" color: It shouts. It does not mean "STOP!"; it means "HEY!"

Good designers take advantage of this attention mechanism without overusing it and watering it down.

Have you ever seen a blue speedometer dial? The right choice is to turn the "hot" unvisited links dark red and leave the visited links distinguishable, but "cool," receding into the black text **[A1.1]**. Red says, "Over here! Hit me!" Blue says, "Been there, done that." Red jumps out. Blue fades into the background. Go to a magazine stand and test this hypothesis for yourself.

Hot red and cool blue links should be standard on all browsers, but they aren't. To compensate, I start almost all my pages with the following header:

```
<BODY BGCOLOR="#FFFFFF"
TEXT="#000000" LINK="#CC0000"
ALINK="#FF3300"
VLINK="#330099">
```

This makes unvisited links dark red, visited links dark purple (which I happen to like better than dark blue; it's a personal preference), and the "active

link" color can be almost anything you like, since you see it only while your mouse button is held down. I hope you will use this formula on your pages, unless you have good reason to do otherwise. Perhaps if enough people set these colors on their pages, browser manufacturers will change their default ways of thinking.

You may have noticed that not a single site in this book has an image with a blue or purple border around it. While visited and unvisited link colors around images are an integral part of first-generation sites, they are so hideous that most reasonable people banned them long ago. Borders ruin the effect of most photographs. If you are relying on them to tell people something, you should consider redesigning. I always set my image borders to zero.

I also use these colors while surfing. I will see them unless the site designer

has specified otherwise. It's much nicer to surf with these colors; you quickly get accustomed to red items being clickable. Change your browser preferences and surf happily!

Underlining

Underlined links are necessary if you are surfing from a black-and-white monitor or if you are colorblind. If you can see colors, you should turn underlining off, and you should encourage people who visit your sites to turn underlining off. Maybe if enough people turn underlining off, the browser programmers will stop making it the "default" setting. Then again, maybe everyone who buys a copy of this book should just send email to *webmaster@netscape.com* and *webmaster@microsoft.com* asking them to turn underlining off at the factory.

Underlining is a traditional typographic proofreader's mark that says "make this italic, for emphasis." People using typewriters didn't have italics, so they used underlining to compensate. In quality typography, underlining simply does not exist. On the Web, if you can see colors, you can safely turn underlining off and live a longer, happier life without it.

Background Colors

Choose anything but gray. As you surf the Web, the best background is either white or a very pale shade of a light color. If you think white is too harsh, use an extremely pale mint green as your default background color, or my new favorite: "wheat." **[A1.2]**

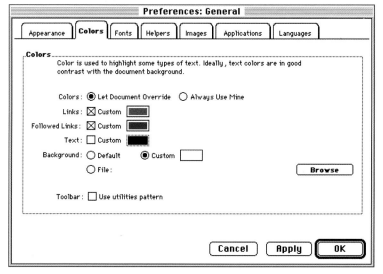

A1.1 Good design starts at your own browser. Make unvisited colors red, visited purplish-blue.

288

Please note: I cannot give you an exact recipe for this color, because I don't know enough about your system. If you have 256 colors, you might not be able to get a light enough color. Use your own judgment to come up with a very pale background color that will eventually "disappear" as you get used to it. These colors should be extremely close to white. If you can't get something very light, stick with white. If you try a light background like this, give it a week before changing it back. It will take a little while to get used to, but you'll be happier in the long run.

Don't set a subtle background color like this on your pages. If it's not in the color cube, many people may see it differently. Always look at your pages with 256 colors to verify a background color. Most of the time, white is best.

Many browser manufacturers have finally figured out that white is the best all-around default color and have begun to ship their browsers with white backgrounds right from the factory. Cleaning up the information highway is a dirty job, but if everyone pitches in, we'll get those gray backgrounds in the garbage can, where they belong.

A1.2 Fewer trips to the Advil home page: Set your background to just barely green, or a light neutral "wheat" color. (Quiz: How many deadly sins can you find on these pages?)

Fonts

As I mentioned in Chapter 5, "Rendering Type," Microsoft offers two excellent fonts designed for on-screen applications. Verdana and Georgia are available for both platforms, absolutely free, from Microsoft's Typography site. These are specially made TrueType fonts that should replace Times Roman and Helvetica (Arial) as your own personal browsing fonts. Download them at www.microsoft.com/truetype, in the core fonts section of that site.